W9-AUX-102

"Engaging and informative. . . . [Elaine] Sciolino so vividly captures [the magic of Paris]. . . . As Sciolino's touching storytelling illustrates, the Seine is more than just a body of water."

—Esme O'Keeffe, *Times Literary Supplement*

"A couple of times a year, a book just simply stops you in its tracks. That was the case with *The Seine*. . . . Elaine Sciolino . . . absolutely nailed the image of how we see this river through Paris."

—Tom Keene, *Bloomberg News*

"Sciolino, a longtime American in Paris . . . takes us along in an engaging travelogue/memoir tracing the Seine's 483 miles from its source to the sea. . . . Readers will enjoy Sciolino's expansive take on the Seine's role in the history and culture of France."

—Maureen McCarthy, *Star Tribune*

"Sciolino writes as a river flows and as Matisse and Monet painted—with beauty, ease and grace. . . . It is her love letter to the Seine."

—Erik Brady, *Buffalo News*

"Elaine Sciolino manages to be both hard-nosed reporter and hopeless romantic. . . . [She] has written a wonderful book."

—Warren Levinson, *Associated Press Get Outta Here!* podcast

"Sciolino helps us fathom the river that defines Paris. . . . She brings us a fresh way to talk about the Seine."

—Rick Steves, *Travel With Rick Steves* podcast

"[Sciolino] shares her love affair with Paris and the Seine with enchanting anecdotes and insights. . . . Francophiles will adore this book, and others may become Francophiles as they read."

—*Kirkus Reviews*, starred review

"Written in an enjoyable journalistic style, the book is both a travelog and a cultural history of not only the river itself but the people who have lived, worked, and taken inspiration from it. . . . For readers who have walked along the banks of the Seine or dream of someday doing so, this love letter to a river is highly recommended."

—*Library Journal*, starred review

"This entertaining account flows along like a love letter to the Seine. . . . Readers will enjoy this engaging and authoritative account, whether planning a trip, reminiscing about past travels, or sitting in an armchair, dreaming of wandering along romantic riverbanks."　　　　　　　　　　—*Booklist*

"*The Seine: The River That Made Paris* is enlightening not only for detailing the ways that, without the Seine, there'd be no Paris as we know it but for its descriptions of the Seine upriver and downriver from the capital, from Burgundy to Le Havre." —Arnie Weisman, *Travel Weekly*

"This beautifully written and deeply personal book captures something profound, not just about the Seine and France, but about people's lives and how important rivers are to them. . . . Elaine Sciolino writes with the authority of a historian, the sleuthing skills of a journalist, and the voice of a storyteller eager to recount the tales of those who have been touched by the Seine."

—David A. Bell, Lapidus Professor of History at Princeton University

"Anyone who, like me, loves and collects books about Paris will be grateful for this wonderful addition. It's erudite and energetic, like the river itself. Read Elaine Sciolino's own story as it emerges from her pages and her travels. I recommend *The Seine* as both a guidebook and a great bedside read."

—Diane Johnson, *New York Times* best-selling author of
*Le Divorce* and *Flyover Lives*

"It seems sometimes that everything that can be said about Paris has been said already. But no one has brought attention and paid tribute to its very heart like Elaine Sciolino managed to do in her latest book. . . . Paris, like New York, is a very diverse, nuanced place, hard to sum up in one book unless you have the talent of Elaine Sciolino. In *The Seine: The River That Made Paris*, she shares stories of her adventures along the most romantic river in the world and in doing so, she invites us to see the river in ways we didn't suspect."

—Gaëtan Bruel, cultural counselor of France to the United States

"Every day, through the windows of my restaurant, I have the sheer pleasure of gazing down at the Seine, awed by its beauty and vitality. In her lyrical and touching book, Elaine Sciolino brings this magical river to life for everyone to experience and enjoy. This is the finest book I've ever read about the Seine, the river that is the most beautiful avenue of Paris!"

—Guy Savoy, chef and restaurateur

"Sciolino's book is light-hearted, energetic and romantic—in a word: fun."

—Phineas Rueckert, *Frenchly*

"A melange of historical vignettes, personal anecdotes and poetic quotes spiced with photos and illustrations, this charming book is both informative and entertaining."

—*Paris Voice*

"Forever the intrepid reporter, [Sciolino's] titanic research reads like a detective novel uncovering lost treasures, debunking myths and revealing secrets."

—*Inspirelle*

"[Sciolino] has come out with an intriguing new book in the finest tradition of story-telling."

—*Global Geneva*

"A brilliantly researched journey down the Seine and a look at French history and contemporary culture."    —French Cultural Center, Boston

"The *New York Times* bestselling author explores every aspect of the iconic river—from its history to its pollution levels to its impact on art and French culture. . . . [I] was swept up with the current of Sciolino's latest. You don't have to have visited France—you just have to want to learn about French culture, history, art, film."　　　　—*The Standard-Times*

"The force of Sciolino's personality lies at the heart of all her explorations. . . . Her enthusiasm and drive are infectious. . . . The book's Afterword, written soon after the fire that almost destroyed Notre-Dame Cathedral in Paris, is particularly touching as Sciolino explains how the water pumped from the Seine was crucial in saving the edifice. . . . [This book] should be recommended reading both for those who love Paris and for those intending to visit France anytime soon."
　　　　—Nick Hammond, *Paris Update*

"Incredible book . . . fascinating."　　　　—WBNY radio

# The Seine

# The Seine

## THE RIVER THAT MADE PARIS

*Elaine Sciolino*

Frontispiece: A back view of Notre-Dame
Cathedral before the fire of April 2019.
JULIE ANN HERBERT.

For information about permission to reproduce selections from this book, write to
Permissions, W. W. Norton & Company, Inc., 500 Fifth Avenue, New York, NY 10110

For information about special discounts for bulk purchases, please contact
W. W. Norton Special Sales at specialsales@wwnorton.com or 800-233-4830

Manufacturing by LSC Harrisonburg
Production manager: Beth Steidle

Library of Congress Cataloging-in-Publication Data

Names: Sciolino, Elaine, author.
Title: The Seine : the river that made Paris / Elaine Sciolino.
Other titles: River that made Paris
Description: First edition. | New York, NY : W. W. Norton & Company, Inc., [2020] |
Includes bibliographical references and index.
Identifiers: LCCN 2019025988 | ISBN 9780393609356 (hardcover) |
ISBN 9780393609363 (epub)
Subjects: LCSH: Seine River Valley (France)—Description and travel. |
Paris (France)—Description and travel.
Classification: LCC DC611.S461 S38 2020 | DDC 944/.36—dc23
LC record available at https://lccn.loc.gov/2019025988

ISBN 978-0-393-35859-9 pbk.

W. W. Norton & Company, Inc., 500 Fifth Avenue, New York, N.Y. 10110
www.wwnorton.com

W. W. Norton & Company Ltd., 15 Carlisle Street, London W1D 3BS

2  3  4  5  6  7  8  9  0

TO ANDREW

*The best traveling companion ever . . .*

*On the road, in life*

# Contents

ENGLISH
CHANNEL

LE HAVRE

HONFLEUR
TANCARVILLE
QUILLEBEUF-SUR-SEINE

LILLEBONNE
VILLEQUIER
CAUDEBEC-EN-CAUX
SAINT-WANDRILLE ABBEY
DUCLAIR
JUMIÈGES
ROUEN

ELBEUF
SEINE

LES ANDELYS
CHÂTEAU GAILLARD

VERNON
GIVERNY

Oise

CONFLANS-SAINTE-HONORINE
CHATOU
ARGENTEUIL
PARIS

BOUGIVAL
VERSAILLES

SEINE
MELUN

FONTAINEBLEAU
MONTEREAU-FAULT-YONNE

Loing

# The Seine

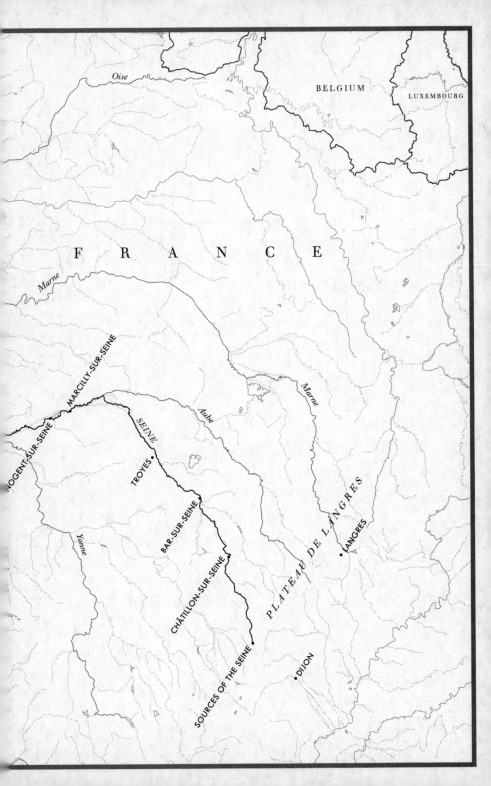

# PART ONE

# The Seine Is France

*Notre-Dame Cathedral framed by the stone underpass of the Pont Saint-Michel.* DARIUS KHONDJI.

# ONE

# Poetry in Motion

*I could spend my whole life*
*Watching the Seine flow by. . . .*
*It is a poem of Paris.*
—BLAISE CENDRARS, "La Seine"

IN THE SPRING OF 1978, I was seduced by a river. I had come to Paris from Chicago to be a foreign correspondent for *Newsweek* magazine. I arrived with no sources, no lovers, no family, no friends, no mission except to start fresh in a city all the world loves.

There had been a husband in Chicago, but he'd announced one day that he was leaving. I let him take the BMW, the butcher block table, the full-sized mattress, the Wassily armchairs, the walnut rolltop desk, the darkroom equipment, and a set of Wedgwood china. I kept the antique brass bed frame, a carpet, and much of the rest of the furniture. Four months later, he remarried. I recounted the story of our breakup over and over until it became as smooth and harmless as a stone worn down by the sea.

I was twenty-eight years old and free to be my own person in Paris.

Like so many Americans, I felt as if I already knew the city, as if I owned it. I had studied French history. I had read about Paris in novels and seen it in paintings. I had heard songs about April in Paris and loving Paris in the springtime and the fall. I had watched movies—oh, the movies—set in Paris.

But I was ill-prepared to dive into the culture of France. My French was so weak that when I did interviews, I had to write out my questions in advance, word for word, and record every conversation to guarantee accuracy. I rigged up a recording device on the rotary dial telephone in my office, a practice that probably violated French privacy laws.

No one told me about French manners and mannerisms. I didn't know that you never discuss personal wealth, religious beliefs, or real estate transactions at proper dinner parties. Or that you should eat hamburgers and pizza with a knife and fork and never take seconds on the cheese course.

I didn't know that wearing a lot of makeup or laughing too loud is considered vulgar. Or that floral prints would identify me as a foreigner or that the uniform for a late Sunday afternoon book party is a pair of well-cut black trousers and a tailored shirt in fine white cotton. Or that it is essential to say *bonjour* to shopkeepers, bus drivers, and people in elevators but impolite to smile at strangers. Or that *"pas mal"* ("not bad") can mean "great!" and "I wouldn't say no" can mean "I'd love to!"

The dollar was at an all-time low against the franc, so there was little money for distractions to relieve my loneliness. I hadn't known to bring a portable typewriter for my new job. *Newsweek*'s Chicago bureau, where I had been working, was a convivial place with a stash of eggshell-blue Olivetti Lettera 22 portables; the Paris bureau was an every-man-for-himself world (the four other correspondents were older men) where self-sufficiency and seniority reigned.

I found two sources of support. The first was "Madame," an elderly French tutor, who gave me conversation lessons every Saturday morning. Her dark apartment oozed Parisian charm, with its crystal chandeliers and fine art. Madame was thin and elegant, smoked filtered Gauloises, and wore Art Nouveau rings set with giant stones. She wrote my homework assignments in turquoise ink with a Montblanc pen.

And then there was the Seine.

People everywhere feel visceral connections with the rivers they love. Mark Twain had his Mississippi; Johann Strauss celebrated the Danube. Russians venerate the Volga, and Indianans sing about the Wabash. Many lovers of Broadway musicals know the words to "Ol' Man River," a tune from *Show Boat*. In Buffalo, where I grew up, my river had been the Niagara, a short, fast-rolling strait between two lakes that does not look, move, or sound anything like the Seine. When I was thirteen, I took ballet lessons in Fort Erie, just across the river in Canada, and I often walked home on the pedestrian lane of the international Peace Bridge. No matter how cold the day, how fierce the snowstorm, I would stop midway across the span to gaze at the river below, abandoning myself to a force of nature beyond my control. Although the bridge was eighteen miles away from the powerful Niagara Falls, the current already ran swift here. The Niagara taught me that a river can dissolve loneliness and catch the heart. And then, in Paris, I moved into an apartment close to the Seine. Most evenings I crossed the river during my walk from the *Newsweek* office, on the rue du Faubourg Saint-Honoré, in the Eighth Arrondissement, to the avenue de la Bourdonnais, in the Seventh.

My half-hour walk took me across the Pont de l'Alma, which links two neighborhoods in the west of Paris: the designer boutiques on the Right Bank and the bourgeois residences on the Left. Napoléon III ordered the city planner, Baron Georges-Eugène Haussmann, to build a stone bridge as a celebration of France's 1854 victory over the Russians in Crimea. But the bridge was too narrow to support the ever-increasing flow of cars and foot traffic. In the early 1970s, it was rebuilt in steel, simple and unadorned. It looks like an overpass on a U.S. highway.

Four stone soldiers stood sentry on the original bridge. Now only one remains, the statue of a bearded Zouave, a colonial soldier from a regiment created in Algeria in 1831 from the Zouaoua, a Kabyle tribe. Dressed in a tasseled fez, blousy pants, and a long cape, he stands with his left hand on his hip, his right holding the end of a rifle barrel. He is the city's unofficial flood monitor. If his pointed shoes are submerged, the river is running high.

ON THE WAY HOME, returning to the habit of my teen years, I would stop midway on the Pont de l'Alma. Confronted with a city so familiar and yet still new and strange, I found comfort in the river's calm and steady flow to its certain destination. Whatever the water level, the Zouave gazed with equanimity over the shimmering stream. At sunset, I watched the light fade from gold to pale yellow to silver and recede into darkness. The streetlights danced in the river's reflection.

I took in the life of the narrow river: the *bateaux-mouches* filled with carefree tourists, the houseboats, the quiet grandeur of the structures on the upper level of the riverbanks, lined with horse chestnut and plane trees, and the proximity of the lower banks to the water. Downstream, the Eiffel Tower peeked out from behind the greenery. Across the river, apartment buildings on the avenue de New York came into view, as did the roof of the Art Deco Musée d'Art Moderne de la Ville de Paris. Directly in front, the Passerelle Debilly, a green metallic footbridge built for the 1900 Paris Exposition Universelle, carried people heading home from work. A half mile away from where I stood was the Pont des Invalides, and beyond that, the gold-colored statues and ornaments of the Pont Alexandre III.

If I listened hard enough, I could hear the voice of the river. In the 1920s and 1930s, when James Joyce lived in Paris, he walked miles up and down the Seine. He was almost always with a companion, as he was nearly blind by then. He would stop at times on the Pont de l'Alma to hear the water move so he could capture its rhythm in his writing. "There's music along the river / For Love wanders there," he wrote in the opening poem of *Chamber Music*.

Even when the Seine was still and silent, I stood on the bridge and reveled in the sounds of life surrounding me: the revving motorcycles, the honking cars, the bells of Notre-Dame announcing the time, the multilingual commentaries rising from the tourist boats, the loud chatter of American visitors who didn't know that in Paris, one's voice should be soft and low.

In *A Moveable Feast*, Hemingway described the Seine as a salve against solitude: "With the fishermen and the life on the river, the beautiful barges with their own life on board, the tugs with their smokestacks that folded back to pass under the bridges, pulling a tow of barges, the great elms on the stone banks of the river, the plane trees and in some places the poplars, I could never be lonely along the river."

Neither could I. I overcame anxiety and loneliness and moved forward in my life, like the Seine in its course. The river allowed me to begin a journey of discovery—of Paris, of the French people, of myself. Its energy pumped deep into my veins; its light gave me strength.

"Everything is going to be okay," I said to myself.

And over time, it was.

*A Chinese bride and groom pose for a photograph near the Seine as part of their nuptial preparations. Before their marriage celebrations, some Chinese couples fly to Paris to be photographed in their wedding finery.* DAVID BROAD.

# TWO

# The Most Romantic River in the World

*She goes to the sea*
*Passing through Paris....*
*And ... walks between the quays*
*In her beautiful green dress*
*And her golden lights.*

—JACQUES PRÉVERT,

"Chanson de la Seine"

THE SEINE IS the most romantic river in the world. She encourages us to dream, to linger, to flirt, to fall in love, or to at least fantasize that falling in love is possible. The light bouncing off her banks and bridges at night can carry even the least imaginative of us into flights of fancy. No other river comes close. The Ganges, the Mississippi, and the Yangtze? They are muscular workhorses. The Thames? Who can name one famous couple who fell in love on its banks? The Danube? It may be immortalized as the world's most recognizable waltz, but its history is one of warring nations.

The Seine's romantic power is rooted in her human scale. Compared with the Nile, the Amazon, or even the Hudson, she feels accessible, narrow enough to track the comings and goings on either side. Her banks are flat, her bridges densely packed and so low to the ground that you can almost touch the water.

Then there is her grandeur. The architectural treasures that line her banks allow her to project power beyond her physical dimensions. The interplay between intimacy and power casts a spell. Painters, poets, filmmakers, photographers, historians, novelists, composers, lovers, and, these days, virtual-reality designers have fallen hopelessly in love with her. Monet painted from a studio boat on the Seine, Matisse and Marquet while gazing down at the river from their Paris apartments. Zola, Flaubert, and Bizet lived in houses along the Seine. Jazz great Django Reinhardt rented a place nearby. Dumas could see the river from his Château de Monte-Cristo.

The Seine, of course, is a woman. She is called *la* Seine, not *le* Seine. Poets and songwriters refer to her as female. She takes her name and her identity from the ancient goddess Sequana, who healed ailing pilgrims at her temple at the river's source.

According to the French rules of geography and grammar, a river that flows into the sea, as the Seine does, should be given the masculine appellation *le fleuve*; many people who live and work on the Seine insist that it is feminine: *la rivière*, which is supposed to refer only to inland waterways. "The old word *rivière* is always used by the people of the water, from bargemen to bureaucrats," wrote Francois Beaudouin, the founder of a museum on barge life in Conflans-Sainte-Honorine, in his book *Paris/Seine*. "*Fleuve*," he continued, is a word that "geographers imposed on the general public in the nineteenth century and that goes against the femininity of Sequana."

THE SEINE EMERGES young and fresh in a field of springs on a remote plateau in Burgundy and grows strong and majestic by the time she reaches the sea, 777 kilometers—483 miles—away. She flows through history: past prehistoric encampments, ancient Roman towns, Viking strongholds, medieval châteaus, monastic abbeys, and World War II battlegrounds. Along her route, she opens herself without hesitation, allowing any riverside town to lay claim to her mystique. Yet her one true love is and always has been Paris, the source of power in France since antiquity. The city arrives slightly more than midway through her journey, giving the Seine her geographic, historic, and symbolic importance.

Long before the invention of GPS—or even accurate maps—the geography of the Seine served as both a practical and an inspirational guide for travelers seeking the heart of France, and so it continued even after the mastery of flight changed humanity's perspective. Look at the Seine from the sky and you find a highway to Paris. Charles Lindbergh, the American aviator who first flew solo across the Atlantic, in 1927, saw the Seine from his cockpit near the end of his transatlantic flight. The river helped guide him safely to Le Bourget airfield near Paris, where a crowd of thousands cheered him. In his memoir *The Spirit of St. Louis*, he wrote, "Down under my left wing, angling in from the north, winding through fields submerged in night, comes the Seine, shimmering back to the sky the faint remaining light of evening. With my position known and my compass set, with the air clear and a river and an airway to lead me in, nothing but engine failure can keep me now from reaching Paris."

Despite her confinement between banks of stone, the Seine becomes one with the buildings and monuments that adorn them. Here she becomes the Seine all of us know, or think we know. "Wherever we are in the world, when we close our eyes and think about the Seine, it's Paris that we see," wrote the poet André Velter.

Life is lived on the river—on barges, pleasure craft, pontoon platforms, decommissioned naval vessels. Afloat on the Seine, you can live, eat and drink, make love, get married, practice yoga, run a business, shop for books, watch fireworks, do a wine tasting, go fishing, dance the

*Bathers sunning themselves on the Right Bank of the Seine near the Pont de Sully and the Île Saint-Louis.* ANDREW PLUMP.

tango. You can attend a fashion show, a concert, a play. You can find a hotel, a psychiatric hospital ward, a film studio, a homeless shelter, an art museum, an architect's showroom—all floating on the river.

The world's most visited cathedral, Notre-Dame, sits on an island in the Seine; the world's most visited art museum, the Louvre, faces the Seine from Paris's Right Bank. Despite a crackdown by Paris City Hall, couples from around the world continue to clamp padlocks to the Seine's bridges as evidence that they long to be locked in love forever. Before they are married, some Chinese couples fly to Paris to be photographed in wedding attire along the Seine. Even worldly-wise Parisians are seduced by the Seine—its geography, history, politics, economics, culture, and, *bien sûr*, its romance.

Philippe Labro—novelist, filmmaker, essayist, columnist, television host—is an urbane Parisian, but he turns downright exuberant when he talks about the Seine. "What's my favorite word in French—*rivière*! River! *Riv-ee-air*!" he said. "It rhymes with *lumière*—light. It moves. It flows like music. It's a sign of life."

Labro was so intrigued by the cultural differences between the Left and Right Banks that in 1984 he made the river the focal point of his seventh and last film: *Rive droite, rive gauche*, starring Gérard Depardieu and Nathalie Baye. "*Rive gauche* meant freedom and liberty and free speech and free sex," he said. "*Rive droite* meant money, politics, scandal, and the power of the media. The Seine became an obsession—it flows through the movie just as it flows through the city. There is movement of place, going from one space to another, and movement of life, from intrigue to love to death. I loved it. I wasn't aware that making the movie was work."

Chef Guy Savoy, whose restaurant has three Michelin stars, became so fixated on the Seine that he invested over €2 million and more than five years of his life to move his restaurant to its banks. Restaurant Guy Savoy now sits at the top of a red-carpeted stone staircase carved with medallions and wreaths in the Monnaie de Paris, the French Mint, which once produced all the coins of the realm.

One morning, Savoy threw open a ten-foot-high window in the main dining room to show me his view. The Louvre was to the left across the river, the Pont Neuf to the right, the tip of the Île de la Cité straight ahead. We were so close to the booksellers on the riverbank below that we could wave to them and say *bonjour.*

"Ah, look at this! It's Paris at your feet!" Savoy said. "There are many beautiful views in the world, but none, none like this one! The first time I saw it, it was like an electric shock. I said, 'I have to be here.'"

In Billy Wilder's 1954 romantic comedy *Sabrina*, Audrey Hepburn explains to a skeptical Humphrey Bogart the magic of a four-mile walk past all the bridges of Paris: "You find one you love and go there every day with your coffee and your journal and you listen to the river."

———

THE SEINE CUTS THROUGH PARIS in a great arc from east to west, touching ten of the city's twenty arrondissements—the First, Fourth, Fifth, Sixth, Seventh, Eighth, Twelfth, Thirteenth, Fifteenth, and Sixteenth. France's two most important islands, the Île de la Cité and the smaller Île Saint-Louis, are at its heart. The arc of the Seine exaggerates the river's size, and connecting canals extend its reach deeper into the city. It loops around the suburbs, enfolding them in a lopsided embrace. "I am the road running through Paris," the twentieth-century author Julien Green has the Seine say.

In Paris, the river is always present, even when you cannot see it. You are on the Left or the Right Bank, defined from the viewpoint looking downstream on the Seine. You are in an arrondissement numbered according to a system that begins on the Île de la Cité and swirls clockwise in a spiral. Street names evoke the river: the rue du Bac is named after the *bac*, or ferry, that transported stone blocks for the construction of the Palais des Tuileries; the rue de Seine follows the wall built by the medieval king Philippe II that led to the river on the Left Bank; the rue des Deux Ponts, on the Île Saint-Louis, connects the Ponts Marie and de la Tournelle. The rue de Bièvre recalls a small river that became a putrid canal flowing into the Seine, until it was covered over in the twentieth century.

How exhilarating to stroll along the Seine with an open spirit and no fixed destination. Take the No. 7 Métro to the Pont Neuf. Cross to the Left Bank and head west, passing the Institut de France, the domed structure that houses the Académie Française, guardian of the French language. From there, return to the Right Bank over the Pont des Arts, the wooden-slatted, iron pedestrian bridge that leads to the Louvre. Seek a moment of contemplation in the Cour Carrée, the sixteenth- and seventeenth-century square courtyard with perfect proportions, hidden at the museum's east end. Walk from there to the entrance on the rue de Rivoli and turn around to treat yourself to a dramatic new view of the Institut de France, framed by the Renaissance pavilions of the Louvre.

The perfect climax is a walk west along the river toward the Eiffel Tower, the most distinctive emblem of Paris and arguably the world's most famous monument. Without the Eiffel Tower, Paris would still exist; without the Seine, there never would have been a Paris. While the river owes the city its romantic aura, the city owes the river its birth, its life, and its identity. The love affair of Paris and the Seine defines them both.

The harmony between Paris and its river is no accident. Parisians left nothing to chance. The Seine has served as a mirror for the city's architectural treasures since the twelfth century, with the construction of the Louvre—first a defensive fortress, then a royal residence, then a museum—and Notre-Dame Cathedral. Paris became the first city in Europe to use its river to put its imposing architecture on display. Over time, the river was contained and landscaped to show off the structures of art and history that line its banks. The Seine allows Paris to present itself as a stage set, with the river cast as the pièce de résistance.

In the nineteenth century, the Seine was plagued by raw sewage, the residents' garbage, putrid smells, and thick mudflats that revealed themselves at low tide. Then, in 1853, Baron Georges-Eugène Haussmann, who was given the title "prefect of the Seine," began to transform Paris, including its riverfront. He and his successors were determined to dominate the river, to channel the waterway into pleasant submission. They lined the Seine with new stone quays to create a single continuous route and built bridges to improve commerce and harmonize both sides of the river. They demolished thousands of decrepit houses—and uprooted thousands of poor Parisians—to create water views and tree-shaded promenades. They constructed locks and dams outside the city to make the river's flow consistent and dependable. The architects outdid themselves. In 1991, the riverbanks earned the honor of being named a UNESCO World Heritage cultural site. That designation applies only to the picture-perfect central area between the

Pont d'Iéna, at the Eiffel Tower, to the west, and the Pont de Sully, near Notre-Dame to the east. This is the Seine of romance; the commercial, industrial Seine farther east is left out.

The Seine can evoke images of exotic places. Toward the end of Marcel Proust's *In Search of Lost Time*, the unnamed narrator feels transported to a faraway place by the river: "It was a transparent and breathless night; I imagined that the Seine, flowing between the twin semicircles of the span and the reflection of its bridges, must look like the Bosporus. . . . The moon, narrow and curved like a sequin, seemed to have placed the sky of Paris beneath the oriental sign of the crescent."

Even when personal disaster strikes, the romance of the river endures. In her diaries, Anaïs Nin tells of receiving an official police order to move her rented houseboat out of Paris. It was late summer 1938, before the outbreak of World War II. Nin sailed away alone, staying on deck in the rain to watch Paris pass by. "I remembered my dream, of sailing for twenty years and all my friends standing on the shore asking me where I was going and when I would be back," she wrote. "Here I was in reality, sailing past the sections of Paris so familiar to me, past apartment houses where I had lived, and streets I had so often explored. But I was not allowed to meditate on how dreams materialize, for the houseboat was taking in water, and I had to man the pump."


WHEN YOU MOVE TO PARIS from far away, it isn't long before visitors start arriving—friends and family who want you to show them the city. Because my first apartment was near the Eiffel Tower, my usual tour started with an ascent to its top, which gave an aerial view of the Seine curving through Paris. When visitors wanted to take the perfect photo of the Eiffel Tower itself, I took them to the place du Trocadéro for a straight-on view of the tower with the river in the foreground. At the place de la Concorde, we circled Paris's oldest monument, a pink granite obelisk sculpted more than three thousand years ago for the

Temple of Luxor in Egypt. It arrived in Paris after a two-year journey on the waters of the Nile, the Mediterranean, the Atlantic, the English Channel, and, finally, the Seine. It was erected in 1836 at the spot where Louis XVI was beheaded during the French Revolution.

At night, there was the requisite river tour on a *bateau-mouche*. It's not a bargain, but a ride on the Seine after sunset is a no-fail crowd-pleaser, and no visitor wants it to end. Movie buffs—and visitors of a certain age—remember that magic moment in *Charade*, Stanley Donen's 1963 romantic thriller, when the murders are not yet solved but Cary Grant and Audrey Hepburn find themselves falling in love on a tourist boat on the Seine. The boat trains its bright spotlight first on a couple kissing as their bodies lean against a tree, then on a second couple sitting on a park bench locked in a tight embrace. Audrey moves closer to Cary, lowers her voice, and says, "Hey, you don't look so bad in this light."

"Why do you think I brought you here?" he replies, then leans in for a perfect ten-second movie kiss. Every time I took a *bateau-mouche* in my early, lonely days in Paris, I thought of Audrey Hepburn and hoped there would be a Cary Grant on the upper deck.

Even Britain's Queen Elizabeth II was entranced by the romance of a nighttime boat ride on the river. When the queen and her husband made a royal state visit to France in 1957, President René Coty invited them on his presidential yacht for a "night promenade," with fireworks over the river in her honor. Dressed in a gown of silver lamé and lace embroidered with diamonds and crystals, a matching stole trimmed in white fox, and a diamond tiara and necklace, the queen waved to the crowd of one million people who lined the riverbanks to see her and pointed out the monuments of Paris to her husband as they passed. A wire service report captured her mood: "She gazed with wonder . . . delighted by the spectacle . . . her eyes sparkling like the diamonds in her tiara."

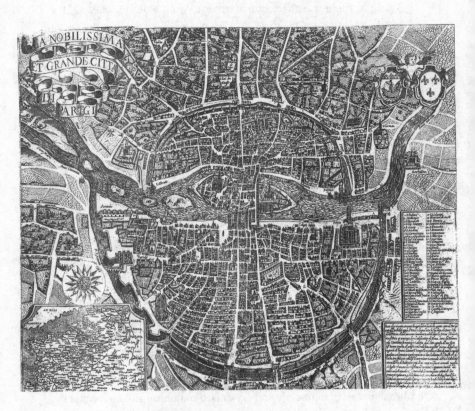

*A map drawn by Mattéo Fiorini in 1550 depicting Paris when it was protected by a wall. Île de la Cité is at the center.*

# THREE

# The Main Street of France

*Here is the entrance to paradise.*

—A VIKING LEADER discussing a plan to
invade France via the Seine, *Vikings*, season three

LATE ONE AFTERNOON in October 1784, a fifteen-year-old military student named Napoléon Bonaparte arrived in Paris for the first time. He came with fellow cadets from a regiment in Burgundy on a cheap passenger barge. They docked at the Quai des Célestins, on the Right Bank, and crossed the Seine at the Pont Marie to reach the Île Saint-Louis, where they dined at a small inn. Later that evening, Napoléon was drawn to a book he spotted at a bookseller's stall along the river. It was the picaresque novel *Gil Blas* by Alain-René Lesage, which recounts the adventures of a naïve but clever young valet who becomes a landowning nobleman and learns wisdom and compassion along the way. As Napoléon had no money, a friend from school paid for it.

From then on, the Seine meandered in and out of Napoléon's life. Although the Seine is not France's longest river—the Loire is some 30 percent longer—it has always had an outsized role in France, as well as in the global imagination. It is a thread running through every significant chapter of French history, and a symbol of the country's identity as crucial as the tri-color flag or "La Marseillaise."

Napoléon intuitively felt the Seine's force, and once he was in power, he altered the river's life, defining it as the national river of France and launching ambitious public works projects to tame and reshape it. He saw it as a romantic inspiration as well as a practical asset and unifier of the nation. In a speech in Le Havre in 1802, he proclaimed its commercial importance as the connector of its three great port cities: "Le Havre, Rouen, and Paris are a single town, and the Seine is Main Street."

During Napoléon's decade and a half in power, he oversaw the construction of three bridges and nearly ten thousand feet of stone quays in Paris. He eliminated about two hundred islands that had clogged the river between Rouen and Le Havre. He started, then abandoned, a scheme to make the Seine navigable westward from Châtillon-sur-Seine, the first substantial town from the river's source, to Marcilly-sur-Seine, where vessels could already travel through Paris and all the way to the sea.

In 1805, Napoléon used the Seine as the basis for street addresses, a system that is still in place today. Numbers start at the point closest to the river and increase as they move away—even numbers on the right, odd numbers on the left. For streets parallel to the river, the numbers get higher as they follow the river's westward course. Whether they are conscious of it or not, Parisians still use the river as their guide. In my long, lazy walks as a newcomer, the Seine was my compass. I loved that I knew where I was going, or not going, thanks to the Seine. If I followed the river, I would never be lost.

After his humiliating retreat from Russia, Napoléon won one of his last battles in 1814 at Montereau-Fault-Yonne, where the Yonne River flows into the Seine. A bronze statue of Napoléon on horseback stands at their meeting point, inscribed with a bold pronouncement: "Do not worry, my friends. The bullet that will kill me has not yet been cast." His enemies captured Paris several weeks later, and Napoléon was

forced to sign the Treaty of Fontainebleau, ending his rule as emperor
of France.

With his defeat at Waterloo in 1815 after a brief return to power,
Napoléon retired to Château de Malmaison, his last residence in France,
near the Seine, before his final exile to the island of Saint Helena, in the
South Atlantic. Six years later, as he lay dying, he dictated a codicil to
his will stating that he wanted his ashes to be buried near the river. His
British captors denied the request, and he was interred more than four
thousand miles away, on Saint Helena. The political winds changed,
and in 1840, Napoléon's remains were carried to Paris along the Seine
in a brightly painted frigate. His body was placed in five successive cof-
fins nested and sealed in a red quartzite sarcophagus in the Hôtel des
Invalides. His words about wanting to rest along the Seine are inscribed
at the entrance to his crypt: "I wish my ashes to rest on the banks of the
Seine among the people of France, whom I loved so much."


ON A MAP, France is veined by 5,000 miles of waterways, 416 inland
*rivières*, and 74 *fleuves* that flow into the sea. The fast-flowing Rhône
cuts through the vineyards and olive groves of Provence; the sandy
Loire is home to France's grand châteaus; the Marne harbors the ghosts
of World War I. The French so revere their rivers that they have named
dozens of their administrative *départements* after them. In the gardens of Versailles, eight bronze sculptures personify the greatest of the
country's rivers and tributaries—the Seine and Marne, the Loire and
Loiret, the Rhône and Saône, the Garonne and Dordogne. But it is the
Seine, the river of Paris, that rules France.

The Seine has been a source of food and water, an irrigator of crops,
and a healer. It has been a killer, a crime scene, and a burial ground. It
has been a sewer and waste dump for towns and cities, farmers and factory owners, tanners and butchers, washerwomen and bargemen. It has
been an attack route in war, a promenade in peace, and a starting point
for global exploration. It has been a practical powerhouse for industry

and a path of transit, ferrying foods across its currents. Finally, it has been the keeper of the secrets of French history.

For two millennia, before the railroads and highways transformed the shipment of cargo, grain moved downriver toward the sea, while wine moved upriver to Paris on barges. An 1809 gastronomic map of France—the earliest of its kind—shows images of the bounty of the river and the land along its shores: trout, catfish, gudgeon, crayfish, eels, squash, pears, eggs, cheese, grapes, partridge, veal, ducks, chickens, pigs, and hares.

The Seine runs through or along the borders of dozens of towns and villages. Three great cities—Paris, Rouen, and Le Havre—serve as the anchors Napoléon evoked. Like blood pumping through the arteries of the landscape, the river's basin feeds a quarter of the country's landmass and population. According to France's National Geographic Institute, the Seine flows under more than two hundred bridges and is fed by forty-five tributaries.

It no longer makes the trip it once did, roaming wildly and freely. Its role as a conduit of navigation, trade, industry, leisure, and beauty physically transformed it. Over the centuries—extravagantly under Napoléon but starting long before him—it has been narrowed, enlarged, tamed, deepened, embanked, dammed, canalized, landscaped, dredged. Its lakes have been filled in, its islands dug out, its swamps drained, its banks lined with concrete. The construction of its quays in Paris began in 1312, and they have been renovated again and again ever since. Some French historians say that when they look at the Seine, they see a botched makeover, like a woman's face that's been lifted too many times. For me, however, it is an organic form that changes color, from molasses to pewter, from emerald to celadon, and turns a hundred shades in between as it works its way to the sea.

Geography has made the Seine an elusive companion. As a body of water, it resists easy categorization. It is hard to measure its length with precision. If the Seine ran in a straight line, its distance from the

*A woman by the*
*Seine, reading a book.*
ANDREW PLUMP.

source to the sea would be 250 miles; because of its capricious twists and turns, it is almost double that length.

THE RIVER STARTS as pure spring water, bubbling up from fissures in an obscure plain in northeast Burgundy. From there, it flows west, cutting a deep trench through the dry chalk plateau of Champagne country and the medieval city of Troyes. It swells as it absorbs other waterways, showing off and then abandoning different landscapes on its banks: cultivated fields, dark green thickets, dense woods, spongy marshes, grassy meadows, white limestone cliffs speckled with black flint. A children's geography book from 1926 describes the Seine as the "most regular and most navigable" river in France, with a gentle drop along its route—only 1,465 feet until it heads triumphantly into Paris. At the city's far western edge, it becomes lazy and winding, looping and twisting and losing its sense of direction as it continues a northwesterly course across the flat country of Normandy. At Rouen, about seventy-five miles north-west of Paris, it becomes a maritime river, deep and wide enough for oceangoing ships. Fifty-six miles farther along, it opens to a large estuary, a huge expanse of water that acts as a transition zone between the river and the sea. At the end of the estuary, the Seine empties into the English Channel at Le Havre.

The official verdict on the Seine's navigability comes from Voies Navigables de France (VNF), the public institution that manages France's eighty-two navigable *cours d'eau*, or water routes, forty-seven of them canals. It publishes trilingual boaters' bibles in French, English, and German, with colored maps showing every curve, island, town, park, bridge, silt deposit, dam, lock, tributary, and rest stop, as well as photos and descriptions of tourist sites. No serious boater would be without them.

Most of the Seine is navigable for small recreational craft. But commercial navigation officially begins at Marcilly-sur-Seine, about a hundred miles from the source and seventy miles from Châtillon. There the Seine takes on a succession of identities: Petite Seine (Small Seine) from Marcilly-sur-Seine to its junction with the Yonne River, Haute Seine (High Seine) to Paris, Basse Seine (Low Seine) to Rouen, and Seine Maritime (Maritime Seine) to the sea.

According to the VNF, a barge of one thousand tons or more can move upstream from Le Havre through Rouen, Paris, and beyond to Nogent-sur-Seine, where the river gets too narrow to accommodate such large craft. The barge would travel precisely 323.83 miles for two days, one hour, and one minute and would transit through twenty-one locks. (There are traffic jams, of course, and boats sometimes line up for hours waiting to pass through the locks.)

Many people who live near the Seine claim that it is an impostor, traveling under a false name. A global geographic convention dictates that when two rivers meet and form one channel—a "confluence"— the river with the stronger annual flow trumps the weaker one and snatches the name. When the Seine gets to the town of Marcilly-sur-Seine, one hundred miles west of the source, it joins the Aube. The Aube is stronger, so it should have trumped the Seine.

Even if the Aube had won the name contest, it would have lost it a bit farther downstream at Montereau-Fault-Yonne, 140 miles north-west of the source and sixty miles southeast of Paris. There the Seine is joined by the Yonne, which is more powerful and nearly twice as wide. So the Seine should have ended in obscurity there, and the Yonne should have been the river that moved on through Paris to the sea.

The French love to argue about their history, and the debate over the name of the Seine continues today. In 2018, the local newspaper *L'Yonne républicaine* stated unequivocally that "according to the rules of hydrography, it is the Yonne that flows in Paris." The article cited scholarly geography tomes as proof of this "injustice."

French geographers point out that the "confluence" rule is often ignored. According to the geographer Yves Boquet, the Rhine River should have been called the Aare, the Mississippi the Ohio, and the Ganges the Yamuna. Maps that accurately measured the flow and size of rivers were drawn only in the mid-eighteenth century, and who would have dared change the Seine's name then?

The consensus among geographers and historians is that the Seine stayed the Seine because of its aura of holiness. Its source was the site of a temple and a place of pilgrimage dedicated to a healing goddess, even before the Romans came and conquered Gaul. Under Roman rule, both the goddess and her river were called Sequana, a Latin name that may have originated from the Celtic (or Gallic) word *siquana*, mentioned in the writings of Julius Caesar.

According to one interpretation, Sequana's name means "sacred river," from the Celtic (or Gallic) words *sawk* (holy) and *onna* (water).

But according to another, it could mean "winding" or "tortuous," evoking the path of a snake, from the Celtic word *squan*. Or *sin-ane* (slow river), or maybe *sôgh-ane* (peaceful river). In any case, the Romans Latinized the name and made it Sequana.

Over time—although geographers do not know exactly when or how—the name Sequana morphed into the word Seine. And the Seine reigned triumphant. "Why weren't one or the other [rivers] considered the mother branch of the river, capable of transmitting the name?" asked Michel Grandin in his 1993 book *Rivières de France*. He answered his own question: "Because the Seine is a sacred river, whose source is of divine origin."

# PART TWO

## Westward from Burgundy

*Signs mark the source of the Seine at the Plateau of Langres in Burgundy. The center sign indicates that the source belongs to the city of Paris.* ANDREW PLUMP.

# FOUR

# The Ancient Source

*The Seine is a silent river. She has no*
*torrents or waterfalls. She sinks and*
*meanders and has great difficulty*
*getting to the sea. She takes her time.*
*I have lived Sequana from the inside.*
*She has touched me and talked to me*
*even in her silence.*

**—ANTOINE HOAREAU**

on the origins of the Seine

THE FRENCH LEARN AS CHILDREN where the Seine begins. They memorize the fact in geography class: "The Seine takes its source at the Plateau of Langres." But the source itself is hard to find. GPS and cell phone service go dead in that forgotten corner of Burgundy. Except for warnings of deer crossings, few signposts dot the back roads that wind through farm fields and tree-covered valleys. No train passes through, and Dijon, the closest metropolis, is about an hour's drive southeast.

Saint-Germain-Source-Seine, the tiny village closest to the springs that give birth to the Seine, is a victim of the erosion of small-town

France. Its church is closed, its cemetery crumbling, its shops shuttered. On paper, Saint-Germain-Source-Seine no longer exists; it has merged administratively with another village down the road. But the people who live in and around it are proud ambassadors of the source of the Seine, especially on holidays. One year, Antoine Hoareau, a self-taught historian of the river's origins who lives nearby, invited me to celebrate Bastille Day with the local community and then see the source with him as a guide. I drove there from Paris with Andy, my husband of more than thirty years and my partner in exploring France.

We sat outdoors near Saint-Germain-Source-Seine's town square, at long tables under a tent, for a three-hour lunch served with a sparkling pink *crémant* to start, followed by a local red. I sidestepped the 60-proof absinthe, but when an older man with a charming smile poured me a double shot of *eau de vie de poire* that he'd made at home with local pears and grain alcohol, how could I say no? The crowd belted out renditions of "La Marseillaise" and the *chanson ban bourguignon*, a regional tune for festive occasions involving hand-waving and clapping. When lunch ended and games of *boules* began, Hoareau was ready for our adventure.

Hoareau, who is in his thirties, works full-time as a city official in Dijon, but the origins of the Seine are his lifelong passion. Since 2003, he has been a leader of the seventy-member Friends of the Sources of the Seine, a group founded in 1992. He has written a short book and participated in television documentaries on the subject.

We drove along a narrow tree-lined road, stopping when we came to a sign that read, "City of Paris, Domaine of the Sources of the Seine." Ignoring the intermittent rain, the three of us followed a flight of concrete steps down a short hill. A ten-acre park with picnic tables, benches, garbage bins, and a gravel walking path awaited us.

"You are now back in Paris," said Hoareau.

Paris? The central point of Paris—located at Notre-Dame—is 178 miles away by car and 157 on foot, so why is a piece of it here? Launching into a history lesson, Hoareau explained that Napoléon III was inspired by the history of the Roman Empire after its conquest of Gaul. Incorporating the source of the Seine into the city of Paris was his way of enlarging the symbolic power of his reign. He ordered Baron Haussmann to define the source of the river and mark the place with a grotto and fountain. In 1864, the Municipal Council of Paris bought the springs and the surrounding land, built a park, planted fir trees, and declared it part of Paris, sort of a disconnected arrondissement. With a budget of about €25,000 a year, Paris pays to mow the lawns, clear the trash, repair the paths, and cut down dead trees at a site that few Parisians visit; only about twenty thousand people in total come each year.

Hoareau led us to the grotto at the far southern end of the site. It was pieced together with stones taken from the surrounding fields and shelters a graceless stone sculpture of a nymph. A local artist, François Jouffroy, chiseled the first statue of her in 1868. A plaque credited

*Stone sculpture of a nymph in a grotto created during the reign of Napoléon III at the "official" spot where the Seine River begins.* ANDREW PLUMP.

Napoléon III with constructing the grotto for the city of Paris, because "Paris owes its prosperity to the Seine."

The 1868 nymph did not fare well. During World War I, according to the Association des Sources de la Seine archives, American soldiers used her for target practice. In 1934, a Dijon sculptor named Paul Auban redesigned and rebuilt her, without noticeable improvement.

The nymph is naked except for a cloth draped over her right leg, her pubic area covered by a bunch of grapes. (We were in Burgundy wine country, after all.) She reclines on a rock in the middle of the grotto. Her breasts defy gravity. She holds a cornucopia in her right hand and gazes over her shoulder.

"Her feet are too big," said Hoareau. "And her hands—they are not even trucker's hands. They're worse! And her expression! She stares at the Seine with a silent, masculine glare."

"You don't like her?" I asked.

"It is not that I do not like her," he said. "But she is a pure invention. We are in the typical style of the nineteenth century. So there has to be a statue of a female creature, with a voluptuous body, posed in a languorous way, with a cornucopia in her hand to symbolize the wealth that the Seine will bring to all the people who live on its banks. Worse, she is confused with Sequana, and she is *not* Sequana."

Even before Rome ruled Gaul, pilgrims came to the river's source to worship at Sequana's temple, traveling with their offerings from as far as the English Channel. They believed the temple was a sacred place, capable of delivering miracles. According to a pagan legend, the pure water rose up from an invisible spring, imbuing the site with supernatural powers.

But that is history, and nothing about the current grotto is authentic. Hoareau pointed to its base, where water bubbled up from a small hole covered with a round metal grate. "That's the 'official' source," he said, his voice dripping with derision. That little hole in a man-made limestone grotto in the middle of nowhere is where the Seine begins? It felt improbable. But it was the most remote location to which the Seine could be traced.

Tourists throw coins into the grotto's pool and make a wish. Hoareau recalled a story from his youth. He and his cousin Anne-Charlotte were fourteen when the euro was about to replace the French franc on New Year's Day 1999. The two teenagers received euro coins already in circulation as presents on Christmas and rushed to the source. "We had a small pouch with the first euros ever made," Hoareau said. "I think we were the first people to throw euros into the source of the Seine!"

I threw a two-euro coin into the pool and wished hard.

From the grotto, a pipe carries the Seine's water underground through a field of grass and moss, until it emerges a few hundred feet away, under a stone footbridge. A caretaker who once lived there built the bridge, the first one encountered by the Seine on its westward journey, and the smallest.

As we made our way from the grotto into the field, we passed a modern sculpture of Sequana, created by a local sculptor named Eric de Laclos. Bits of straw and small plants lay at her feet, offerings, perhaps, from modern-day Druids, descendants of the religious, political, and medical authorities who conducted purification rituals at the source of the Seine in pre-Roman times.

The ground was wet and spongy beneath our feet. Hoareau said that other underground springs moved in a network, flowing not from the mountains but from reservoirs deep below the surface. "Look around," he told us. "The great paradox at the sources of the Seine is that we do not see one gush of water. There's water all around our feet. There is the one we see here, but turn around, and look—there's another spring, at the foot of the little hill there. Then there are two others in the grass." The number of underground springs erupting above ground varies, depending on the season and the rainfall. There are seven permanent sources, but as many as fifteen sources in early springtime.

The site sits in a narrow recess in the limestone Plateau of Langres, which connects the Vosges and Morvan Mountains and dates to the Jurassic period, roughly 200 million years ago. Fresh water flows from higher ground into deep underground reservoirs. Below the soil is a layer of clay and below that a layer of limestone. The limestone filters the water, the clay tightens, and the water forces its way through the surface. When the Seine overflowed during the flood of 2016, an excess of water turned the field into a giant pool.

So the Seine has not one source but many that spring from this concentrated area in Source-Seine. "There is a proverb that says it's the little streams that make the big rivers, and so the Seine starts like that," Hoareau explained. "It is pure, it is beautiful, and it is a little bit magical."

As we walked, the landscape changed from a marshy open meadow into a tangle of reeds, weeds, and trees. Hoareau led us on a narrow path under a canopy of green. Here, the Seine was a collection of clear, shallow pools in an emerald-green swamp flowing into a narrow creek. Hoareau stopped at one of the pools and dared me to drink.

"Is the water clean?" I asked.

"Ah, yes," he replied.

I tried to stall. I knew that half the drinking water of Paris comes from the Seine and Marne rivers, but that water is carefully filtered and purified. "Is this considered the water of the Seine?" I asked.

"It is the water of the Seine, of course! You can drink the water of the Seine here! Ah, yes!"

"Pesticides?"

"There are no pesticides."

Hoareau explained that visitors have drunk from this spring since antiquity. "It is very good and fresh," he said. "We are raised on the water of the Seine. Many Parisians envy us!"

Indeed, this was not Paris, where the river is murky brown much of the time. To prove his point, Hoareau bent over, cupped his hands over a pool of water bubbling up from the ground, scooped, and slurped.

Andy and I followed suit. The water was neither chalky, like Evian, nor metallic, like Aquafina. It was sweet and pure with no trace of calcium or sodium, and certainly no chlorine taste or smell of Parisian tap water.

"You can now say that you drank the water of the Seine at its source!" Hoareau proclaimed.

The water bubbling up from the ground converged into a narrow stream a few feet away, the first evidence of the Seine as a river. "What you're about to do—you're going to physically straddle the river," Hoareau said. "Put one foot on the right bank and the other on the left at the same time." I did so, my feet sinking into the muddy marsh.

The story of the Gallo-Roman temple begins with the Celts—or, since we're in France, the Celtic Gauls, the people who inhabited Gaul before the Romans came and conquered. The Gauls believed that the spring had healing powers. Hoareau led us to a channel made of flagstones that carried water into a catchment basin hollowed out from a stone slab. "You see that bubbling water there, on the stones? Do you realize where you are?" he asked.

I did not. He said we were at an important site of what could have been a small, square temple sacred to the Gauls before the Romans came and built their own. He pointed out a stone at our feet that would have been one corner of the temple, then walked on and pointed out the three others. "It is almost certain—almost—that if we dug here, we could maybe find holes for the foundations of pillars and entrances that would allow us to verify that the Gauls already worshipped at the sources of the Seine." he said. "We could really discover so many things!"

WHEN THE ROMANS CONQUERED the Gauls, they integrated earlier Gallic cultural practices into their own and built a new temple complex on the original site. They enlarged the spring where the goddess Sequana was worshipped into a grand, three-hundred-foot-long healing complex and built terraces, buildings, and courtyards on the marshland. One of the buildings contained small alcoves where pagan priests may have lived and received pilgrims in need of spiritual guidance and medical care.

A narrow, man-made stone trench channeled rivulets of Seine water from its source through the temple complex and into its heart: an oval cement healing basin of water. Pilgrims came to drink and bathe in the water, deposit offerings, say prayers, seek help, and give thanks. There was a dormitory where they could stay and rest for several days. Perhaps they believed that Sequana would appear to them in a dream; perhaps she would deliver them from pain or disease. The temple integrated the ebbs and flows of the river so that it literally wound its way through the architecture. Then it turned and moved toward Paris.

The remnants of the Gallo-Roman temple should be the star attraction of the site. But the sanctuary sits forlorn and forgotten at the bottom of the park, off-limits to visitors and buried under marshy land choked with brambles and reeds. It has been closed to the public since the last archaeological dig, in 1967. Informational panels attached to a low, nondescript metal fence announce a "protected archaeological site" with "access forbidden."

But no one else was around. Hoareau climbed over the fence and told us to follow. "Even if we do not see very much, we have to go and look," he said.

We climbed over into forbidden territory.

As we walked on, Hoareau showed us two steps carved from one block of stone. It was there that a large stone statue of Sequana is thought to have stood. The temple was big business in Roman times, not unlike the shrine of Lourdes in southwest France today. A great esplanade, surrounded with workshops and boutiques, most likely served as a welcome center. Artisans crafted and sold ex-votos—votive offerings—to the traveling pilgrims. These included objects carved from stone and oak, modeled in clay, or hammered in bronze or base metal. They were made to represent parts of the body that needed healing. The pilgrim would explain the location of the ailment, the artisan would fabricate a votive of the affected body part, and then the pilgrim would throw the totem into the sacred pool.

By the fourth or fifth century, the temple had been desecrated and destroyed. The priests and artisans had fled. A century later, Christian church councils campaigned to eliminate pagan practices like the worship of Sequana, wrote Simone-Antoinette Deyts, the archaeologist who studied the site for years, in *Scientific American* in 1971. She quoted a sixth-century directive that stated, "Destroy the springs and the groves they dare call sacred. . . . Be certain you will be cured by no other means than by invoking the cross of Christ."

The church decided that the Seine needed a Christian saint, not a pagan goddess, as inspiration. It identified a local nobleman turned monk named Sigo and called him Seigne, after the river.

As a young priest, Seigne was attacked by seven bandits in a forest that belonged to his father, a wealthy landowner. As the bandits were about to kill him, Seigne got on his knees and begged God to convert them to Christianity. His prayers were answered. They converted and devoted their lives to serving God; some became saints. To give thanks, Seigne built an abbey and church and began a campaign of conversion. He received a large gift of land from his father and invited people living in the area to use it. They cut trees for firewood and cleared forests to plant crops. Seigne became a patron saint of the harvest.

In the town to be called Saint-Seine-l'Abbaye, six miles from the source and the temple, a thirteenth-century abbey of the same name tells the saint's life story through a long fresco, finished in 1504. The paint is peeling, the walls damaged by water. But there he is, pale-faced and serious, with wispy light hair, in his black monk's robes. These days the church is mostly empty; the adjoining abbey is a center for troubled teenagers. An annual local harvest festival in his honor ended long ago. Saint Seigne is a forgotten saint, but the goddess Sequana lives on.

Hoareau is determined to make the source of the Seine known to all. He comes often, hoping to unlock more of its secrets and expand the site to attract more visitors. He envisions a picnic area, a network of walls and passages, an esplanade, and boutiques. The temple site has never been properly excavated for all to see. There is no money from benefactors to restore it, no political will to develop it, no American Friends of the Sources of the Seine the way there are "American Friends" of French national treasures like Versailles and the Louvre. Even if a massive excavation were undertaken, there might be little left to see. In the centuries that followed the destruction of the temple, its stones, even the blocks that made up its pillars, were hauled away and used for local construction.

Hoareau takes the long view. "The original source is hidden somewhere underground, protected and safe," he said. "Nobody will steal it from us. We have only begun to tell its story."

*The Seine in the countryside near its source.* ANDREW PLUMP.

*A Gallo-Roman bronze statue of the healing goddess Sequana standing proudly in a duck-billed boat. This relic can be found at the archeological museum in Dijon.*

GABRIELA SCIOLINO PLUMP.

# FIVE

# The Legend of the River

*When Neptune stretched out his arms to seize her, her body melted into water; her veil and green garments, which the winds blew before her, became emerald-colored waves; she was transformed into a river of that color, which still delights in wandering the places she loved as a nymph.*

—JACQUES-HENRI BERNARDIN DE SAINT-PIERRE, *L'Arcadie*

I CAME FACE-TO-FACE with Sequana in an obscure museum in Dijon. During my visit to the source of the Seine, I had been told her story. Now here she was: a nineteen-inch, sixteen-and-a-half-pound, two-thousand-year-old Gallo-Roman bronze statue encased in protective glass. She stands elegant in a boat, her head inclined, her left leg slightly bent. The prow of her boat is the head of a duck that holds a round object—a pomegranate perhaps—in its long bill; the stern is the duck's upswept tail.

The Musée Archéologique de Dijon is a hidden jewel, housed in a former Benedictine abbey with high stone ceilings and grand halls. It is the receptacle for the region's ancient artifacts, a beneficiary of the French state's policy of leaving some of the treasures of history where they are found, instead of relocating them to Paris. Sequana is displayed prominently in a long, vaulted room and is the star of the museum's collection. "I find her superb," said Frédérique Bouvard, the museum's curator. "She is our Mona Lisa."

The goddess is the most important symbol of the river. Were she to receive the recognition she deserves, she could become the most important female icon in France. But the museum operates with modest ambitions and a small budget: it offers no multilingual audio guides, no museum catalog, and no video telling Sequana's story. Not enough people know about her, although she has given her name to a multinational company that makes paper, a bistro on the Île de la Cité, a wine label, a houseboat moored in Rouen, an association that restores hundred-year-old boats, an office building in a Paris suburb, a folk-metal song, and even to an interior design business run by an Irishwoman married to a Frenchman.

The museum arranged for a private viewing, so that I could see Sequana in all her glory. I was allowed to bring along a photographer. (The last time Sequana had been photographed professionally was about half a century ago.) We arrived one morning for a most unusual unveiling. Two technicians wearing protective gloves unlocked and removed Sequana's heavy glass case. One of them lifted her up and cradled her in his arms as gently as if she were a newborn. He carried her up several flights of stairs and set her on a table covered in heavy white protective paper. "We rarely move her and never lend her to other museums, because she is too fragile," said Sophie Casadebaig, the museum's director. "She hasn't been seen like this for decades."

Slim and small-breasted, Sequana wears a flowing dress that exposes her forearms and part of her chest and falls in pleats to the floor, revealing the tips of her pointed slippers. A sash with an elaborate knot holds the garment in place. A robe trimmed with pearls is fixed to her right arm by five Roman brooches. A large, broad crown partially covers her wavy hair, which is parted in the middle and tied at the back of her neck. Long tresses frame her face.

She is young, with large eyes and refined features, and wears a look of anticipation. Her forearms are outstretched as if in a gesture of welcome. Her right hand once held an object that was lost long ago, said Casadebaig—perhaps a plate, a bowl, or a cornucopia of fruit. "There are so many unknowns about her," she added.

One of the technicians took a fine-haired brush and wiped away loose dust that had settled in Sequana's crevices and folds, revealing her many colors—flat brown, gray, and green; shiny bronze; and tiny specks of white powder where oxidation had taken hold. I moved as close as I could without touching her.

THE FIRST EVIDENCE of the name Sequana comes in eleven ancient inscriptions found on the site of the temple at the source. The cult of Sequana flourished under Roman rule. Her temple complex is believed to have been destroyed in the fourth or fifth century A.D., and over time, Sequana was forgotten. In the middle of the nineteenth century, archaeologists began to comb through the site where the temple complex once stood. It yielded odd treasures, including a large fourth-century terra-cotta vase. Its neck bore an inscription: *Deae Sequana Rufus donavit*—"Rufus gave this to the goddess Sequana." Inside were 120 small bronze votive offerings and more than eight hundred third- and fourth-century Roman bronze coins.

In 1933, Henry Corot, a landowner and self-taught archaeologist from Dijon, and his team were responsible for the discovery of the bronze statue of Sequana that now captivated me. Corot often turned up at the temple site at four in the morning. On the day Sequana was found, some six years after he began excavations, he had become so discouraged that he had instructed his team to clean up the site, and then packed his things up and left.

Antoine Hoareau, my guide to the source waters, told the story: "His men were removing all the gravel and dirt when they hit a large stone slab. Underneath they found two ancient bronze statues. One was a young fawn; the other was Sequana. They ran to the train station and saw Corot as he was ready to get on the train. They yelled, 'Monsieur Corot! Monsieur Corot! We found bronzes. Hurry back!'"

He rushed back. He deduced that the bronzes had evaded him because they had been removed from the temple and hidden nearby to elude robbers. He called the discovery of the bronzes "the treasure of the springs of the Seine!" and described Sequana as "majestic," with "an air of goodness and compassion."

Corot concluded that Sequana had been built in three parts: a base, which had probably been attached with metal nails to a wooden plate; a bronze boat in the shape of a duck, soldered to the base; and the statue of Sequana, soldered to the boat. Corot speculated that the object in the duck's bill might have been what he called "an Alpine gooseberry."

Corot had a grand vision for what the temple site could become. In his formal report on the discovery, he wrote, "There remains much to be done to comb the ancient ground of the Temple, find what is left of its walls, clean the immense pool that stretched from its western façade, so that we can return this Gallo-Roman site, unique in the world, to something of the sumptuous appearance it had in the first centuries of our era."

That never happened.

Instead, the treasures yielded over the years were sent to the Dijon archaeological museum. One is what's left of a large stone statue of Sequana that used to stand in her temple. It was vandalized sometime after Christianity took root in France, and now sits headless and armless in the museum. A modern sculpture, an imagining of what she might have looked like, has been erected at the temple complex at the source of the Seine.

The museum also houses some fifteen hundred ex-votos, votive offerings in wood, stone, and bronze that pilgrims gave to Sequana, hoping her healing energies would cure their illnesses and alleviate their suffering. Some were masterfully sculpted from wood, others mass-produced. One group of offerings consists of four hundred larger-than-life representations of pilgrims hewn from chunks of oak, unearthed in the 1960s—the largest collection of wooden Gallic sculptures ever found. The collection also includes effigies of body parts carved from local limestone or wood: heads, eyes, breasts, arms, legs, and sexual and internal organs that were thought to need healing. Statuettes of women with big bellies and of couples locked in embrace suggest a desire for a child. One figure, with breasts and a penis, represents a hermaphrodite. Statuettes of children holding puppies or rabbits may have been tokens from parents giving thanks. A head without a mouth or ears suggests deafness, and a head wrapped in a towel, migraines. Other statuettes were abstract or decorative, their purpose unknown. There were also small bronze plaques, thin pieces of crudely worked metal, depicting sexual organs, breasts, and stylized eyes.

In 2016, the cities of Paris, Rouen, and Le Havre sponsored Réinventer la Seine (Reinvent the Seine), a competition to develop twenty-three sites along the length of the river. The goal was to create a new way of living with the water. "Entrepreneurs, investors, artists, associations, and others are invited to submit their ideas," the organizers stated. I knew I could never help fulfill Corot's dream of restoring the ancient temple site to its original grandeur. But what if a grand replica of Sequana could be erected? She would be a fitting match to the one-quarter-sized replica of the Statue of Liberty that sits on an island in the Seine in Paris. I decided to enter the idea in the competition.

A pre-Christian healing goddess with no ties to any living religion, Sequana would fit nicely into the official French policy that reveres the republican ideal. She could be the secular version of Joan of Arc, the warrior-martyr, and of Our Lady of Lourdes, the miracle worker. She could be the idealized embodiment of freedom, without the republican weight of Marianne leading citizens to liberty. As Sequana was a healing goddess, we could create an NGO to help women in need of spiritual or physical healing.

I created, printed, and bound a dossier with historical texts, color photographs, and a pitch. I submitted formal applications—one each to the cities of Paris, Rouen, and Le Havre. Paris had the most sites where a statue could be situated, but Le Havre, at the river's end, seemed an especially good fit for a proposal celebrating its source. Over the next few months, I told just about anyone who might help about the Sequana project. Casadebaig, from the archaeological museum of Dijon, was excited about it. She told me that if I wanted to produce any replica of her Sequana—from key chains to a monumental statue—the exclusive reproduction rights belonged to the museum. *Bien sûr.*

THERE IS ANOTHER Sequana story, the fictional tale of "the nymph of the Seine." In the seventeenth century, the playwright Jean Racine composed "The Nymph of the Seine to the Queen," a lyrical poem marking the marriage of Louis XIV to the infanta Maria Theresa of Spain. In the poem, the river nymph, who is not named, both welcomes the queen to France and serves as the voice of the country.

The eighteenth-century writer and traveler Jacques-Henri Bernardin de Saint-Pierre embellished the story. Born in Le Havre and best known for *Paul et Virginie*, a novel of innocent love, Bernardin de Saint-Pierre imagined the origins of the Seine in his 1781 political utopia, *L'Arcadie*. In it he tells the story of a beautiful and high-spirited nymph, Sequana, born to the wine god Bacchus and an unidentified mother. Bernardin de Saint-Pierre injects Sequana into the ancient Greek myth of Persephone (whom the Romans called Proserpine), the daughter of Demeter (or Ceres in Roman mythology), the goddess of the harvest.

There are variations in the story in both Greek and Roman mythology. In one classic Greek version, Persephone is picking flowers in a meadow when Hades, the god of the underworld, rises through a chasm in the ground, kidnaps her, and pulls her down into his kingdom. A nymph who was with Persephone weeps so much that she turns into a pool of salt water. Demeter searches ceaselessly for her daughter, and eventually Zeus intervenes on Demeter's behalf and returns Persephone to her. But Persephone has eaten food in the underground world—a small number of pomegranate seeds—and is doomed to spend her winter months there, returning to the earth's surface only in the spring.

In retelling the story, Bernardin de Saint-Pierre used the Roman mythological names and portrayed Sequana as one of the handmaidens of Ceres (Demeter). Ceres travels the world searching for her daughter, and Sequana helps her when she comes to Gaul. When Ceres eventually succumbs to defeat, Sequana asks for the farm fields that surround them as compensation. Ceres agrees and, in an added gesture, grants Sequana the gift of making wheat grow wherever she walks. Worried that Sequana could suffer the same fate as her own daughter, Ceres assigns the nymph Heva and her team to watch over her.

One day when Sequana is collecting shells and playing in the waves at the seaside, Heva spots Neptune, the god of the sea, swimming deep under the waves. She recognizes him by his flowing white hair, purplish face, and blue robes. Neptune has just come from the North Sea, where he witnessed an earthquake, and is now roaming the seas, checking that his shores are secure.

"Upon seeing him, Heva uttered a piercing cry and warned the Seine [Sequana], who quickly fled to the fields," Bernandin de Saint-

Pierre writes. But Neptune has already spotted Sequana, and, "struck by her grace and her nimble movements, he drove his seahorses onto the shore in pursuit. He had nearly overtaken her, when she called out to her father Bacchus, and her mistress Ceres. Both answered her pleas: when Neptune reached out his arms to seize her, her body melted into water; her veil and green garments, which the winds blew before her, became emerald-colored waves; she was transformed into a river of that color, which still delights in wandering the places she loved as a nymph."

Heva dies of grief from losing Sequana. Her nymphs build a steep cliff of black-and-white stones in her honor. The cliff, two miles north of Le Havre, goes by the name Le Cap de la Hève. It marks the northernmost point of the Bay of the Seine, the place where the Seine meets the sea. Like Heva watching over Sequana, her name-sake cliff protects sailors from shipwreck, its forbidding rock face warning them of danger. The other nymphs who fled inland with Sequana were transformed into the Seine's largest tributaries, the Aube, Yonne, Marne, and Oise, and "all the other rivers that come to the Seine to give their waters to their former mistress," writes Bernardin de Saint-Pierre.

Charles Nodier retold the Sequana myth in an 1836 work, *La Seine et ses bords*. The book includes an engraving of Neptune, bearded and fierce-looking, his feet planted firmly on the ground, his muscular arms wrapped around Sequana's waist. Apparently carried away by lust, he has dropped his trident, which lies on the ground behind him. A terrified Sequana raises her arms high in the air as she struggles to break free. The sky is dark. The sea rushes forward, foaming at their feet.

Neptune's obsession with Sequana continues after she becomes the Seine. Twice a day, he thunders loudly and forces seawater into the river. Sequana so hates her pursuer that whenever he tries to overtake her, she keeps her green river waters separate from Neptune's salty azure sea, "fleeing inland to the fields, retreating to her source, against her natural course," Bernardin de Saint-Pierre writes. Unlike Persephone, who fell victim to her abductor, Sequana escapes.

I find it comforting to imagine that her iron will explains the tides that come twice a day along the Seine—the odd ebbs and flows, the currents, waves, and churning water fighting the powerful sea.

*Jean-Pierre Fleury grows grapes and produces Champagne on his family's thirty-seven acre vineyard near the village of Courteron.* BÉRENGÈRE SIM.

# SIX

# Champagne
# on the Seine

*I live in the Champagne cork.*

—OLD SAYING of the residents
of the historic center of Troyes

I USED TO THINK that "Champagne country" meant the vast vineyards around the cities of Reims and Épernay. The grandest among them have rich histories and lofty labels like Veuve Clicquot, Ruinart, Dom Pérignon, Bollinger. They are situated in the Marne Valley, where most Champagne is produced. But one day my friend Jean-Claude Ribaut told me about a smaller, less prosperous Champagne region two hours' drive south of Paris. "There is a valley and four rivers run through it," he said. "The rivers look like the fingers of a hand. One of them is the Seine."

Champagne on the Seine? The phrase suggests sipping the pale bubbly beverage from a crystal flute on a river cruise. In fact, it is a lush, little-known, and underappreciated grape-growing region en route to Paris from the source of the Seine. Under French law, not just anyone can produce Champagne. The French adhere to classifications and hierarchies as their way of defining excellence. The only sparkling wine in the world that can be labeled authentic "Champagne" must be made from grapes grown on officially designated plots of land in France. Since

the early twentieth century, government-appointed experts have drawn
and redrawn Champagne country. The designated vineyards enjoy a status denoted by *Appellation d'Origine Contrôlée*, or AOC, a coveted, con-
voluted certification that authenticates the content, method, and origin
of production of a French agricultural item. Champagne topsoil must be
light and not too rich, its subsoil chalky, its fields neither too vulnerable
to frost nor too close to forests. Most designated vineyards are on slopes
that face south. The Champagne industry now pulls in $6 billion a year,
and land designated to grow Champagne grapes can be two hundred
times more valuable than ordinary French farmland.

Jean-Claude is one of France's most respected food writers, and when
he offers to take me along on a trip, I never say no. Early one frigid January morning, the two of us went looking for a different kind of Champagne in the Côte des Bar, the main growing area of the Aube region.
We traveled southeast from Paris by train to Troyes, then rented a car
and headed several miles farther southeast to the hamlet of Villeneuve.
After we drove past an abandoned paper-making factory and a church
closed years ago, we crossed a tiny bridge. A narrow, fast-moving stream
with stretches of rapids flowed underneath. It was our first glimpse of the
Seine, still a young river and far from Paris.

In antiquity, the Gallo-Romans drained the marshlands bordering
several rivers around Troyes, including the narrow Seine. In 1115, a mystical cleric, Saint Bernard, founded an abbey at Clairvaux, in the Aube
region to the east. It became a center of learning—and a pioneer in agri-
culture. Its monks were the first in the region to develop a sophisticated
system of vineyards and to produce wine in a serious way; according to a
seventeenth-century text, although it couldn't be determined definitely,
the wines were probably "effervescent."

In the Middle Ages, the Aube became the wealthiest of the Champagne regions. Its wines were sought by the area's dukes and counts.
There was easy transportation to the trade fairs of Troyes, where merchants from as far away as the Rhône and Italy came to buy.

Fortune did not smile on the Aube, however. In 1911, the big houses
to the north, in the Marne Valley, excluded the Aube from Champagne

designation. The *vignerons*—cultivators of grapes to make wine—of the south rioted in protest. An unhappy compromise was reached: the Aube Champagne makers were granted a designation as *Basse-Champagne* or *Champagne 2ᵉ Zone*—"Low Champagne" or "Champagne of Second Rank." It took another sixteen years before the National Assembly passed a law that defined the Champagne regions according to growing conditions like climate and topography, allowing the vineyards of the south to qualify. Nevertheless, the second-class reputation clung to the region. No southern vineyard received the highest designations of *grand cru* or *premier cru*. The Aube *vignerons* found it more profitable to sell their grapes to the big production houses up north.

But in recent years, as the global thirst for Champagne has grown, the southern *vignerons* have asserted themselves and created their own identity. The Champagne makers up north rely on sophisticated blending, produce massively, and evoke big-name luxury. Champagnes from the south have become desirable for their artisanal, creative feel. The southerners tend to be small and independent, making Champagne in their own way, from grapes they grow themselves. They focus on *terroir*, an elusive concept that involves soil, sun, rain, region, and authenticity.

Only about 25 percent of Champagne acreage is located in the south. A tasting tour of southern Champagne houses does not rank on the scale of visits to the huge houses up north, where Champagne domains are lined up one after another, and many are open only by appointments made months in advance. In the south you are more likely to find yourself driving on little-traveled back roads to modest vineyards where you might get a private tour and a tasting conducted by the *vignerons* themselves. You might pass through the village of Celles-sur-Ource, whose entrance is marked by an enormous sculpture of a Champagne bottle made from empty bottles of the wine. Or you might stop in Colombey-les-Deux-Églises, where French president Charles de Gaulle spent the last years of his life and is buried. Then there is Essoyes, where Auguste Renoir and his family lived for many years; a tour of the village includes a tasting in which different Champagnes are matched with images of Renoir's paintings.

Jean-Claude and I first stopped at the Champagne estate of Château

Devaux to meet Laurent Gillet, its owner at the time. The château is a large, eighteenth-century manor house with a tower, a dovecote, and a centuries-old well. A large tasting table with built-in metal spittoons dominates a futuristic white tasting room. As we sampled the vintages, Gillet explained how he came to own the domain, which the Devaux family created in 1846. Jean-Pol Auguste Devaux, the most recent family owner, had no children, and sold it to Gillet, his distributor, in 1987. The manor house was included for free—almost; the condition was that every year, the Devauxs would receive sixty bottles of Champagne.

We tasted several vintages. Among them was a Devaux Grande Réserve Brut made mostly with pinot noir grapes. "Powerful, alive, eccentric," said Jean-Claude. "Very much an acquired taste." It was stronger than much of the Champagne up north, with a distinctive mineral taste. This was not subtle, fruity elegance.

The middle of winter is not the best time to wander through vine-

*A view of the Champagne estate Château Devaux, which has been on the banks of the Seine since 1846.* COLOMBIER MANOIR CHAMPAGNE DEVAUX © OUTSIGN DELAFLOTTE.

yards; the vines have been pruned and look stunted, naked, and gnarled. But Gillet had something special to show us. He led us through the side door and along a path that cut through the garden. We found ourselves standing in front of a long iron railing. Below us was a fast-moving stream. The Seine! We were fifty miles north of the river's source. Here, the Seine is about thirty yards across and only a few feet deep, too shallow for a boat, except perhaps the puniest rowboat. The water was so clear that I could see bright green ferns and reeds and gray and brown stones on the sandy bottom. On the opposite bank was an untamed jungle of trees, bushes, grasses, and shrubs competing for space.

"This is the only Champagne house in France that borders the Seine," said Gillet. "I have friends in Paris who come here and see the water and they ask, 'Is it really the Seine? The same Seine?' For Parisians the Seine is artificial, a regulated flow of dark, murky water channeled into a canal. I tell them here the Seine water is so clean that my father drank from it when he was a boy. I tell them I spent my childhood swimming in the Seine."

Jean-Claude and I traveled deeper into Champagne country with Jean-Pierre Fleury, a friend and neighbor of Gillet's. Unlike Gillet, who bought his way into Champagne, Fleury was born into it. With his ruddy complexion and callused hands, he retains the look of a man who is close to the soil. We hopped into his Audi and followed the curves of the Seine, passing an old grain mill once powered by water from the river. We stopped at the ruins of a *lavoir*, a nineteenth-century outdoor version of a laundromat, where laundresses came to wash clothes and linens by hand. Modern for its time, it was built with a pulley and chain to draw water from the Seine and a stove to heat it.

A serpentine path led us past fields where beets, sunflowers, and corn grow and brought us to the family's thirty-seven-acre Champagne estate near the village of Courteron. The estate stands next to a twelfth-century stone church, closed years ago, but with its bells still programmed to ring loudly on the hour.

For four generations, the Fleury family has grown grapes in the Seine Valley. In 1894, Fleury's grandfather Émile became the first farmer in the region to plant grafted pinot noir vines after phylloxera, a ravenous aphid-like parasite accidentally imported from North America, wiped out almost all the vineyards of France. The grafted vines brought the French fields back to life. Then, in 1911, when the Aube *vignerons* demanded full recognition for their Champagne, Émile Fleury played a key role as the secretary of the movement. "My grandfather was a pioneer and a rebel," Fleury said.

Fleury led us through the main entrance of his "château," an unlit garage furnished with one oak barrel, and into a starkly bare tasting room that held one long table, chairs, and a bar. A refrigerator stood in the corner, and a translucent rock crystal as big as a honeydew melon sat in the middle of the table. On one wall was a photograph of the Fleury family's harvest in 1895. A horse was pulling a plow. "The horse was rented," said Fleury. "We didn't have the money to buy one. Poverty was a way of life for the nineteenth-century Fleurys. It was a time when dinner was three potatoes and a bit of lard."

I later learned more about the poverty of this region in those days from my close friend Julia. Her late husband's Parisian parents retired in the early 1960s to a tiny village not far from the Seine. It was a poor community. "People lived on small plots of land in primitive houses with dirt floors and no appliances or central heating," said Julia. "Every house had a barnyard full of hens, ducks, and rabbits. Some people had a horse that could pull a cart or pull a plow in the vineyards. The region was called La Champagne Pouilleuse—which means 'the lousy Champagne region,' because the soil was so poor and chalky that most crops couldn't grow.

"The big surprise," she continued, "is that you would go into their houses and they'd open a bottle of Champagne. That was the wine they produced and drank. It was such a contrast to the poverty of their lives."

The farmers' fortunes changed when they formed a cooperative to market their grapes. "By the late seventies they were buying refrigerators and washing machines," Julia said.

Fleury had wanted to escape rural life. He dreamed of becoming an astronomer, and at first he refused to go into the family business. But his father ordered him to quit his formal education after high school and stay on the farm. "I was truly upset, truly unhappy," he told us. "But I was the only son. I gave myself over to the vines."

Eventually, he poured his curiosity and love of science into the vineyard. In 1989 he transformed the Fleury vines into a biodynamic enterprise—a first in all of Champagne country. Biodynamic farming, based on principles developed by the philosopher Rudolf Steiner in the early 1900s, centers on respect for the earth's ecosystems, and Fleury has incorporated some of his own theories. He has abandoned the use of horse-drawn plows in the vineyards, instead turning the soil over with hand tools. The grapes are cut by hand. He extols the importance of using cow dung to create "horn manure," which enhances the microbiological life of the earth, and explains that finely ground rock crystals will produce "horn silica," which improves photosynthesis. He does not bottle Champagne when harsh local winds blow or when the moon is full. "There is a connection among the earth, the vines, the sky, and the planets," he said. "It must be respected."

By now, Jean-Claude and I had been tasting Fleury Champagne for more than an hour. Each vintage was better than the one before. All of them held the mineral taste of the land.

Fleury's passion has intoxicated his children. His sons, Benoît and Jean-Sébastien, have joined the family business. His daughter, Morgane, has opened a retail shop on the rue St. Denis in central Paris, where she sells wine—as well as the family Champagne. His wife, Colette, operates a *gîte*—a vacation dwelling for rent—that can accommodate twenty-five people. Its garden is a stone's throw from the Seine. The location offers a place to picnic—and to swim.

I asked Fleury if I could come to the *gîte* and swim when the weather was warmer. I expected him to give me a look that said, "Who is this crazy American woman of a certain age who lives a sophisticated life in Paris but wants to swim in a river?" Instead, he gave me a broad smile and replied, "*Tout à fait!*"—"Absolutely!"

His son Benoît stopped by at that moment, and I asked him if he ever swam in the Seine. "Ah, yes, in the summer," he said. "I often go down for a swim when it is hot and I am done with work. I have it all to myself. The Seine is my private swimming pool."

I knew I would be back.

*The Seine begins to grow in earnest at Châtillon-sur-Seine. The Romanesque Saint-Vorles Church is visible in the background.* ANDREW PLUMP.

# SEVEN

# Paths to Paris

*I forgot everything I was running*
*away from . . . on the edge of*
*the Seine and the forest of*
*Fontainebleau. . . . I felt completely*
*different there, exclusively in love*
*with navigating the river. I honor*
*the river.*

—STÉPHANE MALLARMÉ,
letter to Paul Verlaine in 1885

FROM HER SOURCE until she reaches Paris, the Seine eludes all suitors. Try to follow her course by car, and you'll be lost almost as soon as you start. Set out by boat, and you'll find her early stretches too narrow and shallow to pass through.

You can bike alongside her banks, but this is not the Loire, where devoted cyclists enjoy a 540-mile trail along the river and its surrounding valley, with well-marked itineraries, organized tours, and hotels and campsites nearby. Bike paths line only half the length of the Seine, and many of them are disorganized, badly mapped, and in need of repair.

What about walking? Despite the long arm of French bureaucracy, no agency or travel book has mapped the river's entire pedestrian

length. The best guide to walking the Seine is an official trail called
GR2. There are more than 150 GRs in France—*grandes randonnées*,
or "great hikes," maintained by the French Hiking Federation. You
must consult several books to piece together the Seine trail. Through
research and walking parts of the trail myself, I discovered that GR2
occasionally gets lost in the countryside and forests.

Andy and I set out by car from the Seine's source in the springs of
Saint-Germain-Source-Seine, hoping to track the river's early flow. We
found a back road, but it veered away from the water. In other places,
trees, farms, and private property kept us at a distance.

Outside the village of Chanceaux, about two and a half miles from
the source, a small stream flows under a thirty-two-foot-long stone footbridge. There is a park with tables for picnickers and a walking path.
We followed the path, which crossed the river, moved away from it,
then closer, then out of the river's view. We gave up and decided to find
the Seine's path to Paris in the towns spread along its banks. Road connections are easy, and the elusive river reappears in each town, expanding as Paris gets closer.

That's how we discovered Châtillon-sur-Seine, thirty miles from the
source, and home to one of the most unusual archaeological treasures
of Europe: the Vase of Vix. The Seine flows through the village, splits
around a tiny island, and gets bigger—three feet deep and thirty-six
feet wide in some places. Along one bend, the Seine meets the river
Douix—not really a river but a hundred-yard-long spring that gushes
from beneath a limestone plateau dating from the Jurassic period. Italian aerial attacks early in World War II burned down the historic city
center, but it is a pleasant place, and the town has decorated the bridges
over the narrow waterways with pots of bright flowers. You can climb a
small hill to visit the Romanesque Saint-Vorles Church, which offers a
panoramic view of the town. Behind the church is a cemetery built on
the ruins of a twelfth-century castle.

Few American tourists visit Châtillon-sur-Seine, but more should.
The local museum, once a medieval Cistercian abbey, holds the sixth-

century B.C. tomb of an unidentified Celtic princess who would have been about thirty years old when she died. It was discovered in 1953 five miles away from Châtillon-sur-Seine, near the small town of Vix on Mont Lassois, the highest navigable point on the Seine as it flows downstream.

The princess was buried with a carriage, bronze kitchenware, ceramics, and a heavy, skillfully crafted gold diadem. The tomb also contained a bronze cauldron fit for a giant's cave: the Vase of Vix. At nearly five-and-a-half feet tall and weighing more than 450 pounds, the vase would have held about 300 gallons of wine. It is the largest object of its kind from the ancient world. Stylized Gorgons—with menacing grins, bulging eyes, and snakes for hair—anchor the handles. A line of Greek soldiers and their horses ring the vase's neck. Lions show their claws and muscles. The Vase of Vix is the centerpiece of the museum, and a room has been built around it, with a balcony so that visitors can see it from above. Researchers deduced that the vase, the crown, and other objects were not locally made but originally came from Greece. Their presence in France indicates that the Gauls had rather sophisticated taste and imported goods from the Mediterranean centuries earlier than previously thought.

Later came another blockbuster discovery. In 2007, a team of French and German archaeologists announced that after several years of excavations, they had found a vast, twenty-five-hundred-year-old Celtic fortress town covering 150 acres beneath the Mont Lassois plateau five miles from Vix. There had been a main street leading to an immense palace, houses for hundreds of people, grain warehouses, and water pipes. Panels and photographs in the museum tell the story of the excavation work, which continues every summer. One of its goals is to determine whether Vix was the oldest continuously inhabited community in France and perhaps even the earliest example of urban life in western Europe.

We could have lingered in Châtillon-sur-Seine, but there was so much more to cover. Resuming our drive along the course of the river, we arrived in Troyes, the largest city on the Seine between the source and Paris, and the first one on the route with a significant history of navigation.

Troyes—the name is pronounced "trwah," like *trois*, the number three—has approximately sixty thousand inhabitants. The town is known for its stained-glass windows, andouillette sausage, Gothic churches, sixteenth-century timbered houses, and the world's largest collection of paintings by the Fauvist André Derain. English merchants traded in this area as early as the ninth century, often arriving via the Seine; the expression "troy ounce," a system of tiny weights to measure precious metals and gemstones, is believed to have originated here in the Middle Ages. Troyes also was the birthplace of a twelfth-century poet and monk called Chrétien de Troyes. He wrote *La queste del Saint Graal*, which formed the basis for the Arthurian legends of the quest for the Holy Grail.

As early as the twelfth century, the Seine at Troyes became a marvel of engineering, with a system of canals, aqueducts, and dikes. It supported water mills and opened the area to craftsmen. As Troyes was on the road from Italy to Flanders, it played host to great trade fairs renowned for their tanned animal skins and textiles. The town's proximity to the river, coupled with the poor state of rural roads, meant that many traders chose to use the Seine to travel, transport their wares, and ship purchases to and from Paris. In a coincidental foreshadowing of the region's role in Champagne production, Troyes took the shape of a Champagne cork. Nobility and clergy lived in the rounded head, where the cathedral stood; the lower classes lived in the stem. The town's historic center has retained that shape. Even today, inhabitants of Troyes and official documents often refer to the old part of the city as the Bouchon de Champagne—the Champagne cork.

In the fourteenth century, Troyes became the first town in France to use mills to turn rags into paper. Then, in 1524, a third of the city burned down and was rebuilt with tall, narrow timbered houses, many of which are still standing. As emperor, Napoléon launched a project to make the Seine navigable westward from Châtillon-sur-Seine through Troyes to Marcilly-sur-Seine and chose Troyes as the location for a large port. The project turned out to be more complicated and expensive than anticipated and was abandoned, but Troyes continued to thrive through its links to other towns along the river. In the nineteenth century, Troyes became notable for manufacturing fabric and hats and was celebrated as the center of the French textile industry. The fabric dyes released into the Seine turned its waters red, blue, yellow, and black.

In the twentieth century, the city's network of canals became unsanitary and difficult to navigate; most were filled in. Troyes's historic center escaped damage during World War II, but the town lacked the money to expand. Although textile production declined sharply in the 1980s and 1990s in the face of foreign competition, it is still crucial for the local economy. So is tourism, thanks to the charming old town center and the cycling paths and walkways that line its defunct canal.

Another important site is the synagogue and cultural center devoted to Rashi, an eleventh-century Jewish scholar and one of the most famous citizens of Troyes. Renowned for his commentaries on the Bible and the Talmud, Rashi created one of the first libraries in France. He remains a fixture in Jewish learning. In his writings, he also recorded details of everyday life—how people dressed, washed, cooked, killed animals, made glass—and how Jews interacted with the Christian world. (Jews could own fields and vineyards, Rashi tells us. They could borrow money from Gentiles, have their clothes laundered and tailored and their horses shoed by Gentiles, and own buildings together with Gentiles.)

Over lunch, Andy ruminated about whether Rashi might have celebrated a Jewish custom called Tashlich. "On the first day of Rosh Hashanah, you walk to a body of water and throw in bread crumbs," he explained. "It's a symbol of throwing away your sins and starting afresh. Maybe Rashi threw bread crumbs into the Seine." Then again, maybe he did not. It turns out that there are no recorded references to Tashlich before the thirteenth or fourteenth centuries, long after Rashi's death.

However, Andy later discovered that Rashi wrote about a custom that was undertaken two to three weeks before Rosh Hashanah. Jews made baskets out of palm leaves and filled them with soil in which they planted beans. On the first evening of Rosh Hashanah, they swung the baskets seven times over their heads and then threw them into the river. Some people believe that the custom could have been a precursor to Tashlich. Andy could not determine whether Rashi himself or the Jews of Troyes during his lifetime ever practiced it. But what a lovely thought.

Since the Seine runs around much of Troyes—only the canals run through it—we had to walk to the edge of town to see the river itself. It took some persistence, but we found a path to the Seine. We started on the riverbank near a public swimming pool, across the street from a Total gas station. It was not the prettiest spot.

A metal barrier blocked our way, and a sign announced that swimming was banned: "Danger zone. Strong current. Risk of drowning. Dangerous river bed. Unstable banks." The water itself looked cool, clear, and not very deep. Plants with long green leaves undulated gracefully in the shallow rapids. The rush of water made a lively sound.

We walked under the shade of tall sycamore trees and passed a sports club and a group of men playing *boules*. The river was channeled into two concrete beds, resembling an artificial canal more than a natural waterway. The stone benches lining the unpaved path faced toward the road, away from the unremarkable river.

Near a local university, the river narrowed and made a double curve. We strolled along a shabby path and passed drab apartment buildings and a forlorn post office. A concrete staircase led down to a riverbank and a lane that a sign said was called "The Alley of the Pretty Jump." It could have been a glorious place for a riverside café, but the wooden benches needed painting and repair, and the "alley" was pockmarked with weeds and littered with plastic and paper. "We can see why the Seine doesn't figure in the collective imagination of Troyes," Andy said.

At the other end of the alley, we climbed a stone staircase, and suddenly the Seine was caressing a tiny island. The concrete walls disappeared, replaced by shallow mudbanks covered with stones. Trees made deep shadows on the water. Lily pads sat on its surface. The river had turned tropical.

At Troyes, the Seine is deep enough for canoes, kayaks, and even small motorboats. But the French governmental river authority does not consider the river officially navigable until it is joined by the Aube at Marcilly-sur-Seine, thirty miles away by car. There is little financial impetus to keep dredging the river and maintaining the canal walls, since most cargo traffic now moves by truck and train.

The biggest town between Troyes and Paris is Nogent-sur-Seine, best known these days for its two steam-spewing nuclear reactors. It is also where the geographical areas of Champagne, Brie, and Burgundy come together. A museum in Nogent is dedicated to the sculptor Camille Claudel, who lived there for three years when she was growing up. Later, she destroyed many of her sculptures and is best known these days for her long relationship with Auguste Rodin and, alas, her descent into madness.

Forty miles farther toward Paris, at the town of Montereau-Fault-Yonne, the more powerful and much wider Yonne empties into the Seine. It swells her size and doubles her flow as she leaves Burgundy and crosses into the province of Île-de-France (Island of France), which includes the city of Paris and the surrounding suburbs. From the outskirts of Île-de-France, the Seine is close enough to Paris to feel like a gateway to the city, and then, closer still, an extension of it.

Meandering downstream, the river embraces the forest of Fontainebleau, best known for its château. Fontainebleau was a royal residence from the reign of Louis VII, in the twelfth century, through Napoléon III in 1870. Its 110-square-mile forest, filled with oak, pine, chestnut, and beech trees, borders the Seine for nearly twelve miles as it winds its way west. Part of the château is perched on a cliff a hundred feet above the river. There are trails, but they are narrow, overgrown dirt paths more suited to hiking than a leisurely stroll. This is not the well-paved biking bliss of the Loire, although it is one of the most peaceful spots from which to view the river.

No navigable waterway connects the château to the river. But in 1609 Henri IV came close when he dug a canal to the ru de Changis, a small stream that flowed into the Seine; a carp pond at the château, once part of the canal, still exists. And while living in Fontainebleau, Marie-Antoinette came to like the idea of Seine river travel. One day in 1783, she cruised the river on the Duc d'Orléans's *coche d'eau*, a flat-bottomed "water coach." It had to be pulled by horses on a towpath along the river and could go only as far as the town of Melun, ten miles north of the château and thirty-seven miles southeast of Paris. Never-theless, the queen enjoyed the ride so much that she ordered the same type of boat to be built for her. She may have taken it out on the river during her two final stays in Fontainebleau.

Although most painters of the Seine were drawn to the west of Paris, some found inspiration near Fontainebleau. In the 1880s, Alfred Sisley moved with his family to a village near Moret-sur-Loing, close to the château's forest. From there, he painted more than two hundred canvases. Recently, Moret-sur-Loing and four other nearby municipali-ties created an eleven-mile Sisley walking trail along the banks of the river, with enameled plaques displaying reproductions of his work in the places where he painted. The nineteenth-century artist Rosa Bon-heur also painted along this part of the river. She bought a château and installed a studio; the château is now a museum containing her personal possessions (including a Sioux tribal costume that Buffalo Bill gave her).

Melun itself, which is a bit farther on, originated as a Gallo-Roman settlement on the Île Saint-Etienne, an island in the Seine, and later spilled onto both banks. In that sense, it is a miniature version of Paris, which the Romans first built on the Île de la Cité. Just a few miles away from Melun is a must-see detour: the seventeenth-century château of Vaux-le-Vicomte. With its perfect proportions, it is a masterpiece of

Baroque architecture, more intimate and manageable than the much larger and grander château it inspired: Louis XIV's Versailles.

As the river enters the Paris suburbs, trees, greenery, and private homes make way for factories, graffiti-decorated quays, and high-rise office and apartment buildings. Ivry-sur-Seine is the final town the Seine touches before it reaches Paris, a little more than a mile away. This is where the Seine meets the Marne, a river most famous for the World War I battle thirty miles upstream, where French soldiers and their British allies pushed back the seemingly unstoppable German war machine.

Then come two one-way bridges named after Nelson Mandela. On the left, a large sign for a company with the letters SNB reads *"Matériaux Routiers / Remblais Granulats"* (Road Material / Aggregate Backfill). On the right is a line of working barges at anchor and, behind them, the top of a French mortgage bank building, Crédit Foncier. Infrastructure trumps image. The sight is unspectacular.

But at this point, what does it matter? The Boulevard Périphérique, the highway that rings the city, announces that the traveler has arrived—whether by car, by bike, on foot, or in a boat—at the doorstep of Paris. All that's missing to make this a grand entry point for the Seine is a glorious bronze statue of the goddess Sequana.

# PART THREE

# The Spine of Paris

*An image of the coat of arms of the city of Paris.*
*Below is the motto* Fluctuat nec mergitur,
*"She is tossed on the waves but does not sink."*

# EIGHT

# It Started with a Canoe

*The river . . . provides water which
is very clear to the eye and very
pleasant for one who wishes to
drink. . . . And a good kind of vine
grows thereabouts.*

—EMPEROR JULIAN, *Misopogon*

IN 1991, Paris embarked on a massive urban-renewal project to build
a business complex and a park in the Bercy neighborhood, along the
eastern edge of the Right Bank. When the planning began, no one
gave much thought to Bercy's history.

An archaeologist named Philippe Marquis who was assigned to the
site as an official observer noticed something strange. As construction
workers dug up the earth, Marquis saw unusual black layers in the
sediment. He ordered the project to stop and petitioned the Ministry
of Culture to investigate. A careful excavation revealed that bulldozers
had struck more than six millennia into the past.

About twenty-six feet underground, the workers had encountered
traces of Neolithic wooden huts and jetties, and the remains of ten

long, shallow Neolithic dugout canoes. Some of the canoes were only fragments, others almost intact. One bulldozer had accidentally split a canoe in two. "The site is the most spectacular of its kind ever found in Paris," Philippe Velay, then the archaeology curator at the Musée Carnavalet, said on French television. "It shows that the city is much older than we thought."

I went to see the oldest of these boats for myself in the Carnavalet, the most Parisian of Paris museums. Located in two adjoining mansions in the Marais, it contains hundreds of thousands of pieces of art, furniture, and ephemera, all connected to the city's history. Among its five-star objects are a replica of the Bastille prison carved from one of its stones, the armchair in which the philosopher Voltaire died, some of the original furniture from the cork-lined bedroom of the Right Bank apartment of Marcel Proust, and Napoléon's favorite toiletries case.

When I visited the Carnavalet in pursuit of the story of Paris, Sylvie Robin, one of the curators, was waiting with a set of keys. The museum had closed for renovation; most of its contents had been put into storage. Robin led me through damp, unlit corridors lined with packing crates to our destination: a large, high-ceilinged hall. There, shoved against a wall, was an artifact labeled P06, protected from the elements in a twenty-foot-long glass case, awaiting the arrival of a custom-built, climate-controlled moving container.

P06 is a long, thin length of wood the color of mud. Robin explained that it was one of the dugout canoes known as "pirogues." The Stone Age settlers would use stone tools to carve each pirogue from a single piece of oak. This pirogue was between 6,400 and 6,800 years old, the oldest of the prehistoric boats discovered at Bercy. When it was unearthed, along with other objects from the era, its provenance upended long-held assumptions about the origins of Paris. "As far as we know, this is the first boat that traveled on the Seine," she said. "It is the most important prehistoric object found in northern France in decades. And it was discovered by chance."

The canoe measures about twenty feet long and three feet wide and is big enough to carry ten men, though its sturdiness is a thing of the past. Over time, layers of wet sediment crushed the boat nearly flat. As she spoke, Robin grew more animated, allowing herself to be swept up in the magical retelling of history. "In this boat that sits before us, the very first Parisians went up and down the river to hunt and to trade," she said. "I sometimes imagine what life was like in their settlement, and I say to myself, 'There were once people here who sat down with their basket of chickens and prepared a meal.'"

In that era, the Seine was already a primitive but navigable river with its own identity. It has evolved significantly ever since. Under Caesar's rule, at the start of Paris's recorded history, it still wasn't a single river but more like an archipelago of islands with interwoven waterways that could spread out to a width of about three and a half miles during floods. The riverbanks were broader and their slopes gentler. A swath of the Right Bank was low enough for the river to cover parts of what is now northern Paris—from the place de l'Alma to the Grands Boulevards and the Canal Saint-Martin—before curving around to rejoin the main flow at what is today the Bassin de l'Arsenal and Bercy. The hills of Montmartre, Belleville, and Trocadéro were too high and the river too shallow for the water to reach them.

The poet André Velter called the limestone, sand, gypsum, calcium, and sandstone beneath the prehistoric Seine "the sedimentation of memory." He added, "Secretly, the Seine is still there, united almost in the flesh with the walls and pavestones that were founded on what she abandoned, what she left behind."

Robin explained that the canoes were found at the site of one of the small, cliff-lined waterways at Bercy where nomadic hunter-gatherers passed through, then created encampments. P06 belonged to a people known as the Cerny. They were the monument builders of Neolithic France, located mostly in the Yonne and Seine River basins. Named after a village twenty-five miles south of Paris where prehistoric ceramic shards were collected from a field in the 1960s, the Cerny were the first Europeans to stop wandering and begin to build primitive settlements by the Seine. They grew wheat as their principal grain, and erected monuments for their dead.

Before the canoes were found in Bercy, the accepted history was that the Romans created Lutetia (Lutèce in modern French) on the Île de la Cité in 52 B.C., on a site originally established by the tribe known as the Parisii, the first permanent inhabitants. The discovery in Bercy supported the idea that towns may have existed in present-day Paris much earlier than that. Between a few hundred and a thousand people might have inhabited them, farming, raising livestock, running businesses, fishing, and hunting animals like wild boar, deer, beavers, turtles, and wolves.

Archaeologists at the Bercy dig found more than canoes; they also unearthed nearly fifty thousand artifacts that comprised the necessary objects of a civilization. Among them were hundreds of vases, bowls, and cups—about two hundred of them miraculously intact. Excavators also found flints and arrowheads; a millstone; a polished ax; fishhooks; remnants of tools including handles, picks, hoes, small stones, shells, a carved and polished boar tusk; and a fossil with a carp tail. The jaws of wild boars—probably kept as totems—were hidden at the foot of a wall that would have surrounded the village. The most precious artifact was a five-foot-long hunter's bow in yew wood discovered under a cluster of branches, one of the oldest weapons ever found in Europe.

There was other proof of long-term habitation and family life, including a tomb with the skeletons of two children, ages five and nine, and a three-room, thirteen-by-twenty-six-foot-long house in the shape of a trapezoid. The archaeologists were certain that other houses had existed.

The ancient wood of the canoes survived because it marinated for centuries in layers of wet mud, sand, gravel, and peat in a humid climate without temperature extremes. Dry timber would have disintegrated. The archaeologists' biggest challenge was preventing the boats from crumbling after they were exposed to air. Marquis and his team used a lawn sprinkler to keep the wood wet.

The archaeologists revealed their findings years later, only after they had studied, treated, and stabilized the wood of the canoes. Marquis and his team wanted more time to excavate, arguing that they could have unearthed more of the settlement. In 1993, City Hall officials renamed the street where the canoes had been found the rue des Pirogues de Bercy (street of the Canoes of Bercy). But progress trumped history, and a public park sprang up over the site. In 2000, the city of Paris unveiled the three best-preserved canoes, along with many of the artifacts, and celebrated their discovery as the city's most spectacular archaeological find ever. Paris Mayor Jean Tiberi said the discovery revealed "the soul of Paris."

I wanted to know more. I wanted to see the extraordinary pottery bowls and vases and the archer's bow, but all the objects were hidden away in storage. There is no catalog of them, no public database.

"That's awful," I told Robin. "What a waste."

She disagreed and reminded me of my good fortune. "You are really lucky to see the pirogue today," she said. "If it were not so big, it would have been packed up and gone a long time ago."

As it turned out, my timing was even better than that. The canoe may be too sensitive to permanent exposure to light to ever be put on public display again. I might have seen the most ancient evidence of the origins of Paris in a public space for the last time.

Robin told me that her own area of expertise was not prehistory but the history of France from the Gallo-Roman era through the Middle Ages. That got me thinking that I might have found an ally in my excitement about Sequana. Did Robin know about the ancient bronze statue of the goddess in Dijon?

"Of course!" she said. "She's very beautiful."

"You know her? Really? And the temple?" I asked.

"Yes! But have you been there?" she asked. "It's complicated to find."

"Of course!" I said. I told her about my passion for Sequana standing in the duck-shaped boat. "She is the goddess of healing!" I said. "With all the gloom in the United States and around the world right now, we must have another female healer—like Our Lady of Lourdes, only secular!"

For Robin, however, Sequana was merely a minor goddess of the provinces. In Paris, she said, one celebrates "les Nautes," the armed and powerful river boatmen—the shipbuilders, ship owners, navigators, traders, and warehousemen—who predated the Roman invasion of Paris and won the right of self-government. Their name derives from the Greek word for sailors or boatmen.

"The Nautes are the great emblematic characters of Paris, a Gallic brotherhood," Robin explained. "They were the great bourgeois traders of Lutetia, the armed Gallic boatmen of the Parisii tribe, and when the Romans came to colonize, the Nautes made an alliance with the Romans and took power on the Seine. Suddenly, they became very rich and powerful."

"But they're men!" I told Robin. "I want to celebrate a woman."

Robin laughed. "Yes, but my Nautes are warriors," she said.

She told me I could find vestiges of the Nautes at the Cluny Museum, on the Left Bank. The Cluny, a former medieval abbey built on the ruins of Lutetia's Roman baths, displays, among other artifacts, the oldest Gallo-Roman monument in Paris, the Pillar of the Nautes. A seventeen-foot structure made from four blocks of stone, it was carved with bas-reliefs depicting both Celtic and Roman gods and erected at one of the temples of Lutetia in the first century A.D. It was discovered by accident in 1710, during the construction of a burial vault for the archbishops of Paris in the heart of Notre-Dame.

The pillar sits in the nearly fifty-foot-high vaulted *frigidarium* ("cold room") of the baths. Each of its four blocks is mounted on stands of different sizes, making it easier to see the curved sculpted panels. In 2001, the blocks of pillar were restored, the black grime removed for the first time since their discovery. An inscription written in Latin with some Gallic flourishes revealed the structure's purpose: the Nautes from the city of the Parisii built and paid for the pillar in honor of the god Jupiter, who stands powerful on the pillar with a spear in one hand and a thunderbolt in the other.

Some of the panels had worn away over time, others were complete.

My eyes stopped on the most detailed one: a group of armed Nautes on a ship, floating on a body of water. How strange that one of the first known depictions of the Seine was so modest. The real subjects of the panel were the Nautes in their armor. The Nautes dominate; the river consists of a few simple waves at the bottom of the panel. Without the Seine, the courageous warrior-boatmen never would have existed.

HUMANS HAVE ALWAYS SETTLED and built cities along rivers, drawn to fresh water, fish, fertile land, and the ease of travel on water. The Seine was the servant that made Lutetia.

So much has been written about Lutetia, yet so little is known. The settlement the Romans found when they arrived was a muddy island village surrounded by water, cradled in a bend in the river, and protected by hills on both banks. The Parisii had already called it Lutetia, perhaps after the Celtic words *luh* (river), *touez* (in the middle), and *y* (house), which together mean "houses midstream," or perhaps *luto*, meaning marsh or bog. In 53 B.C., Julius Caesar, the conqueror of Gaul, wrote that it was "a collection of fishermen's huts on an island in the Seine."

Lutetia was a pleasant place to live; the Parisii knew how to make wine and cheese, and they built fishing boats and developed a profitable river trade. Like the tribesmen known as the Sequani, who lived at the source of the Seine, they prayed that the river would make their farming and hunting bountiful. Navigation was so crucial to their survival that their symbol was a ship, which may have been the precursor to the vessel on the Paris coat of arms. They produced their own money, and one

*A coin with an engraving that is believed to be the head of the god Apollo. His head rests on what appears to be a small boat with a curved prow, and his flowing hair evokes an image of waves.*
BIBLIOTHÈQUE NATIONALE DE FRANCE.

Parisii gold coin shows the head of the god Apollo in profile, with thick curls of hair that look like waves. The head rests on what appears to be a small stylized boat with a curved prow.

The Parisii also knew the river's dangers. By their time, the Seine had formed itself into a single river, twice its width today. The area that now includes the two islands of the Île de la Cité and the Île Saint-Louis, still the epicenter of Paris, stretched out as an archipelago of about ten islands. The Parisii drew maps of their settlement, highlighting the sandbanks and flood tides that made it treacherous.

In the Battle of Lutetia in 52 B.C., the invading Romans defeated the Parisii. The Romans discovered that the region's plentiful limestone could be used to make a building material like concrete that was strong enough to support complex structures. They joined the islands to the mainland by bridges and expanded Lutetia to both banks, then built a medium-sized provincial town on a grid design. It started on the Île de la Cité and the Left Bank, with a fortress, a forum, an amphitheater, and thermal baths (which are now below the Cluny). The city spread over 284 acres, with a population of about five thousand people.

THE FIRST IMPORTANT FIGURE to record his love for the city was the military commander Julian the Apostate, who later became emperor. "I happened to be in winter quarters at my beloved Lutetia," he wrote. "It is a small island lying in the river; a wall entirely surrounds it, and wooden bridges lead to it on both sides. The river seldom rises and falls, but usually is the same depth in the winter as in the summer season, and it provides water which is very clear to the eye and very pleasant for one who wishes to drink. . . . The winter too is rather mild there. . . . And a good kind of vine grows thereabouts, and some persons have even managed to make fig trees grow by covering them in winter."

Julian was enjoying his second winter in Lutetia, living happily in an imperial palace on the Île de la Cité, when his troops and the people of Lutetia proclaimed him emperor in the year 360. He made Lutetia the summer capital of the Roman Empire and renamed it *civitas Parisiorum*—City of the Parisii. This name was shortened to Paris sometime between the third to fifth century A.D.

The Parisiis' town on the Île de la Cité was not their only settlement, and perhaps not their original one. In 2003, archaeologists with the governmental Institut National de Recherches Archéologiques Préventives (INRAP) found evidence of a Gallic artisanal trading area from the time of the Parisii in the northwest suburb of Nanterre. Its vestiges indicate a densely populated urban center, more than twice the size of the Île de la Cité settlement. It had cobblestoned streets that ran parallel to each other; houses made of wood, mud, and straw, each with its own well; and drainage ditches that carried wastewater away from the town. The discovery of roasting spits and a cauldron fork suggest that the square plazas were used for communal banquets. Among the treasures found were amphoras, coins, tools, cooking pots, and jewelry, including bronze fibula brooches and bracelets, glass beads, and tubular necklaces that would have denoted high social status.

Since the discovery at Nanterre, archaeologists have debated which site was home to the original settlement: the Île de la Cité or Nanterre. Some of them believe that the site of the origin of Paris is still undiscovered, hidden somewhere in the basin of the river. What remains undisputed is that the Seine, with the Île de la Cité as a power center and natural fortress, became an ideal river for trade, one of the most important crossroads for all of Europe.

LOOK CAREFULLY anywhere in Paris and you will find tribute paid to the powerful river boatmen known as the Nautes on the city's coat of arms. The emblem shows a sailing ship bouncing on the river's waves below a fleur-de-lis design and above the motto *Fluctuat nec mergitur*— "She is tossed on the waves but does not sink." The first official design of a ship sailing on the waves dates back to 1190, when Philippe II offered it to the city of Paris. It evolved into its current incarnation in 1358. The expression *Fluctuat nec mergitur*, which dates to the fourth century, when it was used by the Nautes, was added to the coat of arms in the sixteenth century.

The coat of arms adorns many public buildings, schools, train stations, and bridges. I have found it on the sides of wrought-iron-framed park benches and in a grand mosaic in the Hôtel de Ville Métro station on the No. 1 line. The Eiffel Tower bows to the Seine with a small metal depiction of the city's ship, surrounded by pearl-like light bulbs, on one of its pillars. I have even seen the ship celebrated in a tattoo. The Australian boyfriend of one of my former research assistants had it imprinted on his chest before he returned home from a three-year stint as a Paris tour guide.

*Fluctuat nec mergitur* took on new meaning after the terrorist attacks on the night of Friday, November 13, 2015, when 130 people were killed and more than 400 injured. The Islamic State took credit for targeting eight sites in and around the city, including a sports stadium, the Bataclan concert hall, cafés, and bars. It was an attack on the French way of life, and Parisians responded with messages of defiance and resilience. FLUCTUAT NEC MERGITUR written in graffiti in huge block letters appeared in the place de la République and along the Canal Saint-Martin. *Le Monde* called it a "slogan of resistance." In the ultimate show of solidarity, the motto and images of the seal of Paris were superimposed over the blue, white, and red of the French flag and projected on the Eiffel Tower.

The Seine turns up in other imagery throughout Paris. The symbol of the Paris Transit Authority is the curve of the Seine cutting through the circle of Paris. The curve is shaped like an upturned profile of a woman's face, an official declaration of the river's femininity. A stone fountain in the center of the place Saint-Georges at the corner of my street includes the relief of a *débardeur*, a nineteenth-century longshoreman who collected and sold pieces of discarded wood from the Seine's muddy waters. The Musée du quai Branly looks from the outside like a hodgepodge of mismatched structures set in a lush, exotic jungle, but its six-hundred-foot-long permanent exhibition hall is designed to follow the bend in the river.

A 1930s building on the Quai de Conti, on the Left Bank, features a bas-relief with five allegorical figures evoking the river. Four are burly centaurs: "Religion" holding Notre-Dame Cathedral, "Marine Life" with a conch shell, "Trade" with a caduceus and cornucopia, and "Paris" carrying the city's sailing ship. Front and center is the only human: "The Seine," a tall, naked woman standing ramrod straight. Holding a long oar at her side, she plants her feet firmly in the water and gazes straight ahead, exulting in her power in the heart of the city.

Attached to my key chain is a good-luck charm: a colored enameled double medallion, one with the Paris coat of arms, the word "Paris" written on its sail, the other with the outline of Saint Christopher, the patron saint of travelers. I found it at a neighborhood *vide-grenier*, what Americans would call a yard sale. It cost ten centimes.

Wandering through the Marché Serpette in the vast flea market north of Paris one Sunday afternoon, I came upon still another rendering of the Paris coat of arms—on a secondhand Hermès scarf. The classic silk square is patterned in red, blue, and gold on a black background, with the city's coat of arms in the center and its motto written underneath. Twelve smaller coats of arms—each of them different, separated by images of threaded needles—encircle the main image. It was designed in 1954 and cost €175, about half the price of a new Hermès. Subtler than a Seine-themed tattoo, the scarf was a stylish reminder of the river and all it stands for.

Two years later, Andy found the stall in the flea market. The scarf was still there. He gave it to me for my birthday.

*A view of Paris at night, with the Seine's bridges and the Eiffel Tower illuminated.* © GARY ZUERCHER, GLZ.COM, MARCORP EDITIONS, AND MARCORP-EDITIONS.COM.

# NINE

# The Beating Heart of Paris

*The Pont Neuf is to the city what*
*the heart is to the body: the center of*
*movement and circulation.*
—LOUIS-SÉBASTIEN MERCIER,
*Tableau de Paris*

IT TOOK A BRIDGE to make a city. Henri IV made it happen. The year was 1598. The king had ended the Wars of Religion by signing the Edict of Nantes, a visionary act of reconciliation that gave France's one million Protestants religious and civil freedoms. Twelve years later, Henri would be assassinated. But in that moment of peace, France was united, and Paris was his. He celebrated by fulfilling a dream of his brother-in-law and predecessor Henri III: to build the first bridge spanning the Seine across the Île de la Cité, uniting the three disconnected parts of Paris—the Left Bank, the Right Bank, and the island between them that defined the heart of the city. In constructing it, Henri IV created an intimate, permanent bond between Parisians and the lifeblood of their city, the Seine.

A triumph of design, architecture, and technology, the Pont Neuf

was so revolutionary that Henri IV inaugurated it in 1607 by crossing
it on a white stallion. Today, it is still the oldest bridge in Paris, but it
was so modern at the time that it was given the name "New Bridge."
At 72 feet wide, it was built broader than any of the city's streets.
At 761 feet long, it was and still is the longest of the Paris's 35 main
bridges (there are 37 in all, if you count the ring road around Paris
that crosses the river upstream at Charenton/Bercy and downstream at
Saint-Cloud/Issy).

Before the Pont Neuf, Paris bridges were built at least partially in
wood, which made them weak and vulnerable to destruction by fire and
floods. Since the Middle Ages, bridges were cluttered and weighed down
by houses whose owners paid for the right to build there. For example,
the Pont Notre-Dame, built before the Pont Neuf, was lined with houses
on both sides, which made it too narrow and crowded for traffic.

The Pont Neuf was the first bridge in the city to be built entirely
of stone, making it much sturdier than the other four bridges in Paris.
Instead of houses, there were paved, raised walkways—the first on a
Paris bridge—and the first sidewalks in Paris. The most renowned
Renaissance architects took charge of embellishing it, engraving
twelve low structural arches with nearly four hundred stone masks.
The *mascarons* were relics of a traditional method of warding off
evil spirits; they depicted barbers, dentists, pickpockets, loiterers, and
more.

Henri IV's victory project would turn out to alter the architecture of the city in ways he couldn't have predicted. As part of the
bridge-building project, two small islands, Île du Patriarche and Île
aux Juifs, were joined to the Île de la Cité, enlarging its surface and
making room for the Seine to flow more easily. Even today, the Pont
Neuf has the feel of a bridge that holds the city together.

The Pont Neuf became the most identifiable symbol of Paris, a
sort of Eiffel Tower of the Ancien Régime. It also became a social
and cultural hub for *tout* Paris. People came just to see the river from
a bridge that finally offered unobstructed views. The vista was so

exceptional that the seventeenth-century travel writer François Bernier proclaimed it "the most beautiful and magnificent view in the entire world." On the bridge you could have a tooth pulled, take a fencing lesson, watch a bullfight, enlist in the army. Vendors loudly hawked their goods—hot coffee, chilled oysters, Italian oranges, and live poultry; skin whiteners, wooden legs, glass eyes, false teeth. They competed for space and attention with acrobats, pickpockets, prostitutes, umbrella renters, sellers of secondhand books, and charlatans who hoodwinked passersby with promises of miracle cures.

A dose of bottled water from the Seine would let you live to be 150, they claimed; why not buy some? A seventeenth-century poet who went by the name Sieur Berthod poked fun at their pitch: "I have, Monsieur, a very good remedy. . . . My balm is a cure for stomach indigestion, for eye pain. My elixir is marvelous. It would bleach the devil's skin."

LIKE THE EIFFEL TOWER TODAY, the Pont Neuf became part of the urban iconography, featured in paintings, engravings, drawings, and prints. Some of the first daguerreotypes in the late 1830s used the Pont Neuf as a subject. One image, portraying the bridge's statue of Henri IV on horseback, inadvertently captured a workman resting near its base, making it one of the first photographic images (perhaps the very first) of a living human being.

The Pont Neuf was restored and reconstructed several times. A bronze statue of Henri IV from 1618 (the first equestrian statue erected in Paris) was melted down to make cannons during the French Revolution, only to be reborn in 1818, when Louis XVIII built a copy of the original. The *mascarons* have also been reconstructed since the 1850s, bearing silent witness to Henri's expansive vision.

The structure itself has always been a magnet for celebratory art installations. When Louis XIV married the infanta Maria Theresa of Spain in 1660, for example, they arrived at the Pont Neuf to discover a

one-hundred-foot structure built in their honor on the place Dauphine
just east of the bridge. Atop an obelisk was a tapestry of a chariot
carrying the king and queen pulled by a rooster (a symbol of France)
and a lion (a symbol of Spain), and above that a statue of Atlas carrying
a globe decorated with fleurs-de-lis.

More than three centuries later, in 1963, Greek painter and sculptor
Nonda built, exhibited, and lived on the Pont Neuf in a Trojan horse
he created from steel, wood, and newspaper. In 1985, artists Christo
and Jeanne-Claude covered the bridge in 450,000 square feet of silky
woven polyamide fabric the color of golden sandstone. Nine years later,
the Japanese fashion designer Kenzo Takada decorated the bridge with
thirty-two thousand pots of pink, red, and yellow begonias.

The bridge looks much as it did when Henri first rode his horse
across it. Friends, lovers, families, musicians, and artists still create
their own personal spaces on stone benches built into the semicircular
spaces that once served as stalls selling everyday goods—books, medi-
cines, toys—a precursor of a mini shopping mall. Merchants are still
around, but these days they are selling tours.

The tour guides on the Pont Neuf compete for space as they tell their
stories. One cold Saturday afternoon, two guides led separate groups in
different versions of Henri IV's assassination. They gave performances
in English with enormous verve and varying doses of veracity.

Tour Guide One: "Henri IV gave a little bit of his wealth back to his
people. But Henri IV was murdered. Why kill one of the good kings of
this nation? Yes, he was a good king, but he was a Protestant king who
became a Catholic so that he could govern over a Catholic nation. Eventually one of those fanatical Catholics decided to kill the King. François
Ravaillac was his name. The king was in his carriage. Ravaillac hid
behind a building with a dagger. He opened the door of the carriage
and stabbed the king twice in his chest. One thrust of the knife went
straight to his heart. There you go."

Tour Guide Two: "But, guys, people loved this king. They admired
him. Unfortunately, the king was murdered. Why did they murder

such a great king, guys? Guys, he was a Protestant. This man turned himself into a Catholic. It was as simple as that. Everyone believed in his change of heart except one man: François Ravaillac. . . . François says, No way. Right in front of the guards, he stabs the king over and over. He is able to stab him three times. Three times—in the stomach, the chest, and the neck."

How was Ravaillac punished?

Tour Guide One undersold the gore: "He had to receive the worst punishment possible because he had committed the worst crime. You couldn't just cut off his head. That would have been too easy. It had to be done little by little. I'm cutting the story short. It's called a cliffhanger."

Tour Guide Two oversold it: "He didn't get his head cut off. He got quartered by horses. That means they tied his four limbs to four different horses. They wanted him to suffer, so they chose the oldest and the sickest horses. It didn't stop there. The crowd ripped his limbs off and then rushed to his body and started eating his flesh. To the bone. They chewed, and they swallowed, and they digested his flesh. Enough for disgusting stories!"

The truth is more complicated. Henri IV had been the ultimate pragmatist. He converted to Catholicism to unify France after the Wars of Religion, granted religious freedom and certain civil rights to Protestants, achieved peace at home and abroad, eliminated the national debt, and brought a degree of economic prosperity to his people. Henri had survived two dozen known plots against his life, but this time, as he was traveling from the Louvre to the Arsenal, his royal carriage was caught in a traffic jam on the rue de la Ferronnerie, near the city's main market, and his luck ran out. François Ravaillac, a thirty-two-year-old fanatical Catholic and failed monk suffering from hallucinations, was waiting for him. Ravaillac jumped onto the running board of the king's carriage and stabbed him three times with a kitchen knife he'd stolen from an inn nearby. After a ten-day trial, Ravaillac was condemned to death and taken, almost naked, to the place de Grève, now the square in front of Paris City Hall. His executioners plunged the arm he had used to stab the king into burning sulfur; ripped flesh from his chest with iron pincers; and seared his arms with molten lead and boiling oil and resin before he was drawn and quartered (a punishment reserved for regicides). A frenzied mob tore and chopped his flesh into pieces. One eyewitness said that a woman ate his flesh. The mob carried his body parts through the streets and burned them, throwing his ashes to the wind.

Visitors may not know the history of Henri IV or the Pont Neuf, but many are likely to know about the grillwork around the statue of Henri as a place where couples proclaimed their everlasting love by attaching metal padlocks. They began putting locks on the Pont Neuf after they were banned from doing so on the Pont des Arts, a spindly, fragile

*Lovers' locks on the Pont des Arts. Several years ago, Paris*
*removed the locks and banned people from adding new ones.*
GABRIELA SCIOLINO PLUMP.

footbridge that soon became unable to bear the weight of all this love. Lock vendors would pop up on the Pont Neuf when you least expected them, moving easily among the gaggles of tourists, and flashing their bits of metal with cunning and caution. Eventually, the locks burdened the sturdier Pont Neuf as well, weighing nearly enough to send pieces of the mesh panels crashing onto passing boats below. In 2018, the city fought back by removing the locks and covering the grillwork of the bridge with heavy corrugated plastic barriers. Though the vendors have now moved a few bridges away, some couples still hang their locks on the spaces between the barriers, on the lampposts, and on the heavy iron rings for mooring boats at the bridge's base.

STUDY PARIS THROUGH THE PONT NEUF and the river's other bridges, and you have a mosaic of the city's history and architecture. The Parisii built crude wooden bridges from the Île de la Cité to the riverbanks. Gates and towers closed the bridges and helped defend the island. The ancient imperial Romans built solid bridges of timber and stone in expanding their city, first to the Left Bank, an area that was less likely to flood because of its elevation. In contrast, the Right Bank was a broad swamp. In the ninth century, the Vikings attacked Paris several times. Unlike other invaders, Vikings waged war not on land but on water. Their great military advantage lay in their boats, which could move men and arms quickly over long distances. During the final attack in 885, fortified bridges linking the Île de la Cité to both banks stopped the Viking fleet of seven hundred ships from moving farther upriver. In 886, when the Seine, filled with debris, overflowed and washed away the city's Petit Pont, the Vikings were able to invade Paris. (After a year of fighting, they agreed to withdraw in exchange for seven hundred pounds of silver.)

Long before Henri IV, Parisians thought of their city as three parts: "the island" (the city itself), "the area beyond the big bridge" (the Right Bank), and "the area beyond the small bridge" (the Left Bank).

It was only in the Middle Ages, as the wetlands were filled in, that the city expanded more rapidly and extensively on the Right Bank.

The bridges stretch themselves over the river as if they are posing for passersby. Every one of them has its own story, structure, composition, and character. The Pont de la Concorde, in front of the National Assembly, was built during the French Revolution using stones of the demolished Bastille, "so that the people could forever trample on the old fortress," according to Rodolphe Perronet, the bridge's engineer.

The Pont de la Tournelle, which links the Île Saint-Louis to the Quai de la Tournelle, on the Left Bank, is anchored by a 1928 statue of Sainte Geneviève, the patron saint of Paris. Sitting atop a tall, stark pylon on the southeastern bank of the bridge, she is portrayed as a young woman, her hands on the shoulders of a child who represents the city. Geneviève is one of the most intriguing Parisian saints. Combining ruthless negotiating skills with mystical piety and fasting (she was probably anorexic), she claimed that God told her that Attila and his savage hordes advancing from the east would spare Paris from massacre and destruction. The people of Paris considered her either a lunatic or a fake, until Attila moved south. Then, and forever more, she was heralded as the savior of Paris.

The double-decker Pont de Bir-Hakeim carries the No. 6 Métro high above the Seine, making it the most visually rewarding Métro trip in Paris. For French director, screenwriter, and producer Cédric Klapisch, who celebrates Paris in his films, the experience has a mystical feel. "When I'm crossing the Bir-Hakeim bridge on the Métro, I can't stop myself from having a vision of ecstasy," he said. "There is the Eiffel Tower and the Seine, . . . the Haussmannian buildings, the insane highrises. It's a mixture of time and space. I'm moving forward in beauty."

Then there is the most elegant of Paris bridges: the Pont Alexandre III, a Belle Époque confection linking the Invalides to the Champs-Élysées. Built for the Paris Exposition Universelle of 1900, it was named in honor of the father of the visiting Russian czar, Nicholas II, as a symbol of the emerging diplomatic alliance between France and Russia.

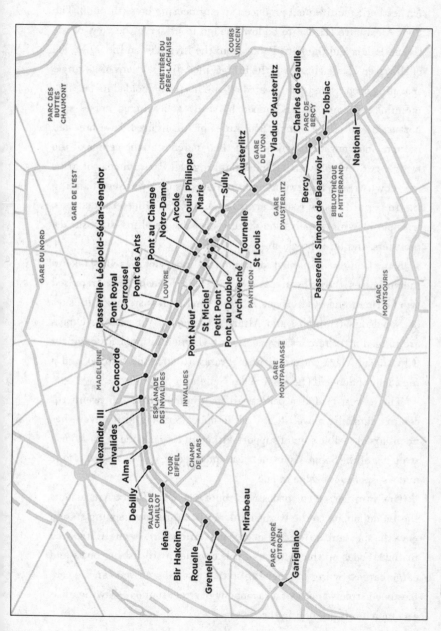

*Within the city limits of Paris, thirty-five main bridges cross the Seine. There are thirty-seven in all if one counts the ring road around Paris that crosses the river upstream at Charenton/Bercy and downstream at Saint-Cloud/Issy.* GLZ.COM.

An aesthetic requirement produced an engineering breakthrough. The Pont Alexandre III had to be low enough to preserve the view of the Grand Palais and the Petit Palais from the Invalides on the other side of the river. Large chunks of the bridge, including sections of its single spanning arch, were prefabricated off-site in strong molded metal. Two monumental stone pillars topped by shiny gold-winged horses support each end of the bridge. Sculptures of full-figured, bare-breasted nymphs look out at the river from their perches at the center of the bridge: two nymphs of the Seine flanking the Parisian coat of arms face downstream, and two nymphs of the Russian river Neva flanking the Imperial Russian coat of arms face upstream. Gilded candelabras, trumpet-blowing angels, lion-taming cherubs, dolphins, starfish, sea monsters, and birds proclaim joy.

Some bridges are named for French military victories. Bir-Hakeim memorializes the Libyan oasis where Free French forces repulsed two German enemy divisions in 1942; Iéna and Austerlitz were sites of Napoléon's triumphs; and Alma, a Crimean War victory. Others are named after famous people: a king (Louis-Philippe), an engineer (Christophe Marie), a president of France (Charles de Gaulle), and a president of Senegal (Léopold-Sédar-Senghor).

The newest bridge, a pedestrian span named after the twentieth-century feminist, novelist, and philosopher Simone de Beauvoir, has no pillars or visible sign of support, although it spans one of the widest stretches of the Seine. Asymmetrical and eclectic, it is an arched bridge and a suspension bridge in one.

One summer, on the pedestrian route where the Pont d'Arcole joins the Île de la Cité to the Right Bank, a virtual-reality viewing station gave the spectator a free, 360-degree panorama of the scene as it looked in 1628. Focus on the Seine, and it is crowded with fishing boats and cargo barges. Swing the viewing station around, and you can see cobblestoned streets and hear a cacophony of street sounds—cawing gulls and merchants promoting their wares.

Bridges are magnets for different sectors of the public. The Pont des

Arts links the Louvre and the Institut de France, home of the Académie Française and the Académie des Beaux-Arts; it's a place for people to picnic. Not far away, the Pont Saint-Louis, connecting the Île de la Cité and the Île Saint-Louis, is an open-air stage for musicians, especially Americans playing jazz. The pea-green late-nineteenth-century Pont Mirabeau, at the western end of Paris, honors Honoré Gabriel Riqueti, the Count of Mirabeau, a leader of the French Revolution's early years. But the bridge is widely known because of one of France's most famous poems, "Le Pont Mirabeau" by Guillaume Apollinaire; it is a place of pilgrimage for writers and lovers of poetry.

I LOVE THE PONT NEUF because it holds a secret. Behind the statue of Henri IV are staircases that descend two flights. They open out onto a spit of land at the westernmost tip of the Île de la Cité, the Square du Vert-Galant. "Vert-Galant" (which can translate to "Old Charmer" or "Gay Blade") was France's nickname for Henri IV. He was twice married, had four important mistresses known as "favorites," countless one-night stands, and more than a dozen—and perhaps as many as twenty-two—children. He is still so deeply appreciated in France that in 2010, to mark the four hundredth anniversary of his death, *Le Figaro* published a special supplement on his life and legacy. The cover declared, "The adventurer, the seducer, the king. Long Live Henri IV!"

Paris insiders use the Vert-Galant as a place to picnic, talk and even sleep. Unlike many other Paris parks, which close from dusk to dawn, this one is open all night long. When the river is high, the branches of the weeping willow planted in cobblestones at the tip of the square caress the surface of the Seine. You can come close enough to reach out and touch the water.

The Pont Neuf is also the subject of my favorite painting of a bridge over the Seine. Unlike so many paintings of the river that depict its water glistening in morning light, *Le Pont-Neuf, la nuit* captures its night magic. Albert Marquet painted it between 1935 and 1939 from his apartment on a quay facing the Pont Neuf and the Île de la Cité. The sky and water are black; the bridge and the cars crossing it shimmer in the glow of yellow and red electric lights. To the north, the ten-story, turn-of-the-twentieth-century department store La Samaritaine reigns over the scene.

During his lifetime, Marquet traveled far to paint—to Italy, England, Sweden, Germany, Morocco, and Algeria—but he kept coming back to the Seine, studying it obsessively for decades through the windows of the different apartments where he lived. One of his constant subjects was the Pont Neuf; he was working on a painting of the bridge covered in snow shortly before his death in 1947. "His balcony was his atelier," Sophie Krebs, curator at the Musée d'Art Moderne de la Ville de Paris, told me when the museum mounted a massive retrospective of his work. The movement, colors, and shadows of the water mesmerized Marquet. Many of his Seine paintings were done in muted grays and browns, in dense fog and under clouds. But in his large canvas of the Pont Neuf, painted as he looked from a window of his sixth-floor apartment on the Left Bank, his final home in Paris, the bright nocturnal lights of the bridge pop. "Look carefully, and you can see that it's raining," Krebs said. "The sidewalk and the roadway are wet. And look at the lights reverberating on the bridge. It's astonishing. There is no equivalent anywhere."

I asked Krebs if she knew the location of the apartment where Marquet painted this view. "On the Quai des Grands-Augustins where it meets rue Dauphine," she told me.

"Do you know who lives there now?" I asked.

"Someone very important."

"Could you find out for me?"

"I don't think so."

I let the matter rest for a few weeks, then asked her again. This time she promised to search the files in case the owner had loaned any personal works or documents to the exhibition, though she thought it was hopeless. But lo and behold, one day Krebs called with the name of the important man living in the apartment. I recognized it. Not only that, I had met the man and his wife at a dinner party years before. The hostess was a close mutual friend. I asked her if she would intercede on my behalf, so I could see the view. *Bien sûr.*

Monsieur and Madame Y invited me over for a drink, under one condition: I had to promise to keep their identities and address secret. I asked if I could bring along the curator of the exhibition. *Bien sûr* once again.

When we arrived, we found ourselves in a long living room decorated in designer modern furniture in shades of beige. Large and important contemporary paintings hung on the walls, framed under a high ceiling. Three tall, wide doors opened to balconies facing the Seine.

The couple invited us into a bedroom and showed us the balcony Marquet loved. "You can see Notre-Dame from here," said Monsieur Y. "There was a photograph in the exhibition of Marquet taken from this balcony!"

I recognized the balcony, with its wrought-iron railing, from the black-and-white photograph of Marquet that had hung in the museum. Standing in the foreground of the photo on a gray day shrouded in fog, he gazes out at the river, holding what looks like a notebook or small sketchbook in his left hand.

On the quay on the other side of the river, I could see the Louvre and the blue flags of Paris Plages, the artificial beach installation that springs up by the river every summer. The Sacré-Coeur Basilica atop the hill of Montmartre rose in the distance. Alas, the right half of the Pont Neuf was blocked by dense green foliage that hadn't been there in Marquet's day. And yes, this was Paris before sunset, not Paris lit up at night.

But it was still Marquet's Seine, at the very heart of the city. And some things about the Seine do not change. A working barge moved slowly upstream. On the Pont Neuf, the bronze statue of Henri IV shone bright in the early evening sun.

*A diver pushing off into the Seine from a diving board at
Pont Alexandre III as part of Paris's bid for the 2024 Summer Olympics.
City officials hope to clean the river enough to hold the distance swimming,
triathlon, and other water events in the Seine.* IRIS SAMUELS.

# TEN

# Clean Enough for a Swim?

*My aunt used to live in Paris. . . . She*
*told us that she jumped into the river*
*once. Barefoot. She smiled.*

—MIA

in the film *La La Land*,

as portrayed by Emma Stone

THE DIVING BOARD on the Pont Alexandre III was twelve meters high—two meters higher than official Olympic standards. But one hot and sunny day in June, the divers plunged, one by one, twisting, jackknifing, somersaulting, and backflipping into the water. Their target was not a pristine, chlorinated diving well but the murky, mud-bottomed Seine.

Paris has prohibited swimming in the Seine since 1923, although the ban is enforced only haphazardly. A trove of black-and-white photographs proves that river swimming continued in the heart of Paris, in full public view, through the 1950s. Afterward, swimmers largely abandoned the river because of the health hazards from chemical and bacterial pollution and the physical danger of erratic currents and boat traffic.

These divers didn't care. Their dives were acts of showmanship and defiance.

"I thought it would be very dirty, but it wasn't bad at all," said Alexis Jandard, a young Olympic hopeful from Lyon. "I felt the pollution of the water a little on my face, but that's all. What scared me was the blackness. You're diving into darkness. You have no idea if you're going to hit bottom."

Laura Marino, a twenty-four-year-old diver living in Paris, said the Seine was pure bliss compared to the pool she had to deal with at the 2016 Summer Olympics in Rio. There, the water turned into an emerald green swamp after a contractor dumped eighty liters of hydrogen peroxide into the diving well. "Everyone says the Seine is dirty, but it was terrific!" she said. "What an honor to promote our sport surrounded by the great monuments of Paris."

The Olympic-style diving event was part of a sixty-million-euro campaign organized by Paris mayor Anne Hidalgo to persuade the International Olympic Committee to choose Paris as the site for the 2024 Summer Olympics. Over two days in June 2017, Paris City Hall put on a show of thirty-three Olympic sports. Command central was the Pont Alexandre III, in the heart of touristic Paris. A floating one-hundred-meter orange running track was attached to the west side of the bridge, the Eiffel Tower strategically visible in the background for the perfect photo frame. It was a publicity stunt on a scale I had never seen in all the years I had lived in Paris.

The most colorful event was a flotilla of hundreds of kayaks and canoes paddling from the waters east of Paris. About a quarter of the kayaks were kid-sized, manned by children with life vests under their oversized white T-shirts. I was crossing the Pont de Sully when I spotted the boats like small dots in the distance. From afar the scene recalled the ninth-century invasion of Paris by the Vikings. As they got closer, the kayaks passed under the Pont Marie, turning the river into an abstract Technicolor painting in motion. Hidalgo met up with them in a kayak of her own. At one point the kids sang "La Marseillaise."

*Young paddlers in a canoe-and-kayak flotilla gather as part of Paris's €60 million campaign for the 2024 Summer Olympics.* ELAINE SCIOLINO.

Paris won the Olympics bid. Big plans for the Seine followed. A government-sponsored study identified potential sites along the river for the triathlon, swimming races, and other water events. After the Games, if the river is clean enough, a total lifting of the swimming ban could follow. "Swimming in the Seine isn't just for the Olympics," Hidalgo said, adding that all Parisians should be able to go for a pleasant dip in their river. Purifying the Seine is part of Hildago's larger crusade to return the river to the people. Throughout her years as mayor, she has fought to create parks, plazas, bike paths, and walkways along the Seine's banks. "Paris must reinvent itself every moment," she likes to say.

Hidalgo's campaign revives the dream of former president Jacques Chirac. During his unsuccessful run for the presidency in 1988, his official platform included a pledge to make the Seine swimmable. In 1990, as mayor of Paris, he repeated the promise on a television talk show. "I have stated that in three years, I will swim in the Seine in front of witnesses to prove that the Seine is a clean river," he said. A few years later, he admitted failure. "I'm not sure the Seine has been getting on too well since I left City Hall," he told a group of schoolchildren. "I shouldn't have made a promise I couldn't keep." Chirac is still mocked for his over-the-top boasting.

THE SEINE WAS ONCE very swimmable. In the seventeenth century, Henri IV went skinny-dipping in its cold waters, and his son Louis XIII and grandson Louis XIV were fans of the bathing it offered—even though they were sometimes dunking themselves in filthy waters. In the eighteenth century, people regularly plunged into the Seine—to wash, to exercise, and to have fun. Parisians swam in floating pools filled with Seine water along the quays and could easily go to the nearby villages of Bercy, Auteuil, and Passy (all now part of Paris) to canoe, fish, and swim; many bathers jumped in nude. Few people, however, knew how to swim properly, so the river was more a place to paddle around in or cool off. After the French Revolution, Paris passed an ordinance banning nude river bathing. *La baignade sauvage*—"wild bathing," as it was called—was still the norm in isolated areas, although bathing suits ruled in places where swimmers might be seen by the public.

The nineteenth-century caricaturist Honoré Daumier poked fun at swimmers (and boaters and fishermen, too). From the window of his studio in an attic on the Île Saint-Louis, he witnessed everyday recreational activities on the river. I found a treasure trove of Daumier's engravings in an unexpected place: the house turned museum where novelist Honoré de Balzac once lived in Paris. The museum director, Yves Gagneux, discovered Daumier's prints at an auction and bought them at a great price. Some of the male swimmers had big bellies and spindly legs, others rail-thin frames, their bodies twisted in grotesque and awkward positions. Daumier had captured the range of their emotions: jubilation, disappointment, foolishness, ridicule, fear, vanity, cowardice. "The swimmers were naked, even if you don't explicitly see that," said Gagneux. "And people in that era were just beginning to learn how to swim. So swimming was a dangerous sport; it was about how people face a cold, hostile place where they can drown." Daumier made light of the challenge of swimming in the river. "For Daumier, the Seine is a place of amusement and little misfortunes," said Gagneux, "We drink there, we get tired, we burn in the sun. He never missed an opportunity to make fun of Parisians."

Many writers and painters celebrated swimming in the Seine. One of Georges Seurat's best-known works is his 1884 oil *Bathers at Asnières*. The canvas shows working-class suburbanites lounging on the river-bank on a hazy, hot summer day while two bathers frolic in the Seine. Bridges and factories in the background evoke the noisy, dirty, and foul-smelling world of progress. The nineteenth-century novelist Gustave Flaubert lived and worked in a grand house overlooking the Seine near Rouen. Swimming in the river helped relieve his hallucinations, con-vulsions, migraines, blackouts, and blurry vision. His disorder was most likely epilepsy, although it was never conclusively diagnosed. In a letter to a niece in 1876, he wrote, "In a little while, I will go and fight like a triton in the waves of the Sequana. . . . Swimming on my stomach, on my back, in the narrows, along the banks of the islands bordered with foliage, I will look like the sea gods depicted in fine tapestries."


FROM ANTIQUITY, Parisians living near the Seine felt blessed. Its constantly moving, unpolluted waters, richly stocked with fish, dem-onstrated the force and goodness of nature and were considered sacred and pure. The water was plentiful and drinkable.

As Paris grew into a major city on both sides of the river, the Seine became a dumping ground for household, industrial, and human waste. Even royals could not escape its odors. In the late twelfth century, Philippe II—a fanatic about cleanliness—was reportedly disgusted by the stench when he opened the windows of his palace on the Île de la

Cité to view the Seine. From the Middle Ages on, tanners' dyes, animal carcasses, and detritus from skinners, furriers, and glovemakers all went into the river. Passing bargemen and traders added their garbage. Putrid water thrown onto unpaved streets or into farm fields inevitably made its way into the river.

In the eighteenth century, the river in and around Paris was known both at home and abroad as a smelly open sewer, so contaminated that parts of it took on the color of what was thrown into it: blood-red from animal carcasses, brown from garbage and excrement, black from tanners' dyes and rot. In a letter in 1771, the English politician and art historian Horace Walpole complained that he had to leave the "groves and lawns and rivers" of his estate outside London for a trip to Paris, "a dirty town with a dirtier ditch, calling itself the Seine."

Wealthy Parisians began to have their drinking water delivered from filtration fountains. But most people had no choice except to drink from the river. "The water of the Seine loosens the stomach, for those who are not accustomed to it," wrote Louis-Sébastien Mercier, the eighteenth-century chronicler of Paris. "Foreigners are scarcely ever spared the inconvenience of a little diarrhea; but they would avoid it if they took the precaution of putting a tablespoonful of white wine vinegar into each pint of water." The reality, however, was much worse.

The practice of dumping waste into the Seine continued without restraint. The river, dirty, disease-ridden, and dangerous, was a place to avoid. In 1808, Napoléon opened a sixty-mile canal to bring fresh drinking water to Paris from the Ourcq River, a tributary of the Marne, northeast of Paris. When the great cholera epidemic of 1832 hit the city, Parisians using water from the Seine were more susceptible to the disease.

Later in the nineteenth century, Napoléon III, his city planner Baron Haussmann, and Eugène Belgrand, their engineer, designed the Parisian water-supply and sewer networks still used now. To provide more Parisians with clean drinking water, they created a system with two sets of underground pipes to separate drinkable from untreated water.

However, waste from factories still went straight into the river. "The Seine, black sewer of the streets, / Loathsome river, fed by gutters, / Dirties my feet," the nineteenth-century writer Théophile Gautier lamented in a poem.

In the twentieth century, with even greater industrial and household pollution, the river became more contaminated. Factory owners cared more about production and profits than protecting the environment. In the 1990s, a scientific study classified the stretch of the Seine that ran through Paris as having one of the highest heavy metal levels in the world—from metals like cadmium, copper, mercury, nickel, and lead. In addition to the scourge of industrial waste, advanced farming methods using nitrates and phosphorous starved the river of oxygen; as more people could afford washing machines, their increased use of laundry detergents further poisoned the water. The river looked and smelled bad.

Cleanup campaigns had started in the 1970s, but it was only in the mid-1990s that France launched a sweeping Seine River basin initiative to restore the river to health. Within a decade, the country spent $13.5 billion on this effort, including the construction of waste-treatment and water-purification plants designed to remove undesirable chemicals. The river slowly began to rise from the dead.

THE SEINE IS a difficult river to clean; Paris is a case in point. The city does not have a sophisticated system of storm drains to channel excess groundwater from streets, sidewalks, and roofs away from the river. Paris's rudimentary drainage system can manage a moderate level of runoff, but it would be technically impossible and financially prohibitive to overhaul the city's network of drains.

Dams help to control the water level when the Seine overflows; reservoirs serve as giant storage bins for excess water. But the system is not fool-proof. When it rains too hard, sewers back up, gutters overflow, and the water pours, unfiltered and contaminated, into the Seine.

Environmental scientists predict that climate change will cause more frequent flooding. The river's current is not powerful enough to flush sediments and sewage to the sea. Waste dumped from boats and industry, high levels of heavy metals, and toxic pollutants from surface run-off, including pesticides, also poison the river. The water purification process begun in the 1990s did not eliminate harmful bacteria like *E. coli*. According to the French Ministry of Health, even today, a swimmer risks gastroenteritis, urinary tract and skin infections, septicemia, and meningitis. The divers in the 2017 Olympics demos were ordered to take antibacterial showers immediately after their short swims.

A major source of water pollution in the Paris metropolitan region comes from lead. Deteriorating lead pipes, metal roofs made with lead, and soil filled with decades of leaded gasoline leak that heavy metal into the river. We once had a major leak in a bathroom in our apartment and discovered that the burst pipe, probably more than a hundred years old, was made of lead.

I HAD LONG WANTED to swim in the Seine. I was convinced I could do it after I watched the divers plunging from the Pont Alexandre III into the river's dark waters with the fearlessness and ferocity of soldiers going into battle. Renegade swimmers in Paris have broken the no-swim rules. In 2015 a group of them organized an unauthorized dive off the pedestrian bridges on the Canal de l'Ourcq, which flows into the Seine. One swimmer reported back that there was "seaweed, but nothing gross." The police broke up the party.

I had my own plan to become a guerrilla swimmer. Even if the river is dark with poisons in and around Paris, it is gloriously clear closer to its source in deep Burgundy. I had glimpsed an opportunity when I'd visited the Fleury family's vineyards in Champagne country, some forty miles from the Seine's origin.

So one July morning, Bérengère Sim, a young French journalist, and I headed to Courteron to learn more about the Fleury vineyards and to take a dip in the Seine. We walked to the family's holiday cottage and into the garden, which stretched about a hundred feet. Fleury's wife, Colette, pushed open the gate in a rickety wooden fence and led us to the water. She showed us the tree with the "Tarzan rope" that her grandson used to swing from land into the river below during the hot summer months.

The water was clear. Looking down from the edge of the grass on the shore, I noticed that the bottom of the river was sandy, not thick and mucky like the floor of the Seine in Paris. Water ran clean and smooth over the stones along the bank. Schools of small black fish swam among speckled underwater weeds.

"It's only about fifteen!" said Colette Fleury, meaning that the water was fifteen degrees Celsius—less than sixty degrees Fahrenheit. That's not much different from the Atlantic coast of Maine in late August, I thought, not too bad.

I hadn't brought a bathing suit—I wasn't sure there would be a place to change. But I stripped down to my T-shirt and panties. Only then did she realize that I was serious. She rushed into her house and came back with a pair of plastic red Crocs that fastened with secure straps behind the ankles, for protection against sharp stones. Just my size. I tested the water temperature with my hand and thought, this could be worse. The Lake Erie of my childhood was a lot colder when we started swimming every summer. I put one foot in the water, then the other.

Then I plunged in. The water was shockingly cold and fresh. Bérengère took a photo with her iPhone. I sent it to my daughters as proof that their mother was not a wimp.

Bérengère was next.

She took a deep breath and jumped in.

What a thrill for us to say later, "I swam in the Seine today!"

*A woman fishing on the Seine in Paris. Cleanup efforts have brought many species of fish back to the river.* IRIS SAMUELS.

# ELEVEN

# The Zen of Rowing and Fishing

*One by one the boats cast off from the landing stage. The oarsmen leaned forward and with a regular swing pulled back. At each stroke of the long, slightly curved blades, the fast skiffs sped through the water making for La Grenouillère and growing progressively smaller till they disappeared beyond the railway bridge and into the distance.*

—GUY DE MAUPASSANT,
"Femme Fatale"

THE TWO FRENCH COUPLES put on striped jerseys and flat-topped boater hats banded in grosgrain ribbon. They tied red kerchiefs around their throats and gave me and my three companions matching boater hats. We were ready to set out from the Île de Chatou for a Sunday afternoon of rowing. Stray clouds relieved the heat of the unforgiving July sun. Along the banks, a wall of trees, including elm, ash, linden,

and willow, turned the water the same Veronese green that mesmerized the Impressionists. Our boats were romantic wooden skiffs more
than a hundred years old.

Renoir would have loved it.

The Île de Chatou, ten miles west of Paris, is so pleasant that after
the Vikings invaded it in 856, they stayed for ten years. These days, it
also goes by a second name, Île des Impressionistes; in 1880 and 1881,
Renoir painted *Luncheon of the Boating Party*, his best-known work on
the Seine, from the balcony of La Maison Fournaise on the island.

I had come to spend time with members of the Sequana Association, an organization of rowing fanatics. For three decades, its members
have bought, restored, rebuilt, exhibited, and rowed some of the most
important boats to have plied the waters of the Seine between the late
nineteenth and early twentieth centuries. I arrived with Laura, my
researcher from Northern Ireland; Heather, a student and varsity rower
at Princeton; and her boyfriend, Chris, who had also rowed competitively
as a Princeton undergrad. The Sequana members had invited us to row
out on the river, though first we would have a French-style "picnic."

We entered a rustic wooden building on the banks of the river, built
to replicate a nineteenth-century *gare d'eau* or boat storage and repair
facility. We opened the door to the smell of wood, glue, and varnish. A
cavernous hall stored old boats in various stages of restoration. Thick
ropes, carefully rolled, hung from the rafters. Dozens of tools, some
with obscure purposes, lined the walls. In the back of the atelier, at a
long dining table covered in blue-and-white checked plastic, our hosts
served a three-course lunch of quiches, salads, sandwiches, fruit pas-
tries, and madeleines. Like the Impressionists at the Maison Fournaise,
we drank chilled white wine heavily sweetened with crème de cassis. I
joked to our hosts that ours was a real-life luncheon of the boating party.

My Italian last name prompted Annie Lesgards, a longtime rower,
to tell me that she, too, was of Italian origin, on her mother's side. "My
family was from a place called Caltanissetta," she said, referring to a
poor agricultural and sulfur-mining city in central Sicily.

"Caltanissetta!" I said. "My paternal grandparents were from Caltanissetta. I've never met a French person whose family came from Caltanissetta. You and I are *paesane*! We are probably related."

Later, I asked how the organization came to be named after Sequana. The word *sequana* is well known here, though not exactly as the name of a river goddess. We were in the region known as Hauts-de-Seine—Alta Sequanae in Latin—a crescent-shaped cluster of wealthy residential suburbs that curves around Paris at its western city limits.

"Anyone who lives here knows Sequana," said Bernard Romain, a retired manager. "From the time you're eight or nine years old and people ask you what you are, you say, 'I'm an *Alto-Sequanais*.' And when the river floods, we say 'Sequana is angry.' Everyone associates the Seine with Sequana."


THE SEINE HAS ALWAYS been a boater's paradise. The river's jousting tournaments of today date back to the Middle Ages, when they were staged for royalty. A jouster armed with a wooden shield and a twelve-foot pole, stands on a boat and tries to knock his opponent into the river.

By the nineteenth century, the river was an experimental laboratory for unusual recreational boats and watercraft. Boaters mounted bicycles on floating wooden structures to make aquatic cycles and developed innovative paddleboats. A *podoscaphe*, for example, was a floating device that resembled a modern-day paddleboard, except that it had two floating pontoons attached like oversized water skis to a base.

From the 1830s on, rowing became a fashionable weekend pastime for both the working class and the bourgeoisie escaping the sweltering city. You could rent boats in places like Chatou, and boating life quickly became so popular that new personality stereotypes sprung up around *canotier*, or canoe-rower, culture. In his caricatures, Daumier often portrayed weekend boaters as unfortunate amateurs struggling with their oars, or hapless rowers who just wanted to get drunk with their friends.

Napoléon III so appreciated the art of rowing that in 1861 he built a 114-foot-long deep red rowing boat modeled after an ancient trireme— a vessel named for its three banks of oars. When launched on the Seine near Paris, it took seventy men to row.

These days, the Seine welcomes sailboats, motorboats, kayaks, rowboats, canoes, water skis, Jet Skis, and paddleboards. The Port de l'Arsenal, located off the Seine near the site of the Bastille, is one of many marinas for pleasure boats, some of them inhabited and permanently moored to create a tiny village.

Voies Navigables de France (or VNF) offers print and online guides with the rules of the river: speed limits, traffic lights, tolls, turning, mooring, and safely passing under bridges, for example. Paris bans boats without motors within its city limits unless there is special authorization; motorboats and yachts may transit through the city if they do not disturb commercial and passenger navigation. Even the Rowing-Club—Société de Régates Parisiennes (Rowing-Club— Paris Rowing Society), is located two Métro stops north of the Paris city limits.

The Sequana Association has a specific mission: preserving the *patrimoine*—or heritage—of historic boats and honoring the memory of Alphonse Fournaise, a master boat maker who founded La Maison Fournaise. Its members study old documents, photographs, and miniature models to make exact replicas of boats that once were and are no more. More than 140 people have paid a forty-euro fee to join (I am one of them), and its collection numbers more than fifty boats.

I first met members of the Sequana Association at a lakeside festival near Léry-Poses, seventy miles northwest of Paris. It was a Belle Époque dress-up affair: more than fifty women wore long dresses with pinafores and wide-brimmed hats with matching gloves, and carried parasols; they paraded before a jury, which awarded prizes to the most authentically appareled. The men wore striped jerseys and straw boater hats.

Sequana launched fourteen boats on the lake that day, the first time it had exhibited so many. Among them was *Madame*, a reproduction of the rowboat that had belonged to the writer Guy de Maupassant, who owned several vessels during his lifetime. The Sequana Association had no original plan or blueprint for the boat, so designers used photographs of him rowing on the Seine in 1889 to build a three-dimensional simulation. A naval architect helped them construct the boat with oak planks and copper nails.

*Roastbeef*, a reconstruction of a twenty-nine-foot-long sailboat Gustave Caillebotte owned for a short time in the early 1890s, was a reminder that he was almost as serious a sailor and boat designer as he was a painter of river life. One of his last designs, *Roastbeef* was a fast boat but, with its 323-square-foot sail, difficult to navigate.

I was invited for a ride in *Suzanne*, a reconstructed steamboat dating from 1882 that is the Sequana Association's jewel. Years before, one of the organization's members had found calcified, crumbling designs for the hull of a steamboat in his family home in Paris. Shortly afterward, he dug up a battered brass steam engine on the family farm in the Gers region, in southwest France. The designs and the engine belonged with each other. Since 2006, when the boat was rebuilt as *Suzanne*, she has traveled more than fifteen hundred miles.

I strapped myself into a bright blue-and-yellow life vest and jumped onto the steamboat. My skipper was Jean Jack Gardais, a retired mechanical engineer and Sequana's president. He was dressed in jeans and a blue-and-white striped sailor's shirt stained with grease. We stood together next to the steam engine, which was housed in a highly polished brass cylinder. The boiling water inside gave off so much heat that sweat poured in rivulets down his face. I asked him how he could stand being so hot. "Hot?" he asked. "Not hot at all."

Several months later, Jean Jack gave me a tour of the Sequana Association's headquarters in Chatou. Its treasures are on display next to the atelier in a boat garage that serves as a small museum. One is a rare yole, a type of rowing boat sometimes equipped with a sail, with a hull made from a single twenty-three-foot-long piece of mahogany. The French state has designated it a national historical monument.

On the day my three companions and I came to row, our hosts chose four boats dating from the first two decades of the twentieth century, pulling them out from their storage racks in the garage. The wooden boats were slightly heavier than today's fiberglass shells, and it took four rowers to lift each one. Then they slid the wooden backs and arm rests of the coxswains' seats into place and rubbed pig fat on the oars to help them rotate more smoothly in the oarlocks. Then they carried the boats down a concrete ramp to the Seine for a "wet launch." That required the rowers to stand knee-deep in the water, two holding each

*Members of the Sequana Association, a group of rowers dedicated to restoring and exhibiting century-old boats, launch onto the Seine from their headquarters on the Île de Chatou.* BERNARD ROMAIN / ASSOCIATION SEQUANA.

boat in place while another climbed aboard and rowed it to a floating dock to pick up the guests. The ramp down to the dock was broken, so we had to step gingerly down a shaky board six inches wide.

Rowing shells are delicate. In both modern and old wooden boats, you must be careful where you step; otherwise your foot might break through the hull. It is easy to dent or crack a modern fiberglass shell, and hundred-year-old crafts made of thin wood are even more fragile.

Sequana's rowers warned Heather and Chris not to treat their antique three-seater like a Princeton racing shell. But once the experienced scullers got going, their enthusiasm took over. "Lightly light!" urged Annie, their coxswain. Heather and Chris shortened their stroke. "See how light and easily it moves?" said Annie. "You don't really need to muscle it."

I was paired with Kareen Sontag, a fifty-five-year-old lifelong rower who holds down a day job as an IT manager. She was rowing our two-seater, *Jako*; I was in the coxswain seat. The construction of the oak-and-mahogany boat was not much different from that of a modern-day scull. Both have sliding seats, oarlocks, adjustable foot stretchers with straps, and rudders with rope steering systems for the coxswain.

I could hear the grinding of Kareen's seat as she plied each stroke, the plop of her oars when she dipped them sharply in the water, and the gurgle of water against the hull as the boat moved forward. Later, Chris said, "When you hear that gurgle, you know that you and the water are in perfect harmony."

We rowed under three bridges—including the same iron railway bridge that Renoir and Vincent van Gogh painted and Maupassant wrote about—and passed old barges docked on the banks. There were boats that served as houses and houses that happened to float. One houseboat was a crumbling wreck, with plastic tarps covering its windowless frames and much of its roof. Annie said its nickname was "the wreck of the *Medusa*," after the tragic nineteenth-century shipwreck immortalized in Théodore Géricault's painting *The Raft of the Medusa*.

We passed what had once been the site of La Grenouillère, a popular boating, swimming, and dining establishment in the nineteenth century.

It had an adjacent floating rest area with a single tree that was nicknamed "the camembert" because of its round shape, Kareen said. Then we came to a house partially hidden behind trees where composer Georges Bizet lived for a short time before his death. When we reached the town of Bougival, the sounds of motorcycle engines and honking horns shattered the quiet. In the 1950s, the construction of Route Nationale 13 near the river had destroyed the tranquillity of the neighborhood. "All the people who owned beautiful houses along the river suddenly found themselves trapped with the permanent sound of traffic," said Kareen.

According to river rules, Kareen explained, barges and working boats have precedence over a pleasure boat like ours. And when a larger boat passes, you turn your boat parallel to the wake; if you try to face it head-on, your vessel might break in two. *Pousseurs*—tugboats that push engineless barges along the Seine—make the biggest wakes. "We are tolerated," said Kareen. "We are the ones who have to maneuver and get out of the way."

Swarms of small dragonflies hovered over the river's surface near the banks; Kareen pointed out the males with bright blue abdomens. "This is a true sign that the river is getting cleaner," she said. "Twenty years ago, they had gone." A large fish jumped out of the water— another sign of the Seine's health. She dipped an oar into the river and scooped up some water to show me how clear it was.

When we reached a lock at Bougival, Kareen stopped. We could make out the remnants of the seventeenth-century Marly Machine on the tiny Île aux Bernaches, in the distance. The Marly Machine was a gravity-defying hydraulic construction with a giant pumping station that Louis XIV built so that the Seine's water could flow five hundred feet up a steep slope to feed his fountains at Versailles.

As we headed back to Chatou, she told me to turn around for one last look. "You are not in the suburbs of Paris; you are in a green forest," she said. "Look at the river and the green trees rising above in the distance, and you are in the world of a hundred years ago."

A group of boys was sunbathing on a concrete dock, partially shaded under a curved plastic roof about ten feet above the water. It looked a little like a bus shelter. Some of them climbed on top of the roof and jumped, one after the other, over and over, into the Seine. Leaning against the dock were their fishing poles, perhaps awaiting the boys' next activity on a Sunday afternoon of sheer joy.

OH, THE PLEASURE that comes with casting a line into the Seine—certainly Ernest Hemingway understood it. He described the lure of the riverbanks in *A Moveable Feast*, his memoir of Paris life in the 1920s. He walked there when he had finished work for the day or needed to "think something out." He liked to take the stairs under the Pont Neuf to the Vert-Galant. There, the Seine's currents and backwaters created excellent places to fish, he wrote. And there, he discovered the fishermen.

They fell into two categories: retirees on small pensions that could become worthless with inflation and enthusiasts who fished in their spare time. The fishermen "used long jointed cane poles," he wrote, with fine lines, light gear, and quill floats. Sure, there was better fishing outside of Paris, but they always caught something.

The Seine was polluted in Hemingway's time, but the fishermen considered the fish healthy enough to eat. The river brought forth a plentiful supply of fingerling fish they called *goujon*. "They were delicious fried whole, and I could eat a plateful," Hemingway wrote. "They were plump and sweet-fleshed with a finer flavor than fresh sardines even, and were not at all oily, and we ate them bones and all."

Hemingway made excuses for why he stayed on the sidelines: he didn't have the tackle; he preferred to fish in Spain; he never knew when he would finish work. In Paris, his fishing pleasure came vicariously. "It always made me happy that there were men fishing in the city itself, having sound, serious fishing and taking a few *fritures* home to their families," he wrote.

The Seine has been fished as long as humans have settled on its banks. Archaeologists have found fishhooks at prehistoric sites along the river. In Gallo-Roman times, carp were introduced into the Seine; this hardy, common species had most probably been imported from Asia by the Roman legions. Over the centuries, fish became an important source of food. In the days when harvesting fish was a reliable way to make a living, men did the fishing, using boats, nets, and traps, while women sold the catch on the riverbanks or in open-air markets in town. John Frederick Smith, in his 1840 book *A Hand Book up the Seine*, describes the glorious bounty that came forth from the Seine in those days: "They fish there the sperling, a delicate little fish, the color of mother-of-pearl, which when taken out of the water smells like violets; also some herrings, shrimps, oeillet, a few capelau, the sea-dog or russet, the lamprey, the pimperneau, very small eels, crabs, flounders, sole, plaice, the green boned orphie, the mullet, the shad, the sturgeon, and the salmon."

Later, observers would write about how drastically pollution had killed off the fish. By 1900, salmon, a marker of the river's health, had disappeared from the Seine; twenty years later, many other species had vanished as well. The twentieth-century writer Julien Green recalled the time he was crossing the Solférino footbridge and saw an ugly sight below: "Hundreds of fish floating on the black water, white bellies turned skywards, poisoned by the filth that pollutes our lovely river." By the 1970s, the river around Paris became so dirty and starved of oxygen that only the hardiest species—bottom-feeders like carp, for example—could survive.

The 1994 book *La Seine: Mémoire d'un fleuve*, a nostalgic overview of what the Seine once was and still is, shows a warning sign from the 1970s that announced, "HERE, River Seine DANGER. Water polluted—poisoned." It adds, "The health of you and your children depends on your common action."

Then the cleanup began, and many species of fish returned. Now local fishing clubs regularly restock the river with fish. The systematic oxygenation of the river helps keep fish alive. "We're improving the quality of water by aerating it for whatever creature passes by," said

Laurent Niquet, the director of the Chatou dam and lock, west of Paris. "We let it breathe, like wine in a carafe."

In the late 2010s, Paris City Hall counted more than thirty species swimming within the city limits, among them survivors like carp, as well as perch, pike, sea trout, shad, rudd, European eel, and even a few Atlantic salmon.


THE CITY OF PARIS mounted an outdoor exhibition on a pontoon boat moored near the Musée d'Orsay to educate passersby about the fish of the Seine. They learned about the history, habitats, reproduction cycles, longevity, and food habits of nearly a dozen species. The northern pike, for example, is a lazy predator with hundreds of sharp teeth. The European eel lives in the Seine but migrates every year across the Atlantic to breed. Small *ablettes* (common bleak) were fished and eaten in the Middle Ages and fried up in riverside restaurants in the early twentieth century. The city bans the human consumption of all fish caught in the Seine, because of dangerous levels of toxins like metals (especially lead), arsenic, and PCBs stored in their bodies, but the fishermen are out there just for fun."

But as part of its campaign to make the Seine eco-friendly, City Hall also promotes fishing and has produced an online map showing the best spots to fish along the Seine and the Canal Saint-Martin. Anyone who wants to cast a line into the water needs a fishing permit, or *carte de pêche*, which can be purchased for a year or even for a day. While fishing for some species is prohibited from January until May (so the fish have a chance to reproduce), fishermen practice their sport all year round.

On a Sunday afternoon visit to the river town of Bougival, I spotted some stone steps leading down to a wooden dock on the river. A young man named Romain Aviron was fly-fishing. He had been born and raised in a rural region of northern France filled with streams, lakes, and rivers rich in fish. He now works as a technician on the mechanical, electrical, and hydraulic systems of the Seine's dams and locks west of Paris. We were only about thirty miles downstream from Paris along the curving river, but the water was almost transparent. Aviron explained the difference between fishing crudely with live bait on a big hook and the refined artistry of what he does with flies. "It's joy to lure a fish with totally lifeless, fake bait," he said. "I must deceive the fish, to make it believe it is chasing something alive." He always throws his catch back into the water.

"So the fish never dies?" I asked.

"Never," he said. "Why would I take away its life when it has made me happy? It's like a game of chess. You don't kill your partner, do you? So I don't kill my fish."

Aviron didn't catch anything that day. But the river made him happy.

Every September, dozens of fishermen and their families and friends descend on Île de la Jatte, northwest of Paris, for a weekend Fish Festival on the Seine. The island is best known as the setting for Georges Seurat's 1884 pointillist masterpiece *A Sunday Afternoon on the Island of La Grande Jatte*. With its natural banks and rich concentration of underwater algae, it is also an ideal place to fish.

Some of the fishermen who came one year were so passionate about the event that they brought tents and camped out with their children and grandchildren. Veteran fishermen offered demonstrations, including angling, street-fishing from a concrete riverbank, predator fishing by boat, and fishing for bottom-feeders. Manufacturers and designers presented their latest fishing equipment and clothing during the festival. Visitors enjoyed free entry to the tiny Musée-Aquarium de la Seine, which displays various species of freshwater fish that swim in the Seine in and around Paris.

The Fishermen's Association of the Hauts-de-Seine department, where the island is located, gave free lessons in a designated zone on the riverbanks. Strict rules governed the competitions, including a no-kill policy that required fishermen to throw back their catch after it was weighed and photographed. "There is a strong connection between us and the fish," said Maxime Cenni, a twenty-year-old gardener who grew up fishing with his grandfather along the Seine. "They come to us, and, of course, we must set them free again." Maxime caught a large but lowly catfish and tossed it back into the river.

His close friend Lionel Pelletier, forty-six, who works for a construction equipment rental company, runs a small fishing club in his spare time. "Fishing is an incredibly social sport," he said. Like Maxime, he learned from his grandfather how to cast a line. He has caught carp, pike, catfish, and the odd plastic bag on the Seine; he was wearing a sweatshirt that read, in French, "A bad day of fishing is still better than a good week at work."

Other fishermen shared their stories. Twenty-year-old Nicolas Vergua said that once, when he went fishing near the Eiffel Tower, he caught a sack of potatoes. A more bizarre story was the one about the fisherman in Paris who in 2013 caught an Amazonian cousin of the piranha known as a pacu. The pacu has a powerful jaw and human-looking teeth and can grow to more than three feet long and weigh more than eighty pounds. A French wire service report said that the pacu is nicknamed "the ball cutter" because it has attacked the genitalia of fishermen; professional fishing websites dismiss the claim as nothing but a fish story.


I CONFESS THAT I have never gone fishing. My closest encounter with the sport was sartorial. In 1979, when I was covering the Iranian Revolution for *Newsweek*, an American war correspondent and part-time boyfriend based in Beirut gave me a khaki-colored fishing vest as a birthday present. He excitedly showed me how it had enough pockets to hold a notebook, pen, tape recorder, small camera, passport, wallet, flashlight, sunglasses, and lipstick; he told me it would liberate me from having to carry a purse into danger zones. I had been hoping for a pair of antique gold earrings from a Middle Eastern souk, or at least a box of fine chocolates and a dozen long-stemmed roses. The relationship ended soon afterward.

*A view of the Pont d'Iéna and the place du Trocadéro
from the Eiffel Tower.* © GARY ZUERCHER, GLZ.COM,
MARCORP EDITIONS, AND MARCORP-EDITIONS.COM.

# TWELVE

# Paris la Nuit

*The sun finally died in beauty,*
*flinging out its crimson flames,*
*which cast their reflection on the*
*faces of passers-by, giving them*
*a strangely feverish look. The*
*darkness of the trees became deeper.*
*You could hear the Seine flowing.*

—GEORGES SIMENON,

*Inquest on Bouvet*

IN THE COUNTRYSIDE, when night falls, the Seine gets lost in bushy trees and wild grasses. She hides in darkness below white cliffs that stretch high up her banks. Not so in Paris. Here the Seine is a city girl, an elegant beauty worthy of adornment. Her banks and bridges were created to be shown, not hidden.

The secret to her success is light.

Because of her slow-moving current, the Seine at night shimmers softly with reflections from traffic lights, streetlights, spotlights above and below the bridges. Light decorates and distorts architectural angles and the whimsical details of buildings and monuments that are lost by day.

In the daytime, the Pont Royal, in the heart of the city, is an unre-

markable, seventeenth-century stone bridge clogged with motor-
ists making their way from the Left to the Right Bank. At night, it
becomes a platform for visual pleasure. Walk north across the river on
the Pont Royal, and the long façade of the Louvre stands on the other
side. To the right, in the distance, the gently lit towers of Notre-Dame
and the dome of the Institut de France appear through the trees. To
the left is the Tuileries Garden, locked behind iron gates and shrouded
in darkness. Farther on, the twin clocks of the Musée d'Orsay and the
curves of the Grand Palais's glass roofs burn bright; the tip of the Eiffel
Tower peeks through. As you approach the end of the bridge, look up to
be greeted by a small sculpture on the Flore Pavilion of the Louvre. It
is a naked nymph by Jean-Baptiste Carpeaux, laughing.

Artificial lighting is expensive, and the buildings of many other
major cities go dark when night falls. Not Paris. Paris spends extravagantly on its public lighting—over $15 million a year. Lighting Paris
requires meticulous planning, trial and error, creativity, and artifice.
Nothing is left to chance.

To celebrate the millennium, the city spent $5 million to decorate the
Eiffel Tower, so that every night, twenty thousand white lights sparkle for
five minutes of every hour, on the hour. Installing the lights involved forty
mountaineers, architects, and engineers, who endured high winds, raging
storms, and attacks by pigeons and bats. The lights continue to delight.

By night, tourist boat rides on the Seine become voyages of discovery. Pleasure boats for dinner and cocktails, for music and dancing
glitter in multicolored splendor. Bridges light up like necklaces strung
across the river. If you arrive early enough, you can be the first in line
for the boat ride and secure a spot in the front of an upper deck. When
the boat passes under the bridges, you can see how the lighting from
underneath reveals the curves and angles of their underbellies.

The river's many bridges at night are a romantic lure. Even the
most absurd fantasy movie scenes seem plausible. Toward the end of
the 2003 film *Something's Gotta Give*, Jack Nicholson, thinking he has
lost Diane Keaton, stumbles out of the Grand Colbert restaurant and

past the Hôtel de Ville to find himself ruminating about life's meaning midway across the Pont d'Arcole. An accordion plays "La vie en rose." A tourist boat aglow in white lights cruises below him. Jack Nicholson—yes, Jack Nicholson—gets tears in his eyes. It starts to snow. Keaton arrives in a taxi to confess that she still loves him. He tells her, "If it's true, my life just got made. . . . I finally get what it's all about. I'm sixty-three years old, and I'm in love—for the first time in my life." They throw their arms around each other and kiss.

The magic lingers even after the city turns off the lights on most public structures at about one a.m. In a Cinderella moment, buildings suddenly seem to disappear. But the streetlamps stay on, muting the colors of the bridges and riverbanks as if they were in a dreamy painting by Matisse or Marquet.

NIGHT IS SO IMPORTANT that the city of Paris spends more than a million euros every year on a one-night celebration of art and culture. Every October since 2002, Nuit Blanche—literally "White Night" and colloquially "All-Nighter"—has lured Parisians into the streets from dusk to dawn with videos, multimedia installations, sculptures, music, and dance. In 2016, the theme was romance, told through a fifteenth-century allegorical fantasy about love—love at first sight, heartbreak, and reconciliation. The setting was the Seine and its bridges, "because of the river's romantic symbolism," Paris City Hall announced. Publicists displayed huge posters showing a red heart on a midnight-blue background with the Seine cutting a curve through it.

In a Nuit Blanche installation about the risk of love running out over time, a giant clock hung from a crane at one of the Seine's ports. At a second installation nearby, intended to evoke the battle for one's lover, zombies hovered overhead. At the Petit Palais art museum, five dancers from the Crazy Horse cabaret, dressed as water nymphs, their naked breasts visible through their sheer costumes, undulated and swayed through plumes of lavender and gray smoke.

At the Pont des Arts, British musician Oliver Beer constructed a multimedia work called *Live Stream*. He mixed live music with real and imagined sounds of underwater life in the Seine. He illuminated the base of the bridge with bright green LED lights that turned the water a murky pea green, making it just transparent enough to allow viewers to see a few feet into its depths. The work was designed to evoke the "mysteries of love." A bit farther on that night, British artist Anish Kapoor showed off *Descension*, an installation that created a swirling whirlpool in the middle of the river. It spanned twenty-six feet in diameter and converged into a vortex that was sucked into the black water. Then the vortex rose to the surface dressed in bright white light, vanished, and reappeared. Kapoor was on hand to explain its meaning. "Love," he said, "is an eternal vortex."

Mayor Hidalgo was the evening's ultimate cheerleader. She called Nuit Blanche on the Seine a "signal to the whole world" to "come to see us, to come to wander . . . to take inspiration, to come to be rocked by this Seine."

Light on the Seine has other manipulative powers. Walking along the river one night after midnight, I spotted two dozen colorful tents pitched in a neat row on the banks below. All was still, except for the silhouette of a man hanging laundry on a clothesline strung between two trees. Bathed in the yellowish glow of the streetlights, the encampment looked at first glance like a tiny village, rather than the makeshift homeless settlement it was.


THE KING OF PARIS lighting will always be François Jousse. For more than a quarter of a century, he was the city's chief lighting engineer, leading a team of thirty decorative lighting specialists. It was under his watch that the lighting of Paris monuments at night became an art.

An engineer by training, Jousse turned to light in 1981, when most Paris monuments were either unlit or illuminated with crude spotlights. His job was to light more than three hundred buildings, bridges, and boulevards every night; this involved choosing the style, color, intensity, placement, and timing of the lighting. The Seine was his preferred laboratory. The structures he lit on the riverbanks were close to the water, so that the visual reverberations were part of his calculation. Jousse memorably demonstrated what light can do when he transformed the nighttime appearance of Notre-Dame. He conceived a new lighting scheme that would allow spectators to discover the cathedral's façade slowly, through the drama of the details.

One chilly evening shortly after the new lighting was installed, he drove me right up to the main entrance of Notre-Dame, so that he could show off the redesigned lighting of the cathedral's south façade. Tourists had to make way for the lighting king to park on the parvis. (He had a special pass.) As we approached, he pointed out the tiny fiber-optic cables tucked into corners and crevices. We entered the cathedral, climbed a private stone staircase to the south roof, and waited for darkness. Just as the sun disappeared, the façade lit up, its pillars, gargoyles, and flying buttresses bathed in bright white. "Look—the light is stronger at the top, so you feel that you are moving closer to heaven," he said. "This is not just a monument. It's a virgin floating above the city."

Jousse is now in his seventies and retired. But his creations and his reputation live on. Standing one evening on the Pont Marie, the short bridge that joins the Right Bank to the Île Saint-Louis, he talked about his vision. His lighting scheme for the bridges that connect the banks to one of the two islands focuses on the connection with the land. This he achieved by outlining the top of the bridge structure with a horizontal line of light.

At the same time, to create a connection between the bridges and the river, he installed lights on the arches below that would illuminate them and make mirror images in the water. "Symbolically, it is to show travel on the river in two ways: a waterway with boats, and a land route with pedestrians and cars," he said. "There is a conflict between them, and light is a way to resolve it, to share space in time."

The structures along the river show off two schools of lighting: the Paris school, which bathes its subjects in warm, even light, and the Lyon school, which uses small spotlights to highlight details for dramatic effect. The Conciergerie, the onetime medieval prison on the Île de la Cité, is covered in the uniform, even glow of the Paris school, as is the Sacré-Coeur Basilica, in Montmartre. The Pont Alexandre III, with its candelabras, cupids, sea monsters, and other decorations, is lit up with the pointillistic precision of the Lyon school. So are the arches and hanging lamps of the Pont de Bercy, the high-relief sculptures on the Pont d'Austerlitz, and the medallions on the *N* monograms, in honor of Napoléon III, on the Pont au Change.

*One of the ornate Belle Époque lampposts on the Pont Alexandre III.* © GARY ZUERCHER, GLZ.COM, MARCORP EDITIONS, AND MARCORP-EDITIONS.COM.

The resulting lighting is complex and elaborate. For bridges with arches, the light shoots out from the pillars (the Pont d'Iéna, the Pont de la Concorde) or the abutments (as in the case of the Pont Alexandre III); for a truss bridge, like the Pont des Arts, the light is diffused; on a steel girder bridge, like the Pont de l'Alma or the Pont du Garigliano, the highlights are linear.

There are practical considerations. The floor of the Pont des Arts is made of wooden cladding; when pedestrians cross, they can see through the cracks to the river below. If the lights were pointed upward, you could lose your sense of balance, so they point downward. Through the cracks in the cladding, strollers glimpse the Seine glimmering as it moves slowly to the sea.

One of Jousse's proudest illuminations is that of the Pont de Bir-Hakeim, which carries the No. 6 Métro line across the river. He took over a project conceived by the Italian architect Italo Rota, who envisioned the installation of sensory lights that would follow the Métro as it passed. But Jousse faced a shortage of funds, as well as scheduling problems: he and his team could work only between three and five in the morning, when the Métro wasn't running. "I thought about his idea long and hard," Jousse said. "Then it hit me! I decided to install lights underneath the Métro tracks." The resulting line of light illuminates the carriages of the Métro as they cross the bridge but is invisible the rest of the time. These days, the city of Paris is more aware than ever of the potential of the bridges to dazzle at night. It has asked architects designing new bridges to integrate lighting into their plans.

The artificial light draws us in, but what can be more romantic than the moon over a river? Gustave Flaubert felt such power when, in 1867, he wrote a letter to his dear friend and fellow writer George Sand: "Sunday night, at eleven o'clock, there was such lovely moonlight along the river and on the snow that I was taken with an itch for movement, and I walked for two hours and a half, imagining all sorts of things, pretending that I was travelling in Russia or in Norway. . . . I thought of you and I missed you."

THE POWER AND MAGIC of light on the Seine at night reminded me of the faster-flowing river of my childhood, the Niagara, and its powerful falls. Years ago, when I was living in Washington, D.C., and my daughter Alessandra was twelve, I took her to Niagara Falls. After dark, the falls were dressed up in a changing wardrobe of iridescent colors. We called on the technician responsible for the display. He led us onto a lookout that held his instrument panel and, like the Wizard behind the curtain in Oz, showed Alessandra how to do it.

She turned knobs and rushed out to the balcony to view her work, then rushed back in to change the colors. She colored the falls in rainbow hues; patriotic red, white, and blue; and what the technician called "bridal white." When the lights went off, he gave her a signed document that read, "This will certify that Alessandra on February 9 lit up both the American and Canadian Horseshoe Falls in the colors of the rainbow. The above recorded person now becomes an official 'Illuminator of Niagara.'" A kid's magic moment.

The Niagara is fierce and angry, the Seine slow and easygoing. But at night they evoke similar emotions: the wonder and joy that well up from watching their transformation in light.

*Passerelle Simone de Beauvoir with the Parc de Bercy on the Right Bank in the background. A pedestrian bridge, it opened in 2006.* © Gary Zuercher, glz.com, Marcorp Editions, and marcorp-editions.com.

*A fireworks display by Chinese artist Cai Guo-Qiang during Paris's annual October event, Nuit Blanche. Guo-Qiang's show,* One Night Stand, *was a pyrotechnic celebration of the sexual fantasy of having a one-night stand in Paris on the Seine.* THIERRY NAVA—COURTESY CAI STUDIO.

# THIRTEEN

# What's Sex Got to Do with It?

*Photographing couples on the banks of the Seine in spring—what a cliché! But why deprive yourself of the pleasure? Every time I encounter lovers, my camera smiles; let it do its job.*

—WILLY RONIS, photographer

ONE OCTOBER NIGHT a few years ago, the city of Paris celebrated sex. It happened in the most public of places: the middle of the Seine between the Musée d'Orsay and the Louvre.

*One Night Stand* was a "conceptual pyrotechnic explosive event" by the Chinese artist Cai Guo-Qiang. Cai doesn't create with acrylics or pastel; he paints with explosives. He once ignited a six-mile-long fuse to lengthen the Great Wall of China, so that "extraterrestrial intelligence on faraway planets will be able to see it." For the opening ceremony of the 2008 Beijing Summer Olympics, he choreographed fireworks that more than a billion people watched on television.

This time, he used fireworks displays to evoke the ultimate Paris

sex fantasy: a one-night stand on the Seine. The river, he said, was the
"eternal witness of the romantic history of France" and a setting to
"present an adventure into the night."

Writers and filmmakers have long coupled fireworks and sexuality.
In James Joyce's *Ulysses*, Leopold Bloom masturbates while fireworks
fill the sky and a young woman named Gerty MacDowell exposes her
underwear. (The scene helped ban the book's publication in the United
States and England.) For the 1955 film *To Catch a Thief*, Alfred Hitchcock beat the censors by cutting to fireworks when Grace Kelly and Cary
Grant were about to make love. (It remains one of the steamiest no-sex
sex scenes in movie history.) Times change, and in the twenty-first century, fireworks suggesting sex certainly don't shock the French. Paris City
Hall commissioned Cai's work of art for an official Nuit Blanche festival.

*One Night Stand* opened at midnight with the sounds of sex—heavy
breathing, gasping, and moaning—woven into a contemporary musical composition and broadcast across the river by loudspeaker. Rhyth-
mic drumming and what sounded like a monkey's mating call added
auditory texture. Next, a pyrotechnic display sent fireworks into the
air. The act lasted twelve minutes, estimated to be the length of time
the average French couple needs to climax, Cai Studios claimed in
a press release. Purple fireworks spelled out in English, "One Night
Stand" and "Let's Play."

As if the symbolic evocation of intercourse were not enough, Cai
transformed a *bateau-mouche* into a "love boat" where fifty couples
from around the world had sex inside translucent red tents. The couples were given the option of either turning off the lights in their tents
to copulate privately or turning them on to reveal their silhouettes in
motion. To share the bliss with the crowd, the lovers could press a but-
ton signaling operators in small boats nearby to send a fifteen-second
spurt of bright white fireworks into the air.

A minute of blazing silver fireworks acted as a "good-bye kiss."
Another message in purple fireworks followed: "Sorry Gotta Go." The
Seine swirled in purple, pink, and midnight blue. Then the sky lit up

with a finale of white, green, red, and purple bursts that shot up to 164 feet. Spectators crowded the banks and cheered. Even Bertrand Delanoë, then mayor of Paris, came out to watch the show.

Such an overtly sexual fireworks display (paid for with taxpayers' money) would never happen over the Potomac or the Hudson, or any river in the United States. But here in Paris, it was considered sheer pleasure. And, *bien sûr,* art.

PEOPLE SEEKING PHYSICAL SATISFACTION and personal liberation have often come to Paris. The Seine is part of the seduction. One of the most famous songs about the river, "La Seine," portrays the river as the city's paramour: "The Seine is a lover / And Paris sleeps in her bed."

French writers have found romantic inspiration in the river, illustrating their characters' intimacy and sensuality by setting their stories on its banks. In his 1869 novel *Sentimental Education*, Gustave Flaubert's characters find themselves sharing a meal along the river. "That evening they dined at an inn on the banks of the Seine. . . . They were served a chicken with its legs and arms spread, an eel stew . . . rough wine, hard bread, and blunt knives. . . . They felt almost as if they were in the middle of a journey, in Italy, on their honeymoon."

In Émile Zola's 1886 novel *The Masterpiece*, lovers Claude and Christine share an enchantment with the river that fuels their desire. They walk arm in arm along the quays, dazzled by the wharves and vessels and massive river barges. "The soul of the great city, rising from the waters, wrapped them in all the tenderness that had ever pulsed through its age-old stones," Zola wrote. Later, Claude, half-mad, drags Christine back to the same place on the Seine with the hope of rediscovering its magic: "There he stopped again, his gaze fixed upon the island riding forever at anchor in the Seine, cradling the heart of Paris through which its blood has pulsed for centuries."

In French literature, some writers portray the Seine as a curvaceous

woman; some even see a woman in the architecture. "Now it seems difficult for me to believe that others, venturing into the place Dauphine from
the Pont Neuf, should not have been overwhelmed at the sight of its triangular formation, with slightly curved lines, and of the slit which bisects it
into two wooded spaces," the surrealist—and sexist—André Breton wrote.
"It is, without any doubt, the sex of Paris that is outlined in this shade."

THE SEINE ONCE MEANT sexual liberation. But you had to leave
Paris to find it. After the construction of a railroad line to the western
suburbs in 1837, city dwellers began to flock to riverside pleasure pavilions known as *guinguettes*. The strict social mores governing city life
were left behind. In the countryside, Parisians ate simple fare, drank
cheap wine, and danced to live music. Millionaires mingled with artists' models; seduction was expected. One diversion was a *promenade sur
l'eau* (a river excursion) in a canoe; it could include swimming naked
among the reeds and under the hanging branches of willow trees.

In 1869, Monet and Renoir painted side by side at La Grenouillère
("The Froggery"), one of the most famous *guinguettes*. It was named
after the young and free-spirited female swimmers who frolicked in
the water like frogs. Optimistically promoted as "Trouville-sur-Seine"
after the seaside resort in Normandy, it featured a spa, a boating establishment, and a floating café. It was so fashionable that Napoléon III,
along with his wife, Eugénie, and their son, once visited.

In his short story "Femme Fatale," Guy de Maupassant painted a
dark portrait of La Grenouillère. "The place reeked of vice, corruption,
and the dregs of Parisian society . . . ," he wrote. "Cheats, con men, and
cheap hacks rubbed shoulders with under-age dandies, old roués and
rogues, sleazy underworld types once notorious for things best forgotten
mingled with other small-time crooks and speculators, dabblers in dubi-
ous ventures, frauds, pimps, and racketeers. Cheap sex, both male and
female, was on offer in this tawdry meat-market of a place."

Renoir's much brighter view of *guinguette* life, in his painting *Luncheon of the Boating Party,* captured the free-spirited mingling of the social classes at La Maison Fournaise, overlooking the Seine, and the joy of a glorious sunny afternoon meal on the terrace among friends. At the *guinguette,* Renoir felt liberated. "I was perpetually at Fournaise's," he wrote about his time spent there in 1869. "There I found as many splendid girls to paint as I wanted. One wasn't reduced as today to follow a little model in the street for an hour, only to be called a dirty old man in the end."

La Grenouillère closed long ago. A tiny museum struggles to preserve its memory. La Maison Fournaise, by contrast, is still a working restaurant, in what is now a prosperous suburb. At lunch on the balcony immortalized by Renoir, you will find yourself surrounded by business executives and families celebrating birthdays and anniversaries.

These days, the Seine in Paris is not really an inviting place for lovemaking (unless perhaps you live on a houseboat or check into the ultra-cool floating hotel named Off). Sex on the Seine sounds better in theory than in practice. The bridges are too public for copulation, and the romantic nooks under the bridges sometimes provide shelter to rats as large as cats. Even prostitution is not widespread along the Seine, as it is in more deserted areas such as the Bois de Boulogne on the western edge of the city.

With its open riverbanks, the Seine also invites predators. Bérengère and Joanna, two young women who worked with me, said that even in daylight, men harass women on the riverbanks. "You sit along the banks with your friends looking at the water, and men passing by feel they have the right to sit down next to you and start a conversation even when you don't want anything to do with them," Bérengère said. "It happens everywhere in Paris, but by the Seine it's scary." The women agreed that they would never walk along the Seine after a late-night party.

For gay men, the banks of the Seine have long been a place for cruising and a sexual refuge. In Blake Edwards's 1982 film *Victor Victoria,* Robert Preston plays Toddy, a struggling middle-aged gay impresario who waxes lyrical about Paris. "Along the banks of the Seine," he sings, "just take a walk now and then, you'll meet some interesting men: Gay Paree!"

Edmund White's 2001 book *The Flâneur* recounts his wanderings in Paris. He describes the best stretches of the Seine for cruising, as well as his own experiences, in passages that struck me as raw and vulgar the first time I read them. It was only when I came to know the power of the river—and after I got to know him—that I appreciated the sheer pleasure he took from these brief and random encounters.

When White arrived in Paris, forty-three and "fairly young-looking," he'd "cruise along the Seine near the Austerlitz train station under a building that was cantilevered out over the shore on pylons. Or," he continues, "I'd hop over the fence and cruise the pocket park at the end of the Île Saint-Louis, where I lived. There I'd either clatter through the bushes or descend the steps to the quay that wrapped around the prow of the island like the lower deck of a sinking ship. . . . I had to step over the giant rusting rings on the quayside to which boats could be roped—though I never saw a boat moored there. When the *bateaux-mouches* would swing around the island, their klieg lights were so stage-set bright that we'd all break apart and try to rearrange our clothing."

White evokes the memory of an "ardent, muscular lad" who went home with him several times but never told him his name or gave him his phone number. The young man said only that he was kept "in great style" in a townhouse in the Marais by a German businessman who looked a lot like Edmund. White admits that this behavior was not mainstream. "Of course, most people, straight and gay, think that cruising is pathetic or sordid," he writes. "But for me, at least, some of my happiest moments have been spent making love to a stranger beside dark, swiftly moving water below a glowing city."

FILMMAKERS HAVE EXPROPRIATED scenes of dark embraces interrupted by bright lights on the Seine. In that special moment in *Charade* when Cary Grant and Audrey Hepburn are falling in love on a *bateau-mouche*, the lights are illuminating other lovers. Nothing is left to chance. The script itself spells out what happens next: "A searchlight near the boat's bridge has gone on and now begins sweeping the river banks. On benches by the water's edge, lovers are surprised by the bright light which suddenly and without warning discovers them in various attitudes of mutual affection. Some are embarrassed, some amused, and some (the most intimate) damn annoyed. One even shakes his fist at the light."

The lights are indiscriminate; a *bateau-mouche* spotlight can reveal secrets. An acquaintance told me how a friend of hers, a Parisian woman in her sixties, learned of her husband's infidelity that way. One night, the husband, also in his sixties, happened to be passionately kissing a much younger woman on the banks of the Seine when they were caught by the piercing spotlight of a passing *bateau-mouche*. Shortly afterward, a television channel that had been filming from the boat aired a frothy feature on how tourists love to kiss on the banks of the Seine. The wife was watching the program and recognized her husband. She confronted him. They divorced.

FOR A MONTH every summer since 2001, sensuality and sexiness—if not sex—is officially sanctioned at a makeshift beach along the Seine. For a city dweller with no access to a house in the country, Paris Plages (Paris Beaches) serves as an egalitarian alternative. Until recent years, the city trucked in two thousand tons of sand to this urban riviera on the Right Bank, which attracts millions of people and has spawned copies around the world. (The city still brings in dozens of palm trees.) Paris beachgoers line up for free massages, dance lessons, games of *boules* and volleyball, trampoline jumping, and wall climbing. Deck chairs, outdoor showers, hammocks, and beach umbrellas are free. Cafés, restaurants, and ice cream stands offer refreshments. Corporate sponsors pick up much of the bill.

With transplanted beach culture come beach rules. Several years ago, the exposure of skin and the presence of "perverts and voyeurs" pushed Paris City Hall to enforce a ban on full nudity, bare breasts, and even thongs. "The behavior of the public must be in accordance with good morals, tranquillity, security, and public order," the ruling stated.

The police threatened to issue thirty-eight-euro fines to bathers who refused to cover up. "Heat wave or not, appropriate dress is required," proclaimed a front-page article in the newspaper *Le Parisien*. "This is a space of freedom, but if people want to see breasts, they should go to the Lido or the Moulin Rouge," said Yvan Hinnemann, a manager of Paris Plages.

Police officers and guards patrol the beach, although the rules are often stretched. Just as many men as women wear thongs that reveal their buttocks; the consensus seems to be that only bare-breasted women are at risk of a citation.

The truth is that the Seine—like many other settings in Paris—is ideal for seduction. You might have no intention of kissing the person you're with, or no hope of getting kissed back. But on the Seine, in the thrall of the bridges, dark water, and shimmering lights, it might happen. It's a place to fall in love, rekindle love, or bear witness to love.

An American friend of mine, Elizabeth Stribling, looks down at the Seine through the tall casement windows in the bedroom of the pied-à-terre she shares with her husband on the Île de la Cité. She opens the heavy drapes to revel in the romantic riverside stage set before her. "I see young lovers," she says. "I see old lovers, too. In Paris, there are a lot of old people just as amorous as the young ones. It's one of the things I love most about this river."

Her words echo those of the American novelist Sherwood Anderson nearly a century before: "On a bridge over the Seine—a young working man with his sweetheart. . . . They stood with arms about each other looking up the river. Occasionally they kissed, oblivious to the thousands of people passing, seemingly equally oblivious of them."

Tour guides on the *bateaux-mouches* say the Pont Marie is the lovers' bridge. The story goes that if you make a wish as the boat slips under the bridge and keep the wish secret, it will be granted. There are different versions of the story. One summer night, I took Laura and Heather, two students who were working with me in Paris, for a boat ride. As we approached the bridge, the recorded voice of a tour guide announced: "If you're with the person you love, kiss him or her under the bridge, make a wish, and your wish will come true."

Although her boyfriend was an ocean away, Heather closed her eyes and made a wish. A feeling of harmony filled the night. The Paris air was still hot, but it felt cooler by the Seine, and even though it was late, hundreds of people sat along the stone riverbanks and at the Vert-Galant park, at the tip of the Île de la Cité. We could see a party on the roof of a houseboat moored on the Right Bank, and dancing in the stone amphitheaters of the Tino Rossi Garden on the Left. The sun had set, turning the sky the palest of blue and the water a deep gray-blue with dark, rippling waves. Then the sky became a shade of rose and the Seine the color of gooseberry syrup, as Flaubert had described it to George Sand in a letter in 1866. The moon, yellow and full, hung low in the sky.

SHORTLY AFTERWARD, the luxury brand Chanel gave the river a starring role in an elusive game of seduction. In a black-and-white ad for Chanel's J12 ceramic unisex watch, French comic actress Camille Cottin and television and film actor Syrus Shahidi flirt and gaze into each other's eyes on the Pont Louis-Philippe in Paris. It is dusk, and the river shimmers silver in the reflection of the streetlights.

"Let's go," says Cottin.

"Yes, let's," Shahidi replies.

Cottin shouts "Taxi!" to the driver of a motorboat passing below, but Shahidi hesitates. Cottin decides to go alone. Clothed in a tight-fitting dark sweater, mini-shorts, and high heels, with the black Chanel watch on her wrist, she steadies herself on the bridge's stone guardrail, raises her arms above her head, and dives into the water with a crisp somersault. She swims to the boat, climbs in, and speeds off with the driver, who wears sunglasses and a boater's cap, leaving Shahidi behind.

"Diving into water," says Chanel in its online promotion, "has never been so alluring."

*A postcard depicting the 1910 flood in Paris. After months of heavy rainfall, the Seine overflowed and inundated much of the city, including every city bridge except the Pont Neuf and the Pont Royal.*

# FOURTEEN

# The Seine Also Rises

*Paris was swimming.*
—HELEN DAVENPORT GIBBONS,
an American writer, when the
Seine flooded Paris in 1910

As long as history has remembered the Seine, it has flooded. In May 2016, the rains came once again. The Seine swelled, churned, turned mud-brown, overflowed its banks, and flooded the land. Paris City Hall closed roads and turned off the lights along the river. The Louvre hauled priceless art out of its basement and into safer storage facilities on higher ground.

Boat travel in the city came to a halt. Floating restaurants and clubs on the river were submerged; some were destroyed. Basements, parking lots, and tunnels filled with water. Underground Métro and intercity train lines near the river shut down. Thousands of people were evacuated from towns around Paris. An eighty-six-year-old woman was found dead in her flooded home in a town nearby. On Friday, June 3, the Seine reached its peak, rising more than twenty feet above sea level, the highest level in thirty-four years. That day, there was only one person to call: my old friend Mort.

Mort Rosenblum is a book writer and former war correspondent who lives on a decommissioned British naval vessel on the Seine. It is 54 feet long, much smaller than a *Freycinet*, the classic 126-foot working river barge built to pass through the river's locks that works well when renovated as a residence. His is a fast military craft designed for the high seas. I know the name of Mort's boat, but he likes to keep it secret. He made one up when he wrote a memoir, a quarter century ago, about his river life.

The majority of the houses on the Seine are refitted barges, but like Mort's naval craft, there are odd and rare floating residences, including centuries-old wooden sailing ships and at least one Chinese junk. Looking down from a bridge, you cannot help but wonder what it is like to live on them.

Mort is in his early seventies, but he still wears his jeans low on his narrow hips and his hair wild and woolly. He has written books on subjects as diverse as chocolate and olive oil. He shares his life with his wife, Jeannette, but since her job often takes her on the road, the boat is very much his world. He loves cats and the same Cohiba cigars that Fidel Castro smoked. He is allergic to mold and dust mites, and the boat is full of both, so his asthma kicks up from time to time. When he talks, you must pay close attention to what he says; sometimes his words tumble out so fast that they trip over themselves.

In 1987, he was living in the perfect fifth-floor walk-up in an old building on the Île Saint-Louis; then his landlord found a better tenant and threw him out. He was the Paris bureau chief for the Associated Press back then, and when a British colleague and his wife decided to sell their boat and move back home, Mort bought it.

"It took only one lunch on deck," he wrote in his memoir. At the time he knew nothing about boats, describing himself as "a son of Arizona desert and a klutz with wrench or varnish brush."

Mort and I met for the first time in 1978, when he was still living on land. I had just arrived as a correspondent for *Newsweek*. At the Associated Press, he ran a large operation one floor below our bureau at 162 rue du Faubourg Saint-Honoré, close to the Élysée Palace and the luxury clothing boutiques, one of the swankiest journalistic addresses in town. Those were the days when many American foreign correspondents flew first-class, enjoyed generous allowances, and had expense accounts to dine at three-star Michelin restaurants. Mort was a veteran globetrotter who had covered wars—in Vietnam, in the Congo—and headed bureaus in Kinshasa, Lagos, Kuala Lumpur, Jakarta, Singapore, and Buenos Aires.

In contrast, I had been writing about the drought in Kansas and pork belly futures in Chicago. Later I would return to Paris, after a stint in Rome and two decades in New York and Washington, as bureau chief for the *New York Times*. But during that first sojourn in the city I was green, and Mort was generous with his knowledge.

Mort is a living encyclopedia of the Seine. All good journalists are storytellers; Mort is a great one. He gets a laugh when he talks about his life on land, when his clothes didn't smell bad and he had a warm, dry apartment in a charming old building with fireplaces and a rose garden on the terrace. He will tell you about the summer of 1992, when the water was warm, the oxygen level low, and a thousand tons of fish died and rotted in the river. He remembers the Piscine Deligny, an outdoor floating swimming pool moored near the Musée d'Orsay, where—until it sank in 1993—women went topless and men sometimes swam in the nude.

At the time of the 2016 flood, Mort and I hadn't talked in a few years. I dug up an old cell phone number for him and dialed.

"Meet me on the boat," he said.

"Can't we meet on dry land?" I asked. "How about if I buy you lunch?"

"You need to experience this moment!" he said. "Come along topside. If you want to see the Seine, you have to come out onto the Seine."

The boat doesn't have a fixed address, although it has been based in and around the Port des Champs-Élysées since the 1970s. He moors it alongside other houseboats. It has a hull of double teak planking; a living room with mahogany cabinets and built-in benches and bookcases; a kitchen with a three-burner gas stove, a mini-refrigerator, hand-painted Portuguese tiles, and heavy copper pots; a portable air conditioner; a functioning toilet; a tiny bathtub; a small bedroom; and a furnished deck overflowing with potted red geraniums.

Mort has decorated the space with trophies and trinkets from his travels: a hand-carved sailboat from Vietnam, a large crab shell from Brittany, a collection of wooden pipes. Over the years, he has learned how to install water pumps, replace oil joints, rewire cabin lights, and varnish decks. He has bought fire extinguishers, life vests, buoys, and deck furniture. He has learned the tricks of navigating the Seine: how to swing away from silt deposits that form at the bend of a curve, watch for telltale debris and ripples that could be hiding rocks, and shimmy in and out of locks.

To get to his boat, Mort told me to take the Métro to the Solférino stop, cross the footbridge in front of the Quai d'Orsay, then turn left. "I'm four boats toward the place de la Concorde," he said. "You'll see a chair on one side of the wall that's connected to a ladder on the other side. You climb onto the chair, swing over, and come down the ladder. Then there's a gangway. Walk slowly. It's almost sitting in the water. The river's steady, but don't move too much. It's precarious."

Flooding has always been part of life in the Seine basin. The Marais, on the Right Bank, was once a giant swamp (*marais* means "swamp"). Grégoire de Tours, the sixth-century historian and bishop of Tours, described a catastrophic flood in 582 that inundated hundreds of acres. A book about the life and miracles of Sainte Geneviève described the flood of 814 as God's punishment of the people of Paris. In the thirteenth and fourteenth centuries, believers marched in a procession through the flood-ravaged parts of the city and appealed for the saint's help. In 1658, shortly after flood levels began to be precisely recorded, the Seine's waters rose to twenty-nine feet above their normal level, covering more than twenty-eight hundred acres—over half the surface of the city. The floodwaters washed away the Seine's Pont Marie, even though the bridge was built of stone.

In the modern era, Parisians have measured floods against the great one that came in the winter of 1910, when the Seine overflowed, and the City of Light was submerged in chaos and darkness. Torrential rains soaked the soil. The river rose twenty-eight feet above its normal level. The sewers failed. The river that had breathed life into Paris drowned its streets, houses, museums, and shops. It flooded twenty thousand buildings. All but two bridges—the Pont Neuf and the Pont Royal—were totally submerged. There was no electricity, no Métro. For forty-five days, parts of the city were transformed into a lake of filth and debris, as far north as the Gare Saint-Lazare. Parisians navigated the streets in rowboats and on wooden walkways. The Eiffel Tower, built on a foundation of sand, shifted three-quarters of an inch. But Gustave Eiffel was a wizard of engineering. He had also built his creation on hydraulic pumps, and the tower moved back into place when the floodwaters receded.

After that flood, the city constructed reservoirs upstream to help manage the Seine's water level. Now six large dams hold back excess water during winter and release it during the hot, dry summer months. The porous, permeable rock of the Seine's basin absorbs some of the water, which reduces the risk of flooding. But when the rains came in 2016, the dams were full, the soil saturated. Nothing could stop the flow.

I DONNED AN ANORAK, jeans, a small backpack, and rubber-bottomed work shoes. I headed out, following Mort's directions, and found the upper quay at the designated spot. The quay held rows of densely packed houseboats. Three boats can be parallel-parked on the river at one mooring. They can share water and electrical power lines. If you happen to live on the third boat out, you must climb over the decks of your two neighbors to get to dry land. Mort lived on the third boat. He waved from his deck, clambered across his neighbors' decks, crossed a flimsy metal walkway connected to the land, climbed up a vertical metal ladder bolted into the quay, and stepped over a stone barrier onto an old chair that filled in for a stepstool; with another stride he reached the sidewalk. We took the same route in reverse to get to the boat. The flood had knocked out Mort's water and electricity. Jeannette was away. It was cold and dreary. The boat smelled of diesel, damp, and cat.

Usually, the river in Paris enjoys a steady stream of traffic: *bateaux-mouches*, the sightseeing giants; smaller, more agile tourist boats like those run by the Vedettes de Paris; low-slung working barges; tugboats; motorboats. The traffic is so dense that if you live on a houseboat, you feel it moving. The wakes from the larger vessels can cause your boat to shudder and sway and can topple your balance. But these were not normal times. The water had risen too high for boats to pass beneath the arches of the bridges. Now the only boats on the river were those of the Brigade Fluviale, the river police.

Life on land appears different when you look at it from a river, even more so when the river is swollen. Usually the stone walls along the quay block the street-level view of the Right Bank. But the water had lifted Mort's boat so high that the obelisk on the place de la Concorde was entirely visible.

The Seine is a slow river, only now the water was moving fast. It swirled in spirals, flowed backward, and kicked up waves. Paris's detritus went by: tree trunks, wooden planks, car tires, tin cans, air conditioners, fans, plastic bags, bicycles, and bottles, so many bottles—wine, beer, water, and baby bottles.

Tourists had been gathering on the banks and bridges to record the swollen waters with their cameras and smartphones, clustering around the city's unofficial water gauge, the statue of the Zouave on the Pont de l'Alma. Water reaching the statue's toes shows that the river is running high; water reaching his thighs shows that the river is unnavigable. The year 2016 was truly remarkable: the water rose to his hips. During the great flood of 1910, when Paris nearly drowned, it reached his shoulders.

Despite all his years covering disasters, Mort said he had never seen the river this high. "One night I'm sitting on my deck drinking a glass of wine, and the ducks are swimming by, and everything is perfectly normal," he said. "And the next morning I wake up and it's like Noah's ark! It's a sign. This is not supposed to happen. Anyone who doesn't think global warming exists has to have his head examined."

Mort almost lost his car to the river. As the water rose, he moved it to higher ground and thought it was safe. Then he received an urgent call from Jeannette, who had seen the car featured in an online warning notice from the small port association representing houseboat owners. The water was drawing nearer to the vehicle. Mort put on waders and walked through waist-high water to get to it. Exhausted, he managed to move the car to still higher ground.

*A scene of a lamppost in Paris during the 2016 flood.* ANDREW PLUMP.

"It was already going underwater," he said. "Half an hour more and it would have been too late."

"But how did you get it to start?"

"It's a Volkswagen."

Houseboats are not unique to Paris, of course. But no other houseboat community has views of the Eiffel Tower, the Louvre, and so many long strands of bridges connecting the riverbanks. When I'd first moved to Paris, I'd gazed down at them from the Pont de l'Alma and wondered who were those people perched on *chaises longues* on their decks, sipping white wine and watching the sun as it settled into the river. I've never fantasized about living on a houseboat, but a few glorious nights? Living on a houseboat, you belong to the romance of the river. You belong to Paris at its heart.

The French live on boats along many of the country's rivers, but the densest community is in the Paris area on the Seine, where more than thirteen hundred residential boats are officially registered. They fit into two categories: working boats that have been transformed into homes, and motorless houses floating on pontoons.

The same social and cultural divide between city and suburban life translates to life on the water. In lower-end areas, like the Canal de l'Ourcq, which feeds into the Seine in Paris, some houseboats are little more than shabby dinghies for two. Some of the poshest floating houses in France are docked in the upscale suburbs west of Paris. They have their own street addresses, mailboxes, and independent electrical, gas, and water lines. There's little water traffic in their neighborhoods.

Along a narrow river path near the Club Nautique, in the suburb of Sèvres, are dozens of elaborate floating houses. Rosebushes, palm trees, and evergreens embellish some of their decks. Inside are Persian carpets, leather furniture, and pale wood paneling. An inspection of one home revealed a Weber grill and a tall Christmas tree heavy with ornaments; another boasted enough neatly stacked firewood to last the winter; still another had a modern eat-in kitchen, with picture windows looking out at the river. *Sinbad* was a floating house with a brass anchor door knocker; *Bel Ami* was a mansion of a barge, with a small, inflatable Zodiac boat and a motorboat tied to its side (perhaps recalling Maupassant, who gave the name *Bel Ami* to a boat he owned and a novel he wrote); *Light II* was a modernistic construction of white and gray angles, with an abstract painting hanging in the front hallway.

Years ago, I heard a dramatic house-on-the-river tale of woe from Pierre Bergé, the longtime partner of the designer Yves Saint Laurent. One summer in the 1960s, Bergé rented a shabby-chic houseboat on the Seine. He was seeking a weekend refuge with Saint Laurent, who had suffered a severe nervous breakdown. The designer had just returned from hospitalization in a military facility, where he had endured powerful drugs and electroshock therapy.

The houseboat they rented wasn't a boat at all—it was a real house that happened to float in a classy and quiet neighborhood: off boulevard du Général Koenig in the rich western Paris suburb of Neuilly. "The Seine boat was my version of a house in the country," Bergé said. "Our lives are cluttered with too many things. On a boat, you're stripped to the essentials. It was marvelous."

The friend who had rented Bergé the floating house was oblivious to its seaworthiness. "I would tell him, 'The boat is not in a good state,'" Bergé recalled. "I would say, 'The boat takes in water.' His answer was always the same: '*Ah, bon?*'" One Sunday night that summer, a three-deck canasta game heated up. Saint Laurent, Bergé, and two of their friends were so deep into meld making and point scoring that they didn't bother to eat or drink. Nor did they notice what was happening around them.

That night the boat was taking in water. A lot of it. A team of river police patrolling the Seine noticed. The police ordered the men to stop their game and evacuate. They watched from shore as the houseboat sank.

*Houseboats in the Port de l'Arsenal, in Paris off the Seine.* ANDREW PLUMP.

———

BUYING A HOUSEBOAT in Paris requires a huge investment of time and money. A luxury houseboat can cost as much per square foot as an apartment on land. France is notorious for—and perversely proud of—the complex and contradictory, mysterious and mind-bending bureaucratic hurdles and red tape that confound even the most patient supplicant. Houseboat ownership takes this centuries-old tradition to a new level. The process of buying a houseboat starts with a twenty-eight-page guidebook from the governmental authority Voies Navigables de France. The guidebook asserts that houseboats along the Seine are pretty and make Paris "most attractive." But buying one is not an endeavor for the faint-hearted: "Occupying a site on the public domain of the river is precarious, revocable, and non-transferable," it warns.

Complicated procedures involve six different agencies for document registrations, certification of navigation, inspections, insurance, and obtaining a sailing license. A houseboat cannot be sold with a parking place—that is public property. The wait for a berth in Île-de-France, which includes the area in and around Paris, can last years. There was a time when living on a houseboat was a comparatively cost-effective way to set yourself up in Paris. That would change in 1994, when the VNF and the Paris port authority imposed a housing tax, a mooring fee, and a contract of occupation. With those added costs, the fantasy of renting a berth in a prime location in central Paris with an unobstructed view of the Eiffel Tower turns out to be expensive.

In recent years, though, Airbnb has made it easy to rent a houseboat in Paris for a temporary stay. A large, floating house that sleeps eight might cost three hundred euros a night. The promise of romance is one of the selling points. As one rental website explains in its promotional material, "What can be more romantic than dining on the deck of an authentic ship, while feeling the energetic city around you?"

———

MORT RARELY PULLS his boat out of its berth and onto the river these days. It would take too long and be too much trouble. He spends his winters back in his home state of Arizona, where he teaches journalism, and his summers at his olive farm in southern France. Even though he lives in Paris for only about four months a year, Mort usually keeps the boat unoccupied when he is away. He once lent it to his sister and her children for their vacation. Another boater hit Mort's boat, and the fuel-pump switch malfunctioned. His sister didn't know how to fix it, and a flood of oil poured into the main living area, covering the floor and soaking a precious Oriental carpet. It took three days to clean up the mess; the smell of oil lingered for weeks.

Mort is convinced that as climate change accelerates, the river will become ever more vulnerable to flooding and a less desirable place to call home. "The boat is getting to be kind of a mess," he confessed. "And Jeannette wants to be more settled." He also laments the gentrification of the boat-dwelling class—many lawyers and businessmen, fewer artists and writers.

When I asked Mort if the river had changed him, he swatted away my question.

"Hard to say, you know? Because I don't know what I'd be otherwise. I have to have a home in Paris," he said.

"But so much of your work is outside of France," I said.

"So much energy and knowledge pass through Paris. And I love it on the boat. I mean, look, I'm sitting there, and it is rocking back and forth, there is beautiful light, all the windows are open, there is a breeze, I've got this beautiful bottle of wine. . . . I'm in the middle of the city, you know, and I'm always in the elements."

I asked him if he needed a place to stay until the river's waters receded.

"*Je ne quitte pas mon bateau,*" he said. "I don't leave my boat."

*Grain in a cargo barge at the capital's main port at Gennevilliers.* © HAROPA—PORTS DE PARIS AGNÈS JANIN.

# FIFTEEN

# A Bend in the River

*Don't worry. You will see the world.*
—JEAN, a bargeman, to his bride,
Juliette, in the 1934 film *L'Atalante*

RIVER BARGES DATE BACK to antiquity. The Seine was already a busy commercial river during the Roman invasion of Gaul. Julius Caesar reported that Labienus, one of his best lieutenants, captured fifty barges at the port of Melun and used them to advance northwest in his successful attack on Lutetia. In the Gallo-Roman era that followed, merchants used the Seine, and a network of other rivers and streams, to deliver tin, lead, and grain from the English Channel to France, and to move commodities like Spanish oil, Italian marble, and French wine and pottery up to the British Isles. In the early Middle Ages, barges transported blocks of highly polished, white building stone from Caen on a stretch of the Seine to erect churches throughout Normandy.

Over the centuries, water continued to be the most practical way to move people and goods, as transporting overland by road was painfully slow and expensive. Grain shipments were particularly important, because bread was the anchor of most people's diets. By the sixteenth century, barges did most of the hauling along the Seine, even moving exotic goods, like a dark reddish wood that originated in Brazil, to Rouen for dyeing cloth bright red and purple.

By the eighteenth century in Paris, the Seine was a living organism—chaotic, dirty, crowded, and intense. Dyers tinted silks, fabrics, and hats from a quay on the Île de la Cité; families worked together, washing and cleaning animal organs for sale; washerwomen on designated laundry boats used the polluted Seine water in an often futile effort to clean clothing and linens; vendors set up stalls on the quays to peddle lottery tickets; floating grain mills clogged the river. Merchants sold fish, fruits, and vegetables from floating shops on the river and fixed stalls on its banks. Barges sometimes had difficulty passing through and docking in the city.

Operators of river barges made a decent living carrying goods as varied as sand, coal, grain, stones, iron, metals, salt, and wine. However, when railroad lines were built in the nineteenth century, barge commerce spiraled downward. The trend accelerated after World War II, as rail and highway transport boosted economic growth. By the early 1980s, the barge industry was doomed. The Socialist government of President François Mitterrand poured massive sums of money into the state-owned railway system, expanded the network of highways, and subsidized overland freight traffic. The bargemen, fiercely independent and isolated from mainstream society, had neither a lobby in parliament nor a union to protect them. In 1950, there were fifteen thousand *bateliers*—bargemen who haul cargo along the Seine; today there are only about a thousand.

But the spirit of the barge world lives on, celebrated at Conflans-Sainte-Honorine, the Seine port and traditional French capital of the *bateliers*, located at the confluence of the Seine and Oise Rivers, twenty-five miles northwest of Paris by car, thirty-four by boat. Hundreds of *bateliers*, most of them retired, live there, and they revel in celebrating the lives they once led on the river.

Every year, Conflans recalls the joys and sorrows of barge life with a two-day festival of boat excursions, tours, exhibitions, music, dancing, and speeches by local officials. The French navy and the port authority of the cities of Paris, Rouen, and Le Havre send recruiters.

The most poignant event the year I attended was a performance by the choir of the Clos de Rome, an assisted-living residence that caters to *bateliers* and their families.

THE CHOIR CONSISTED of seven women ranging in age from seventy-three to ninety-three. Their hair was neat and cropped short; they wore what they called "Sunday dress," sober black pants or skirts and white tops fancy enough for churchgoing. They mounted a tented stage at the end of a day so hot and humid that the river seemed ready to boil over and the pink cotton candy puffs turned liquid in their paper cones. But the choir is the living memory of the songs sung on the river for more than a century, and the crowd had been waiting for them.

I had always understood barge life as a man's world. It hadn't occurred to me that there were barge*women*, as strong, tough, and resilient as their husbands (even though this group looked like the gentlest of grandmothers).

Miguel Biard, the forty-seven-year-old maestro, told the crowd he had grown up as a fourth-generation *batelier* and wanted to celebrate the men and women who lived and worked on barges. He had pieced together lyrics from his grandfather's notebook and from navigation diaries found in the Conflans museum. The songs, set to well-known melodies, told stories of hard labor, protests, and injustice.

"These songs are about real events that happened during everyday life on the barges," Miguel said. "They are part of our river heritage. I have nothing against people on land, but today we are in the world of the water." He used the word *terriens* when he referred to "people on land"; the word translates to "terrestrials" and also to "landlubbers."

A rotating disco ball sent beads of white light falling onto the stage. An accordionist behind a curtain began to play. The singers gripped their sheet music, smiled wide, and sang loud. The first song, "Dans nos péniches," a singsongy tune that made you want to dance, dated from 1904. I heard the words "rich" and "happy" and assumed it extolled the pleasure of barge life. Only later did I learn the full lyrics: "On our barges, *mesdames* and *messieurs*, we are neither rich nor happy. . . . The only thing we eat is work."

"The Tribulations of the Canal Saint-Denis," the song that followed, told the story of bargemen who lived on the canal and rented horses to haul barges that weighed as much as 250 tons. When there were no horses, humans had to pull those barges into the docks. Miguel said that some of his singers had pulled barges as an everyday chore and praised their hard work; the crowd burst into applause.

The third song "Le Batelier," from the 1950s, celebrated the freedom that came with barge life. The *batelier* "is happy to live this way. He is the only master aboard his boat. . . . He loves his kind barge-woman as much as his beautiful river."

Spectators clapped to the beat. When the singers finished, the crowd cheered, and the choir started up again. Miguel treated the women like rock stars. "I want to introduce these elderly barge ladies!" Miguel said. "Liliane, who remembered these songs, from the boat *Notsa*! Reymonde, from the same boat, because she is Liliane's sister. Monique, a lady of the land, but who sings well and has her place in this choir. Ginette, of the boat *Gima*. Olga of the boat *Pirée*. Nicole of the boat *Épinoche*. And Simone. Which boat, Simone?"

I waited until the stage cleared, then introduced myself to Miguel. He said he had abandoned the barge to become an archaeologist. His mother, Arlette Renau, had spent her childhood and much of her adult life as a *batelière*—a female barge worker—and was at his side. I asked if we could meet again. Arlette said she would welcome me into her home even though I was "a lady of the land."

The day was hot, the air still, when I called on Arlette in the working-class village of Veneux–Les Sablons. She lived with six cats in a small, functional house at the confluence of the Seine and Loing Rivers, near Fontainebleau. She welcomed me into a space that served as both dining and living room. She had hot and cold running water, a modern shower and toilet, and brand-new kitchen appliances. There was no central heating; a wood stove warmed her home. Several small, framed oil paintings of boats hung on the walls, bearing witness to the years she and her family lived and worked on the river. She received no pension for her barge years.

Arlette grew up knowing that she would continue the barge life of her parents and grandparents. She would have been born on the river had the Germans not invaded France in 1940 and seized the family's barge for use as a tank transporter. To give his wife and children a place to stay during the Occupation, her father bought the house where she was now living. He spent two years as a prisoner of war. When he came home, he bought another barge. The family returned to its itinerant life, hauling heavy cargo, like sand and coal, along the river. Arlette should have gone to one of the special state-run boarding schools for children of barge people, institutions run with military efficiency and without love. Arlette's parents rejected that option and decided instead to keep their children on board.

Arlette spent her childhood on the boat, going barefoot and wearing whatever she liked. She taught herself how to read and write. "My father thought school was a waste of time," she said. "His world was work. But he was curious and cultivated. My father always told me, 'If you want to learn, observe nature. Everything is there, you'll understand.' "

"Yeah, but when you had to go to the bank and deal with a banker, nature didn't help," Miguel interjected.

"Did you suffer?" I asked.

"I never saw it as a sacrifice," she said. "It was freedom. The happiest time of my life was when I was a child being with my parents. How awful, school! I never could've gone to boarding school. I would've run away. Or killed myself."

Arlette's mother took her as *matelot*—first deckhand—on a barge when she was only twelve; Arlette's father navigated a second barge with her brother. When Arlette went out among those she called "people on land," she was mocked for not speaking or writing proper French. "I was wild," she said.

She became pregnant at twenty by a bargeman and married him even though she did not love him. She almost lost Miguel, her youngest, to kidney cancer when he was two years old. A young niece drowned in the Seine after she slipped off the wet deck of Arlette's boat. The insular culture created its own complications. "It was a family operation," she said. "It was forbidden to take a barge out alone, so you had to have a partner with you. That meant a bargeman couldn't survive if his wife didn't work with him. Women did everything a man did."

"Women had to do all the household chores, too—shopping, cooking, cleaning the cabin, taking care of the kids," Miguel said. "The man never did any of that. My father never changed or washed a diaper." Addressing his mother, he added, "When you were very pregnant, you had to carry buckets of water down to the hold."

"Yes, but that was in my day," Arlette said. As a bargewoman for twenty-two years of her adult life, Arlette drove the boat, emptied the oil tank, chopped wood, maintained the engine, scraped and painted the hull, and bailed out water—sometimes by hand. "I once had to spend all night taking an engine apart!" she said.

Arlette swept the cargo hold clean after every delivery, sometimes encountering dangerous substances like lead, sulfur, and soot. She breathed in fine cereal dust and poisonous asbestos. She became ill when lead ore was loaded onto the barge. But in those days, health issues were not the bargeman's priority, and she loved the freedom of barge life. The deck became a playground for her children. When it was loaded high with sand, they would dig holes and build castles. "I adored every minute of it," said Arlette. "It kept me positive in life no matter what."

Then life became unbearable. Arlette's husband suffered from depression and physically abused her. She broke one of the unwritten rules of barge culture when she divorced him. As they owned two barges, she tried to go it alone on the other one. But without a helpmate, and struggling to support her children, she fell deep into debt. She was forced to live on land, in a small apartment subsidized by the state. She earned what she could cleaning factories and houses. "I felt like a bird in a cage," she said.

For Miguel, her son, nothing about this life was ever romantic. He was born on the barge and sent away to state boarding school between the ages of six and fifteen. At twenty-three, he abandoned barge life to pursue a more conventional path. "When you stand on the banks of the Seine in Paris, the work of a bargeman looks like a picturesque profession," said Miguel. "You cannot imagine how hard the life is."

Over time, the roughness wore him down. "You didn't keep garbage on the boat—it smelled bad," Miguel said. "You used the river as a garbage dump. You did your business in a chamber pot and threw it into the water."

When the bargemen docked, "You weren't super-clean because you were still working, and your hair wasn't cut and combed nicely like landlubbers'," Miguel said. "Frankly, sometimes we were disgusting. We made campfires, we yelled, we played music, we made noise. We ate, drank, and fought a lot. We went to nightclubs at the age of twelve and to streets where prostitutes worked."

Petty theft was part of *batelier* culture. The dockworkers were complicit. They trafficked in cigarettes and whiskey. They would slit open a fifty-pound bag of sugar and fill up a jar for the family of a favorite bargeman.

"My father did not do that," said Arlette. "The only thing we did was salvage what we could from scrap piles—bolts, brackets, screws, stuff like that. When I was a kid, I walked around looking for things to take. Since I was a kid, no one did anything to stop me."

"*Terriens* were afraid of you," said Miguel.

They also called the bargemen names: *manouche*, slang for "gypsy," and *caoutchoucs*, meaning "rubbers," because of the heavy rubber boots they wore on board. The bargemen themselves had cliques. Loire bargemen looked down on Seine bargemen. "They called us 'the black jaws,' because we carried so much coal," he said.

IN 1934, screenwriter and director Jean Vigo made *L'Atalante*, a landmark film on the world of the *batelier*, released just after he died of tuberculosis at age twenty-nine. The Gaumont studio cut the film to make it more marketable, but film historians preserved Vigo's original footage. When I saw it at the Cinémathèque film center in Paris, it had been restored and remastered to its original glory, with the enthusiastic sponsorship of Gaumont.

The standing-room-only crowd was transported into a world of fantasy and hardship, of love and broken dreams on the Seine barge named *L'Atalante*. The viewer can feel the cold dampness of the river at night, the claustrophobia of the living quarters, the powerful allure of life on land in Paris. François Truffaut once said that Vigo achieved poetry with this film. Martin Scorsese called Vigo a "visionary."

The film tells the story of Jean, the captain of a traditional 126-foot-long river barge, who marries Juliette, a peasant's daughter. There is no wedding party or honeymoon. Juliette is still in her wedding dress when Jean takes her to the barge where they will live with a first mate, a cabin boy, and a passel of cats.

Vigo's camera lingers over scenes of daily life in the cramped, indoor spaces of the barge, even as the vessel plies its way through bucolic settings. Juliette soon finds barge life suffocating. One night when the barge is docked in Paris, Jean takes his wife to a bistro and dance hall. A peddler-magician sings to Juliette about his chic Parisian wares, and they dance. Furious, Jean drags her back to the barge. But Juliette longs to see Paris at night. She slips away, planning to be back on board before Jean awakes. Discovering that she is not there, Jean falls into a rage, unmoors the barge, and leaves Paris. Juliette is left alone in the city.

Juliette loses her money to a purse snatcher and has to take a menial job. In her absence, Jean falls into a deep depression. But the Seine is pure and clear, a means of entering an imaginary world of peace and wisdom. Juliette once told Jean that by opening your eyes underwater, you could see the face of the one you love. He jumps in and, swimming with his eyes open, deep below the surface, sees a vision of her, smiling, in her wedding dress.

The first mate eventually finds Juliette, and she returns to start her life with Jean anew. In the film's final shot, the barge, seen from above, looks sleek and triumphant as it moves with confidence along the river.

THESE DAYS, Conflans-Sainte-Honorine preserves two pillars of traditional barge culture: a floating Catholic church for the *bateliers* and a museum dedicated to their history. Since 1932, the church, Saint Nicolas of the Batellerie Chapel, has inhabited a converted barge named *Je Sers*—"I Serve." Moored along the quay among the barges of *bateliers* who have made Conflans their floating retirement community, the chapel has a small library, a multipurpose recreation and meeting room, a kitchen and dining area, and cabins that function like a small dormitory. Alcohol and drugs are banned on the premises.

An adjoining barge serves as the chapel's floating self-service laundromat, where visitors wash their clothes and hang them on lines on deck. Local shops and supermarkets donate food for the meals that the volunteer church staff members prepare, feeding as many as 130 people a day. No one in need is turned away. On the day I visited, four Tibetans were playing table tennis; they were not bargemen but refugees seeking asylum. "If people have difficulties, they can always find a roof and a meal here," said Sister Marie-Rose, a volunteer from the Little Sisters of the Assumption.

The Musée de la Batellerie (Museum of Barge Navigation) opened in 1967 in a nineteenth-century mansion on a hilltop overlooking the gentle landscape of the Seine Valley. Despite its small size, it is considered the most important museum devoted to the history of inland navigation in France. Among its treasures are miniature wooden barges, maquettes that explain the history of barge life, and a collection of old black-and-white photographs that bear witness to daily life on the river.

The most impressive feature is a corner containing rows of periodicals

REMORQUEUR PRÈS DU PONT DE BERCY.

that the museum's Association of Friends publishes. One issue was dedicated to a bargewoman who wrote the following passage about her life: "To be a seafaring woman, you have to know how to read, write, count, swim, paint, varnish, run, jump from a boat onto land, eat in seven minutes. . . . You must be resistant to cold, heat, storms, humidity. You must have no fear of danger. . . . If you are sick or expecting a baby, your daily workload doesn't change."

She could have been describing Arlette.

*A nineteenth-century engraving of a tugboat near Pont de Bercy.*

THE SEINE BASIN is still a transit route for more than twenty million tons of freight every year. But barge people agree that the life of the old-fashioned *batelier* is over. There are two different worlds now: the nostalgists and the futurists. For both camps, the changes are permanent—and pervasive. The isolation and loneliness that came from months on the water have receded, along with the kind of closeness that comes from insularity. Now anyone can connect on Facebook and communicate online. There's even a blog for retired boatmen. "All the nomads are now in contact," said Arlette. I couldn't tell if she was celebrating a sign of progress or lamenting a lost way of life.

Many of the old-timers and their offspring who are still working have moved on to navigating the big tourist boats of Paris. When I took a week-long luxury cruise on the Seine, I met Stéphane Humbert, an ex-*batelier* who has made it as a cruise-ship captain. He was a fourth-generation bargeman from northern France, near Nancy. From the ages of six to sixteen, he was forced to live away from his parents in a boarding school. "It was very, very hard, as much for the parents as the kids," he said. "You did everything on your own from the time you were six. You washed alone. You dressed alone. You made your bed alone. You ate alone. To sleep alone—in a great dormitory with a hundred and fifty kids—was really hard. It's like the military, except you are a kid. You learn to manage on your own very quickly. Otherwise you don't survive."

When it was time for his much younger sister to be put into a boarding school, his parents could not face the rupture. They quit the profession, and his father went to work as the captain of a cruise ship. Stéphane followed suit. As a ship's skipper, when he is called on to mingle with the guests, he wears a uniform that looks a world away from his difficult youth: a white dinner jacket, black serge trousers with crisp creases, a black bow tie, and shiny black dress shoes.

There is a new generation of *bateliers* with bigger, newer boats and cutting-edge technology that navigates the river for them. They have one-thousand-square-foot living spaces with toilets and showers. "They laugh at the old ways of the river bargemen, even if they have descended from four generations of sailors," said Miguel. "Their goal is to earn a good living, not to reminisce about the lives of their parents."

"Before, you had to know how to steer a boat," said Arlette. "You had to know the interactions of the boat with the current, the wind, the height of the water, the reports from the bridges and the locks, as the ancients say. Even with artificial tools, we still had to 'feel the water.' We had to feel the boat. We walked with the vibrations. Now anyone can steer a boat, because there is radar and an engine in front and another one in the back."

These days, river transport is praised as "green." *Bateliers* and environmentalists point out that it takes twenty-five fuel-guzzling trucks to carry merchandise that would fit on one barge. Paris proper is no longer the big working port it once was, but Haropa, the institution that governs the port complexes of Le Havre (Ha), Rouen (Ro), and Paris (Pa), is expanding and integrating its activities. Most of the growth involves "giants of the sea"—ships that each contain up to ten thousand twenty-foot containers, not barges. The goal is to make the Seine the heart of a transportation network that connects markets in and around Paris to more than seven hundred international ports. Increasingly, container ships deliver goods from around the world, including finished products like furniture, appliances, electronics, textiles, and toys.

Paris's main port complex—and the largest river port in France, with canals, loading docks, basins, warehouses, and quays—occupies 954 acres in Gennevilliers, just northwest of the city. One day when I visited, a multistory gantry crane moved brightly colored containers emblazoned with names like Hanjin, Yang Ming, Evergreen, and Cosco from ships to a docking area along the river.

The Franprix supermarket chain, with financial support from the city of Paris, uses a much smaller port area near the Eiffel Tower as part of its "Franprix Enters the Seine" initiative. By 2018, Franprix was moving goods for three hundred of its outlets in and around Paris via the Seine. That same year, the French transportation giant Bolloré Logistics, also with government support, launched a once-a-week, eco-friendly commercial-freight river shuttle between Le Havre, on the Atlantic, and Bonneuil-sur-Marne, southeast of Paris.

AS THE BARGE WORLD changes, Miguel is rushing to preserve the past. Working with a filmmaker, he made a documentary about his family's life. He had precious raw material: in 1924, his grandfather bought an early movie camera to record the everyday life of bargemen and built a darkroom deep in the barge he'd named *Go-Ahead*; his son Freddy, also a *batelier*, continued to film. They left behind hours of raw footage.

Miguel screened the film, *Aboard the* Go-Ahead: *Memories of Sea-*

*men*, at a weekend festival in the port city of Rouen. It interspersed old footage with current interviews Miguel had conducted with his mother Arlette, Freddy, and Freddy's wife, Marie-Noelle. "You always see the bargemen from the water's edge, but never from within," he told the audience. He said it had taken years to convince Freddy to turn over the footage and for him and other family members to share their stories. The interviews marked "the first time I ever heard my uncle Freddy speak to 'terrestrials,'" Miguel joked.

On the day I visited Arlette at her home, she said she took comfort in the fact that her barge had been bought by a person who loved it, that she hadn't been forced to sell it for scrap. "To tear apart a boat for scrap is to tear apart the heart of the sailor," she said.

But she continued mourning the loss of her life on water. "In my house, I feel nothing, I hear nothing," she said. "With the double-glazed windows, I can't even hear the rain. When I was in the boat, I could hear the wind. I could hear the fish coming onto the raft! The landscape was always changing, the weather, too. There was the magnificent fog. I saw misty landscapes, the mist that formed tears on your face. It was fabulous. The boat was freedom."

Her voice trailed off. She started to cry. I reached across the table and took her hand. She didn't pull away.

"It is life, and we must turn the page," she said. "But a house? A house is a completely different way of life, even if it is at the edge of the water. I do not have blood in my veins. I have water."

She teared up again. "When I die, I want my ashes to be put into a bag and thrown here, in the Seine," she said. "Right out here in front, in the river."

Out the front window, beyond the red geraniums in the window boxes, is the Seine and the place where it meets the smaller Loing. A fitting place, I thought. A bend in the river. The river that had bent her, the river that had pulled her up straight again, the river that had never broken her.

*Actress Audrey Hepburn on a boat on the Seine while filming the 1964 film* Paris When It Sizzles. © VINCENT ROSSELL.

# SIXTEEN

# Scenes on the Seine

*All Parisians know instances of
serenity and grace: crossing the Seine
and looking to the left and the right
and saying to themselves, "Ooh la!"*
—CÉDRIC KLAPISCH, filmmaker

IN THE FANTASY WORLD of film, it is perfectly normal for lovers to dance along the banks of the Seine. One of the most romantic dance scenes in movie history comes when Gene Kelly takes Leslie Caron in his arms in the 1951 classic *An American in Paris* and sings George and Ira Gershwin's "Love Is Here to Stay." Sixty-five years later, director Damien Chazelle paid homage to that scene in *La La Land*.

In *An American in Paris*, Kelly plays Jerry Mulligan, an ex-GI struggling to be a painter, and Caron is Lise Bouvier, a young French woman working in a perfume shop. They fall madly in love. One night, he leads her down a stone staircase on the banks of the Seine. It is a pretend Seine, created by MGM in a Hollywood studio. The water is a few inches deep, and a painted one-hundred-foot cloth stretched around the soundstage gives the illusion that they are really in Paris. As the

Seine shimmers in white and golden light against a midnight-blue sky and the backdrop of Notre-Dame and the Pont de l'Archevêché, Kelly bursts into song. They dance. They kiss. They walk arm in arm along the riverbank. The sound of moving water breaks the silence. Caron is involved with a man she deeply admires but does not love. She runs away, leaving Kelly behind. But as this is Hollywood, and Hollywood-plus-Paris usually means happy endings, they will meet again.

Chazelle, who grew up in the United States as a fan of American musicals, loved the film and its daring, avant-garde experimentation with song and dance. He set *La La Land*, his 2016 musical comedy-drama, in Los Angeles, then inserted a surreal love scene in Paris. In the scene, Mia, an aspiring actress (Emma Stone), imagines what life would have been like if she and Sebastian, a would-be jazz pianist (Ryan Gosling), had stayed together. Mia wears a flowing white cocktail dress and high-heeled pumps, Sebastian a dark suit. String music serenades as they stroll, holding hands, through a tunnel onto the banks of the Seine. They walk along the quay, which is covered in a carpet of rose-colored leaves; they pass a boy in short pants holding a red balloon, a young couple on a bench about to embrace, and a flower seller handing a bouquet to a sailor—all of them immobile as if frozen in time. A river of deep blue and silver pebbles sparkles. On the other side of the Seine is a backdrop of Paris painted with broad strokes in a palette of blues, oranges, and yellows that evokes Van Gogh. They waltz off the quay onto what seems to be the surface of the Seine itself, an expanse of blue-and-white liquid light that blends into a dark sky with stars. It's clearly fake, but it doesn't matter.

Chazelle told *Entertainment Weekly* that although he set the film in Los Angeles, he crammed "a combination of a bunch of things I love" into the scene—the look of leaves in fall, a clock set to midnight that recalls the 1924 French short film *Paris qui dort*, "when a magician casts a spell and the entire city freezes." And, of course, the river, "which reminds me of *An American in Paris*, when Gene Kelly and Leslie Caron dance by the Seine."

Such a scene would seem ridiculous in most places in the world, but along the banks of the Seine at night, it looks just right.

Paris is where the real and the imagined become serendipitously intertwined. More than any other art, cinema knows how to play on the myths and fantasies that Paris creates, capturing reality but also distorting, enhancing, and magnifying it. Paris's City Hall is conscious of this power, and is determined to document, preserve, celebrate, and promote the city's stardom in film. On any given day, an average of twenty films, documentaries, commercials, and television series are being shot somewhere in Paris, all with official permission. Even in the imagination, Paris, and the silver ribbon of water that curves through it, delivers.

FAIRY-TALE ENDINGS just seem to work better in Paris. The French poke fun at American directors who make Paris-on-the-Seine predictably sweet. When *Mission: Impossible—Fallout* was released in 2018, the daily *Le Figaro* mocked the seduction scene between Tom Cruise and Vanessa Kirby, noting that it is set along the Left Bank with shots of Notre-Dame, the booksellers on the quays, and a barge "that passes by at exactly the right moment." The newspaper concluded, "The cliché of romantic Paris that is much appreciated by American filmmakers still has a bright future." But Cruise's photograph made it onto the paper's front page that day, with a story that ran two full pages inside, under the headline, "*Mission Impossible* Declares Its Love for the Capital." Sometimes Parisians need the view of naïve outsiders to appreciate what is theirs.

There is no official count, but probably tens of thousands of films have been shot in Paris or made about Paris. And just about every film set in Paris includes a shot of the river. "Anytime there's an aerial view of New York City in a film, you see skyscrapers, and anytime there's an aerial view of Paris, you see the Seine," said Régis Robert, the head of research at Paris's Cinémathèque Française. "Thanks to movies—especially American movies—the Seine is the best-known river in the world."

The Cinémathèque is a sculptural, limestone-clad space designed by Frank Gehry and located in the Bercy district in eastern Paris. Largely financed by the French government, it features exhibition halls, a multimedia library, screening rooms, and a world-class collection of films, photographs, costumes, decor, cameras, posters, scripts, drawings, and postcards. When I visited it, Robert and his team became my guides to the history of the Seine in film.

In 1896, the Lumière brothers used the panoramic technique—the art of moving a camera along a fixed setting—to capture the grandeur of Paris in footage of the banks of the Seine, the place de la Concorde, the Eiffel Tower, and the Arc de Triomphe. The Seine became the ultimate testing ground for the panoramic shot. "The frame was always fixed," said Robert. "You set the camera in one position and then move on a boat along the river." Thomas Edison, who made motion pictures commercially viable, demonstrated the panorama effect to the world at the Paris Exposition Universelle of 1900. His *Panorama of the Paris Exposition from the Seine* was a six-and-a-half-minute caress of the river's banks filmed from a steamboat. Even today, one of the best ways for a tourist to film the river in Paris is to point a camera at the shore from one of the *bateaux-mouches*, which serve as grand, gliding dollies for millions of phone cameras.

Directors just can't stay away from some of the vistas. "You see the Eiffel Tower and the Pont Alexandre III bridge all the time in film," Robert said. He mentioned a few movies with shots of the Belle Époque bridge: the 1985 James Bond thriller *A View to a Kill*, Eric Rohmer's 1995 *Les rendez-vous de Paris*, Woody Allen's 2011 *Midnight in Paris*, and Christopher McQuarrie's 2018 *Mission: Impossible—Fallout*.

I asked the Cinémathèque team to recommend a filmmaker or cameraman who could explain how to film the Seine. One of its members said, "There is only one person who understands the light of the river. Darius Khondji."

I had interviewed Darius, a French-Iranian cinematographer, a few years before, for a profile I wrote about him in the *New York Times*. We had talked in the kitchen of his eighteenth-century house near Saint-Sulpice Church, drinking espresso from white china cups trimmed in gold. All the lights were turned off. A dim light crept in from outside. It was too dark for me, just right for him.

"I have always been sensitive to light, and I love to play with natural light," he said then. "The light of the day. The blue light of darkness. The light of the city. The light of the seasons. Feeling physically assaulted by certain light."

His feel for natural light served him well when he was filming *Midnight in Paris*. He and Allen had a tight schedule for filming in the city, and it was overcast and raining much of the time. Fortunately, the two men share a visual sensibility: they dislike bright sunlight. "We went out in the street shooting, and it started raining, and we were chasing the rain," Darius said. "We loved it."

The Seine bookends the film and moves in and out of the narrative. The story begins with more than three minutes of Paris in picture-postcard framed shots, as if the camera were making urgent, passionate love to the city from dawn to darkness. The Eiffel Tower, the Champs-Élysées, Notre-Dame, the red windmill of the Moulin Rouge, the staircases of Montmartre, and the Seine. There is no dialogue, just the soulful sound of "Si tu vois ma mère" by the late American jazz saxophonist, clarinetist, and composer Sidney Bechet. You expect the opener to end, but the images and music keep coming. By the time the movie starts, you are filled with an overwhelming longing to get on the next plane to Paris.

In the last scene, Gil Pender (Owen Wilson), a screenwriter who dreams of becoming a novelist, runs into Gabrielle (Léa Seydoux), an alluring young French antiques dealer, on the Pont Alexandre III. It is night, and raining. "Paris is at its most beautiful in the rain," she tells him. He agrees, and they walk off together. You are left with the impression that Gil will settle down in Paris, move in with Gabrielle, learn to speak French, and write great novels.

Darius is forever filming and hard to pin down. But during one of his brief stays in Paris, I caught up with him again. We met for a stroll along the Seine at the Quai Malaquais, in the Sixth Arrondissement. We walked down a cobblestoned ramp at Port des Saints-Pères and went east, under the Pont des Arts and the Pont Neuf, which crosses the Île de la Cité. The path along the Seine there is narrow, uneven, and little used by pedestrians, except for the occasional lost tourist.

"I love this," he said. "It's all poplars. The light of the sky penetrating the trees turns the water green! And look—the trees make shadows on the stones."

He pulled out his iPhone, locked his legs in place about two feet apart, and began shooting still photos—of the river, the bridges, the quays, the cobblestones. He explained that he always zooms in slightly to make the wide angle of an iPhone more like a 40-or 50-millimeter lens. "I want to make it like a reproduction of the human eye," he said.

As we walked, the sun burned hot and high above us, flattening the landscape with bright light. Darius was frustrated. "Here we are at the worst moment of the day," he said. "We are seeing the most romantic river in the world in her worst light!"

As if on cue, the sun hid behind a cloud. "Ah, see the blue in the distance beyond the green," he said.

"What blue?" I asked.

"You don't see the blue?"

"No, I see green and brown and gray and silver—not blue."

"Are you color-blind, Elaine! The reflection of the poplars in the water is green, and the reflection of the sky is blue!"

I stared hard into the distance. And then, I could see it. A blue that started silvery and turned darker the more I looked. It was the blue of a Corot painting.

"The Seine, it is forever changing and showing off the reflections," he said. "The light plays tricks and makes magic. Gray, gray brown, gray green-blue, dark blue against the blue sky. The bridges, the stones, the banks change and move with the river."

As we walked, Notre-Dame appeared in all its glory, perfectly framed beyond a curved arch of the Pont Saint-Michel. "You don't have this view with the Thames, or the Hudson, or the Tiber, or the Danube, or the Guadalquivir," he said. "You don't have it with any other river in the world."

Under the Pont Saint-Michel we found a long stone bench against the wall. A cool breeze passed through. A *bateau-mouche* with a guide speaking in Chinese passed us, splashing waves against the stone quay. A tourist from Guadeloupe played his saxophone for us. We sat for a moment, and our voices echoed as we spoke. "We had Gil Pender walking on the other side of the river," Darius said of an important scene in *Midnight in Paris.* "Why didn't we have Gil Pender walking here? I've lived in Paris for most of my life, but I never walked here before. It's a perfect set."

As we approached the Petit Pont, with Notre-Dame at street level above us, Darius told me to turn around and face west. The sun was moving in and out of the clouds behind us. "You see the light makes shadows of the poplars, and the people in the distance are in darkness, and the Seine is so green it zings."


THE SEINE IS IDEAL for many tricks of cinematography. In one classic cinematic view of the Eiffel Tower, it is filmed not straight on but at an angle from the eastern part of the Right Bank, with the river and its bridges in the foreground and the tower in the distance. This is a predictable but pleasing way to let viewers know that the setting is Paris. I have lost count of the films that contain this shot. Even the goofy 2006 remake of *The Pink Panther* includes it.

The banks of the Seine at the bottom of stone staircases offer a ready-made stage for a fantasy scene. A picnic. A kiss. A breakup. A catch-up. The identification of the Seine with romance is at its most literal in *Love in the Afternoon,* Billy Wilder's 1957 classic. In the opening scenes, couples kiss passionately in front of fountains and on tour boats on the Seine. "Paris, France," Maurice Chevalier declares in his voice-over, "is just like any other big city—London, New York, Tokyo—except for two little things. In Paris, people eat better. And in Paris, people make love, well, perhaps not better, but certainly more often."

French filmmakers have used the Seine as more than a decorative backdrop. In *La vie d'un fleuve* ("The Life of a River"), a twenty-four-minute documentary made in 1932, Jean Lods traces the river from its source to the sea. Lods, who joined the French Communist Party, tells the story through the lens of laborers who worked on or near the river. The film opens with a tiny spring, and then a creek flowing amid weeds at the Seine's source. An old farmer plows his land with a horse and hoes it by hand. Sheep and cattle graze in open fields. Two men fish from a rowboat. A husband and wife struggle to tow their barge into a lock. Then comes Paris, with the Eiffel Tower, fishermen, and hundreds of swimmers and sunbathers. From there on, the industrial Seine takes over—a factory spewing smoke from giant smokestacks, steam shovels moving rocks, forklifts transferring bales onto ships. The Seine widens dramatically at the estuary, and *L'Atlantique*, an ocean liner, sails westward toward the Americas. The message is clear: that trickle of a river grows to become the France that is a global maritime power.

Joris Ivens's 1957 black-and-white film *La Seine a rencontré Paris* ("The Seine Meets Paris") uses a poem written by Jacques Prévert as a voice-over. Here, the Seine becomes a unifier, a key to understanding Paris. Wine, wheat, wood, and bricks are piled high in barges along the Seine. When a line of workers move bricks onshore, one pile after another, you can feel their burden and almost smell their sweat. "The Seine is a factory," the narrator states, reading from Prévert's poem. "The Seine is work."

The film observes boys playing on a stack of logs, a dog jumping into the river, girls in a circle singing, the sights and sounds of traffic, people sleeping, eating, walking, fishing, and splashing on the riverbanks. "There once was the Seine," the narrator continues. "There once was life. . . . A river with eddies, sewers, and, every once in a while, a drowned person, when it isn't a dead dog, with fishermen who never catch anything."

At the end, a lock opens wide to reveal the river flowing downstream to the open sea.

With its bridges and banks, the Seine has become a favorite backdrop in adventure films. The 2011 film *The Intouchables* opens with a car chase along the Seine at night. In *The Bourne Identity* (2002), Matt Damon takes to the roof of the building that was once La Samaritaine department store to track Chris Cooper as he stops on the Pont Neuf. In *Inception* (2010), director Christopher Nolan creates a dream sequence where the characters play with reality. Mirror images give the impression that the Pont de Bir-Hakeim, near the Eiffel Tower, goes on forever.

The chase scene is key to the 2007 animated film *Ratatouille*, when Skinner, the greedy, paranoid head chef of the restaurant Gusteau's, chases Remy, the rat and aspiring chef, through the streets of Paris. Skinner jumps on a red scooter, races along a quay of the Seine, tumbles down a set of stairs, then chases Remy on foot across the decks of two barges. The scene ends with Skinner falling into the river as Remy escapes.

In my view, the most daring, real-life moment in Seine film history comes in the heart-stopping 1976 documentary, *C'était un rendez-vous*, an eight-minute film shot in one take by director Claude Lelouch. Lelouch hops into his Mercedes early one morning at Porte Dauphine, on the western edge of Paris, with a camera attached to the car's front bumper, and races around Paris at breakneck speed. He plows through red lights, goes the wrong way on one-way streets, ignores cars, buses, and pedestrians, and ends up in a romantic encounter at the top of Montmartre. For twenty-five seconds along the way, he speeds along the Seine. He starts with a skid across place de la Concorde. Just as he is about to cross the river at the Pont de la Concorde toward the Assemblée Nationale, he swerves left and accelerates along the Quai François Mitterrand. Lelouch passes two cars at the Pont Royal, and heads straight for the side of a bus as he approaches the Pont du Carrousel. Two statues at the northern end of the bridge come into focus just before he makes another screeching left turn through an archway and onto the place du Carrousel, in front of the Louvre. (Lelouch was arrested for failure to stop at red lights after the first screening of the film, which was banned and for years shown only surreptitiously.)

Other directors film the Seine for slapstick comedy. In the remake of *The Pink Panther*, Steve Martin, playing the clueless Inspector Clouseau, inadvertently sends Kevin Kline, lying on a gurney, his body swathed in bandages, crashing through the window of a hospital and into the Seine. In *Irma la Douce* (1963), Jack Lemmon emerges from the river as an unfazed English gentleman, umbrella first. The Seine was so polluted that Lemmon was given several immunization shots, including one for tetanus, before shooting the scene. He later called it the most disgusting thing he ever had to do in a movie, according to IMDb, the online film and television database.

Sometimes the fantasy world of film can invade real life. *Camille Claudel* (1988), about the sculptress who had been Rodin's lover, was filmed in an apartment on the Île Saint-Louis made to look like Rodin's atelier. In one scene, Isabelle Adjani, who plays Camille, becomes so angry and despondent that she takes a sculpture she has made of Rodin's foot and throws it from a bridge into the Seine. A few years later, a team of frogmen from the river police found it at the bottom of the river. It had some sort of signature on it. They thought it was a real treasure. Then they got the bad news: it was only a movie prop.

*Every summer, the city of Paris turns parts of the Seine's riverbanks into "Paris Plages"—urban beaches.* ANDREW PLUMP.

*A night-time image of La Seine Musicale, the ultramodern concert hall on Île Seguin just west of Paris.* NICOLAS GROSMOND.

# SEVENTEEN

# River of Song

*The Seine sings, sings, sings, sings,*
*Sings all day and all night,*
*Because she is in love*
*And her lover—it's Paris.*

—**"LA SEINE,"** a popular song from 1948

SINGING IS NOT an everyday habit in Paris. It's unusual for a Parisian to spontaneously burst into song in the middle of a conversation at work. So I was surprised when Juliette Jestaz, the curator of manuscripts and engravings at the Bibliothèque Historique de la Ville de Paris, a repository for more than two million books, manuscripts, documents, and maps about Paris history, began singing to me. Jestaz is a quiet beauty. On the day we met she was wearing a long, loose, gray flannel skirt, a burgundy-colored turtleneck, and matching flats. Her brown hair, streaked with fine strands of gray, was pulled into a low bun, her face untouched by makeup. The office where we met was piled high with books and papers crammed into heavy cardboard file boxes. A large, dark tapestry hung on one of the walls. The crystal chandelier was unlit.

The singing began during a conversation about the library's resources. I told her I was looking for unusual facts and stories about life on the Seine.

"Have you found any songs?" she asked.

"Not many," I said.

She asked if I knew "Les Ricochets," written and sung by Georges Brassens, the twentieth-century singer-songwriter and poet. I told her I didn't. Without another word, she began humming the 1976 tune. Then she sang: "I was only eighteen, just leaving my hometown one fine day . . ."

Her voice was pure, sweet, and practiced. The song recounted the story of a young man who arrived in Paris for the first time and headed straight to the bridges of the Seine, where he fell in love with the first Parisian woman he met. She broke his heart, but he was not sad.

I had come with Joanna Beaufoy, a young British scholar with a passion for songs, and we asked if Juliette knew any others.

"Of course," she said.

Jestaz singled out "La Seine," a 1948 love song and probably the best-known song about the river. This time, Joanna joined in as Jestaz sang. Jestaz explained that the library owned a large collection of songs about Paris, some of them in the form of small printed scores that were sold on the street so that people could sing along with a street singer.

Rivers and songs. Songs and rivers. Rivers belong to all of us, and to none of us. They nourish and betray. They remind us of misery and of bliss. It is no wonder that composers have put words about rivers to music, probably for as long as songs have been sung. The Danube inspired Johann Strauss's waltz; the Mississippi, "Ol' Man River." In 1941, folksinger Woody Guthrie wrote twenty-six ballads for a movie about the Columbia and the benefits of hydroelectric dams. The Seine is rich in material for song: a river on a human scale, it provides a perfect setting for sunrise and sunset, a means of livelihood, an association with romance, love, life, and death.

A 2004 scholarly essay by Martin Pénet analyzed 123 twentieth-century songs inspired by the Seine in Paris. He classified them according to subject: sites and monuments (21), bridges (20), upstream and downstream from Paris (19), the river in general (18), quays (18), water traffic (13), floods (10), and bathing (4). But songs about the Seine originated centuries before. In the Middle Ages, poems were sung, not read, and these became the earliest documented songs about the river. The medieval French poet Eustache Deschamps, for example, composed a ballad extolling the clear waters of the Seine in Paris as a source of fertility:

> *She is the city crowned above all others . . .*
> *Situated on the river Seine,*
> *Vines, woods, field and meadow.*
> *All the wealth of this mortal life.*

In 1635, a general proclamation banned singing in public. Songs could be subversive, filled with rumors, gossip, political protest, and criticism of the ruling classes. The intrepid ignored the ban, many of them singing in code to avoid arrest. The most sensitive meeting place was the Pont Neuf. All the social classes mingled there, making the bridge a dangerous place to sing a song and the best place for spreading it.

As in poetry, rhyming is important in song, and "Seine" is a great word for lyrics. In French it is pronounced "sen" and rhymes with *reine* (queen), *sereine* (serene), *peine* (trouble), *sirène* (mermaid), *souveraine* (sovereign), *veine* (vein), and almost with *aime* (from the verb *aimer*, to love). It is a homonym with *scène*, to mean "scene," as on a theater stage. In French, the two words are sometimes used interchangeably. In 2017, La Seine Musicale, a modernistic concert hall, opened on the Île Seguin, on the Seine. When spoken, the hall's name can mean both "Musical Seine" and "Musical Scene." In English, Seine is sometimes mispronounced "sane" and is coupled with the long *a* sound, as in ABBA's song "Our Last Summer" ("Walks along the Seine / Laughing in the rain").

Joanna gave me one of the most thoughtful Christmas presents I've ever received: a CD containing a score of famous songs about the Seine, tunes that she had found and digitized. The CD included peppy songs like "La Seine" from the 2011 animated film *Un monstre à Paris*, set during the great flood of 1910. In the film, an inventor transforms a flea into a giant monster, Francoeur, a gifted singer who performs in a cabaret alongside a feisty female star, whose voice is that of actress Vanessa Paradis.

Oldies like Léo Ferré's 1952 interpretation of "Le Pont Mirabeau," Apollinaire's classic 1912 poem about the loss of his muse and lover, Marie Laurencin, are inspired by the Seine. The bridge represented freedom and peace for the couple, and when Laurencin ended the relationship after five years, Apollinaire wrote of a heart broken by love's fickleness. Ferré turned the poem into a waltz of melancholy: "All love goes by as water to the sea / All love goes by / How slow life seems to me / How violent the hope of love can be." It is a masterpiece of the French chanson.

There are songs of love, friendship, nostalgia, danger, loss, longing, political protest, work, and death. The Seine in song is often represented as a woman courted by various lovers (France, Parisians, visitors). In the song "Paris a rencontré la Seine" ("Paris Met the Seine") by Serge Reggiani, the Seine is Paris's fiancée, and her bridges are her rings ("For the Seine is a lover / and Paris sleeps in her bed"). In the poem turned song "Quai de Béthune," Louis Aragon, a founder of France's Surrealist movement, sees the Seine as a blonde who makes love to the Île de la Cité. (True to the Surrealist tradition of nonsense and mystery, he doesn't explain why she is blond.)

In "Les Feux de Paris," a Louis Aragon poem sung by Jean Ferrat, the Seine becomes carnal on "obscene mornings," opening at the Île de la Cité's place Dauphine "like a woman with crazy eyes" and her legs spread apart. (Why are there so many comparisons of the Seine to a woman with spread legs?) Ferrat also sings songs about the Seine belonging to all of France—from Burgundy to the sea. "Don't act so cocky, Paris," he croons in the 1961 song "Regarde-toi Paname," which uses a slang name for the city. "I wouldn't want to hurt your feelings / But you can see the Seine flow / From elsewhere than the foot of Notre-Dame."

The Seine's seductive power cuts across nationalities. In 1959, the Kingston Trio, an American folk group, sang a song called "The Seine" written by Brooklyn-born Irving Burgie (a.k.a. Lord Burgess). It came out as a ballad of singsongy syrup. A song with a similar title, "La Seine," tells the story of a love affair that ended at the river; it was a hit in France and the United States. When the great French vocalist Maurice Chevalier sang it, he enunciated every delicious syllable—the river was *eur-eu-seh* and *ad-ven-toor-eu-seh* (happy and adventurous). The best line comes when the Seine reveals herself as a woman who can't stop singing about the city she loves: "The Seine sings, sings, sings, sings, / Sings all day and all night, / Because she is in love / And her lover—it's Paris."

Doris Day offered a perky, English-language version, replacing the words *"Elle roucoule, coule, coule"* with "She's cooing, cooing, cooing." Dean Martin sang it slow and sexy. ("Someday I know / She'll come to Paris again, / And I'll find her again where I lost her, / By the lovely river Seine.") Only one false note: both Doris and Dean pronounced "Seine" as "sane" instead of "sen." Josephine Baker and Bing Crosby insisted on authenticity, singing "La Seine" in French. Bing did it in 1953 with strong violins and horns for the album *Le Bing: Song Hits of Paris*, in which he gamely sang every single song in French. An actress playing a South Vietnamese cabaret singer sang a half-English, half-French version in the 1968 war film *The Green Berets*, starring John Wayne. There are versions in German and Swedish.

Dean Martin returned to the Seine in 1955 with his English version of the 1913 French song "Under the Bridges of Paris." There was also a version by Eartha Kitt and an instrumental arrangement that featured in the 2004 film *Shall We Dance?* But Dino, the king of croon! How he seduced with that liquid languor. Never mind that the underbellies of the bridges could be dirty, smelly, and damp. Who wouldn't want to follow Dean Martin (or at least his voice) down to the lower banks of the Seine, where no one could see? He clearly laid out his intentions: "How would you like to be / Down by the Seine with me . . . / Under the bridges of Paris with you . . . / I'd make your dreams come true."

America was happy in the mid-1950s, and the English words written for "Under the Bridges of Paris" reflected the country's mood. But take a look at the original French lyrics:

> *Worn down by poverty*
> *Driven from her home*
> *We see a poor mother*
> *With her three small children . . .*
> *Under the bridges of Paris*
> *The mother and her little ones*
> *Come to sleep there near the Seine*
> *In their sleep they will forget their pain*
> *If we helped*
> *All the truly suffering people a little*
> *No more suicides or crimes at night*
> *Under the bridges of Paris.*

The French version is a reminder that the Seine does not always carry happiness. Indeed, suffering and sadness infuse the only opera that uses the Seine as its stage set: Giacomo Puccini's *Il Tabarro* ("The Cloak"), a tense, fifty-minute, one-act thriller, the first in a trio of his one-act compositions. Puccini based the opera on *La Houppelande*, a long-running play he saw in Paris in 1912; it concerns the murder, by a jealous barge owner of his wife and her lover, on a barge on the Seine. Puccini puts the river itself at the heart of *Il Tabarro*. "La Signora Senna [Lady Seine] should be the true protagonist of the drama," he wrote in a letter to Giuseppe Adami, his librettist.

Adami's version has one, not two murders. It tells the story of a love triangle involving Michele, the fifty-year-old barge owner; his wife, Giorgetta, a Parisian half his age; and her lover, Luigi, a handsome, twenty-year-old longshoreman who works for Michele. The scene is Michele's barge, moored on a bend in the river near Notre-Dame. The libretto describes the barge's cabin as pretty, with painted green win-

dow frames, pots of geraniums, and a cage of canaries. Laundry hangs
on clotheslines. In the overture, strings and woodwinds swirl solemnly,
ominously, to evoke the river's murky flow. Tugboats sound their whis-
tles loud and harsh as they roll past.

Giorgetta, bereft over the death of her infant son the year before,
longs to return to life on land. "The air of my Paris is life and joy
to me!" she sings. " . . . 'Tis no life for a woman, in that dark, dingy
cabin. . . . We cannot live forever on the water!" Michele is miserable
when he realizes that his young wife has fallen in love with Luigi and
no longer cares for him. He overhears her arranging a love tryst with
Luigi and pleads with the river to end his misery.

> *Flow, eternal river, flow!*
> *Like your deep and mysterious waters!*
> *Anguish pervades my soul endlessly!*
> *Pass on, eternal river, pass on!*
> *And drag me in and engulf me!*
>
> *Your waves soothe so many sorrows!*
> *You have marked the end of so much misery!*
> *Forever calm, you flow, never halted by pain, fear*
> *or anguish!*
>
> *Forever flow on, forever continue your lament!*
> *Are those the moans of icy corpses?*
> *You carried thousands of dead in quick succession*
> *toward their end, on your slimy arms!*
>
> *Are those the sorrows you quelled by choking*
> *their last breath in your whirlpools?*
> *Mysterious and dark waters, flow on and pass*
> *over my broken heart!*
> *Wash away my sorrow and my bitter pain!*

*Make my destiny yours, and if you cannot give*
*me peace, then let me die in your waters!*

Michele grabs Luigi, forces him to confess his love for Giorgetta, and strangles him. He hides the body under his black cloak. When Giorgetta returns to the barge, Michele pulls off the cloak, and Luigi's body falls at her feet. She shrieks in horror and falls on the body of her dead lover.

Puccini wrote *Il Tabarro* and the two other one-act operas for the triptych's world premiere at New York's Metropolitan Opera house in 1918, shortly after the signing of the World War I armistice. Puccini's *La Bohème* and *Tosca* had already made him famous, and the performance—with more than forty curtain calls that night—was a smash hit. Puccini would have attended, but there were still too many mines in the Atlantic to allow a safe crossing.

In late 2018, I attended the Met's performance of the trilogy celebrating the centenary of its premiere. *Il Tabarro* was staged somber and grim and set in 1927 Paris. The curtain rose with the cast frozen in place. Michele's deteriorating, blood-red barge was moored on a dark channel off the river, across from a row of decrepit factories; a tall crane was poised to unload cargo, and a metal footbridge spanning the stage carried pedestrians overhead. The sun set, night fell, and the red sky very slowly turned black. Baritone George Gagnidze, as Michele, sang plaintively about longing for the river to liberate him in death. Even though Michele would soon commit murder, at that moment he was a sympathetic figure. There were not forty curtain calls, but the performance, nonetheless, received a rousing standing ovation.

I DISCOVERED SONGS connected to the Seine hidden away in the Bibliothèque Historique de la Ville de Paris. Some books and documents were so obscure that the library's digital catalog did not list them. A librarian brought out printed and handwritten treasures one by one, among them a large twentieth-century scrapbook compiled by a collector of centuries-old papers. The collector had copied out many of the poems and songs in longhand. One was an extract from a 1661 songbook apparently performed by a blind street singer known as Le Savoyard, who boasted of his own talents: "A singer blessed with such a powerful organ and such a deafening and loud voice that even if I had drunk only two fingers of *eau de vie*, if I sang on the Quai des Augustins, the king would hear me all the way from the windows of his Louvre palace."

Another document was a 1939 arrangement of Francis Poulenc's "La Grenouillère," a nostalgic ode set to a poem of Apollinaire's about the restaurant and place of leisure on the Seine. Poulenc drew inspiration from his childhood memories of time spent in boats on the Marne. "I of course thought of those lunches in straw hats painted by Renoir," he wrote, evoking the most famous of Renoir's paintings on the Seine, *Luncheon of the Boating Party.* "It is the bumping together of the boats that provides the rhythm from start to finish of this tenderly haunting melody."

The piece of music was so meaningful for Poulenc that he commanded its would-be singers, "Do not sing it if you do not believe it."

*Nineteenth-century novelist Émile Zola with his camera on the Seine. Zola became a passionate photographer late in life.* © ASSOCIATION DU MUSÉE ÉMILE ZOLA.

# EIGHTEEN

# Capturing the Moment

*I was on a river boat at night when Paris looks so beautiful and we're passing the Eiffel Tower. How did I make a really original, great picture of the Eiffel Tower? It was thanks to the river. I consider it my Seine masterpiece.*

—*National Geographic* photographer
**WILLIAM ALBERT ALLARD**

LATE IN LIFE, the novelist Émile Zola became a passionate amateur photographer. He took more than six thousand photographs from 1894 until his death in 1902. He owned at least ten cameras, including some of the earliest Kodaks, and experimented with wide angles and panoramas, glass plates and film, small and large formats, paper of different textures. Zola perfected a shutter-release system so that he could take photographs of himself. He made his own contact sheets and developed and printed photos in darkrooms installed in the basements of his homes.

Zola took photographs for his personal pleasure; they were not intended for public display. It was only in 1953, more than half a century after his death, that *Life* magazine published a small selection of them, revealing to the world that the literary realist had also been a realistic photographer.

Zola discovered photography years after he moved into what would become his main home. In 1878 he took the money he earned from his novel *L'Assommoir* and bought a small two-story house facing the Seine in the village of Médan, west of Paris. Over the next few years he expanded it into a comfortable villa on a large plot of land where he developed wooded parks, stables, chicken coops, a garden, and a greenhouse. He also bought part of the Île du Platais, an island in the river, and built a chalet there.

Every morning at seven-thirty, Zola walked his dog, Pinpin, along the river valley. At nine sharp, he entered the high-ceilinged room where he did his writing, its twelve oversized windows imbuing it with the stark light and airy openness of an artist's studio. Zola sat at a long desk in a high, straight-backed, upholstered armchair and fastidiously wrote four pages in four hours. When tempted to put down his pen, he found resolve in the Latin of Pliny the Elder painted in large script above the fireplace: *Nulla dies sine linea* ("No day without a line"). Just about every afternoon after writing, Zola left the house he shared with his wife, Alexandrine, to spend time with Jeanne Rozerot, the other woman in his life and the mother of their two children. He and Jeanne took long walks together along the Seine. Alexandrine was deeply wounded when she learned of the relationship, but the two households continued an uneasy coexistence.

On the day I visited Zola's house, I sat, in a similar armchair, in the spot where Zola wrote. The tall stained-glass windows before me opened to the garden and, just beyond it, the railroad tracks that carried trains west from Paris, a thick row of trees, and the Seine.

In much of his fiction, Zola painted the Seine darkly. His photographs, by contrast, are clear and bright. They explore the power of light, which he called "life itself." After a visit to Rome in 1894, he wrote, "My visual memory has a power, an extraordinary vividness. When I evoke the objects I have seen, I see them again the way they really are, with their lines, forms, colors, odors, and sounds. It is the ultimate materialization: the sun that illuminated them almost dazzles me." A few years later, he stated that visual memory is best preserved in photography: "You cannot claim to have truly seen something if you have not taken a photograph revealing an array of details that could not otherwise have been noticed."

Zola photographed family life with his wife; his double life with Rozerot and their two children; his friends; his dogs; his travels abroad; scenes of Paris in the 1890s; and the Seine. He took black-and-white panoramic views of the river. In one, the Seine stretches across the horizon, beyond the trees and broad lawns of his estate. A view of the quiet river shows the Île du Platais and two rowboats on the shore, apparently waiting to take him, and perhaps his friends, to the island. In 2017, the estate of Zola's grandson auctioned off thousands of his prints and glass plates, five of his cameras, photo albums, and even white linen laboratory coats embroidered with his initials in red. The museum in Médan houses most of Zola's photographs, and a small number can be found at the Musée d'Orsay.

THE SEINE LENDS ITSELF to photography. In the first half of the nineteenth century, Paris was the cradle of photography and the first city in the world to create a photographic record of itself. Two Frenchmen, Joseph Nicéphore Niépce and Louis Daguerre, gave birth to this new art, inventing printing techniques and experimenting with primitive cameras. Niépce and Daguerre became partners, and in 1839, Daguerre unveiled the results of a new process, the daguerreotype. Among the first daguerreotypes to be publicly displayed were images of the Seine—starring the Pont Neuf and the Île de la Cité. One of the first panoramic views of Paris was a view of the Seine and several of its bridges taken in 1842 by the photographer-painter Charles Nègre from the top of the Church of Saint-Gervais. Three years later, photographer Frédéric Martens used a panoramic daguerreotype camera to capture a 150-degree shot of the Seine and its banks from the Salon Carré, in the Louvre.

By the time Zola was shooting pictures, early Kodak cameras were in vogue. The new technology dovetailed with Impressionism in painting, aiming to catch fleeting moments in time. Zola's camerawork was done in the countryside, but even he was lured to Paris. There, the river of the goddess Sequana reveals herself to the camera in all her sophisticated glory. The city's landmarks and monuments revel in their intimate visual relationship with the water, while the bridges and stone banks give the river a unified structure. Light plays with the water and reflects off the stones in infinite shades of gray.

Twentieth-century photographers used the medium to capture daily life along the river. At the turn of the century, Louis Vert photographed dockworkers unloading a barge and women grating cheese; Eugène Atget photographed dog shearers, lampshade sellers, street musicians, and mattress makers. (The filler for the mattresses—wool, hair, and feathers—arrived by barge.) The photographers also experimented with landscapes in black and white. Among the most well-known photographs are Atget's 1923 albumen image of two houseboats on the glasslike surface of the Seine in Paris, with the Conciergerie in the shadow and light of a winter day struggling to pierce the thick fog, and Henri Cartier-Bresson's 1952 view of the triangular tip of the Île de la Cité, dreamy and sensual, riding the river between the two halves of the Pont Neuf.

The Seine never becomes a cliché in photographs. In 2014, Sun Honglei, one of China's most famous actors, and Wang Jundi, a Chinese musician and opera singer, decided to get married in Paris. A professional film crew from China recorded the event, including the couple's poses on the riverbanks. They started a trend; the Seine has now become a backdrop for wealthy young Chinese couples who travel to Paris for pre-wedding photographs before the real celebration back home.

THE SEINE OFTEN PRESENTS greater challenges for the photographer than for the painter. The painter may aim to capture the moment but always has the luxury of whimsical approximation. The photographer starts with concrete techniques, struggling to capture and frame the rhythm of the flowing river through the lens at a precise moment.

The twentieth-century French photographer Willy Ronis explained the process. He told an interviewer from the newspaper *Libération* of standing on the Pont d'Arcole on a January day as a convoy of gigantic barges went by. As the last barge was passing, he spotted two children playing on the empty deck, aimed his camera, and hoped for the best.

"The most overwhelming emotion of my life was what I felt in 1959 when I took this photograph . . . without being sure if I had managed to pull it off," he said. "It was a shot that I could not repeat. If I had pressed the shutter a tenth of a second later, it would have been all over. We are often late in our perceptions, because we're not birds of prey. We've lost those instincts. Between the time I took the shot and when I plunged the film into the developing tank bath and took it out in the darkness to put it in the fixing agent, and then a minute and a half afterward, seeing it shimmering in the bright light, I came close to having a heart attack." An instinct had compelled him to wait for exactly the right moment, and he'd turned it into art.

Ronis died in 2009, at the age of ninety-nine. I once met his friend Jean Claude Gautrand, an expert on photography and a photographer himself. I was then writing a monthly online column called Lumière for the *New York Times' T Magazine* and met Gautrand for a story about a ten-pound, 624-page photographic opus on Paris he had edited. His modest apartment on the city's eastern edge was decorated with dozens of antique cameras and hundreds of photography books, some of which he had written or edited.

His book *Paris: Portrait of a City* examined more than 160 years of the city's history. He spent three and a half years deep in archives, libraries, and private collections, sifting through hundreds of thousands of files, finally settling on just over five hundred photographs. They documented demolitions and building projects that had transformed the cityscape, key events in Paris' history, and quotidian scenes of pleasure and of suffering: on the streets, in cafés, parks, and the river. "I was born here," he said. "Paris is my universe."

Among the book's photographs were some taken by Zola of the Exposition Universelle of 1900 from two flights up the new Eiffel Tower. One shows the Pont d'Iéna, over the Seine, thronged with pedestrians. You can see the Romanesque-Moorish Palais du Trocadéro, razed in 1935, blurry and dreamlike in the distance.

WHAT VISITOR TO PARIS doesn't like to memorialize the trip with a photograph taken from one of its bridges? A classic shot captures Parisians on the bridge, seen from behind, gazing at the Seine. You don't always see the river, but you know it is there. And you wonder what the people are thinking. The bridges themselves are powerful photographic images, as the painter Richard Overstreet discovered some years ago. Richard, an American married to a Frenchwoman, has lived in Paris for decades. His passion is painting. "It's my second breath," he likes to say. But at one point in his life, he put down his paintbrush and picked up a camera. "I needed to go from a turpentine-framed studio to plein air," he explained.

He said he had "always been drawn to the panoramic format in all art forms." Painted dioramas from the nineteenth century, decorative folding screens, the wide format photographs of Jacques Lartigue and especially the widescreen images of CinemaScope, Cinerama, Panavision, VistaVision—the wider the better. "I decided to try my hand and eye at it, so I rented a Fuji panoramic camera that takes in expansive horizons without fish-eye lens distortions," he said. "I had only one subject in mind: the Seine, that I crossed over daily, winding its course through Paris in a beautifully broad berth, horizon to horizon. And its bridges, marrying Left Bank to Right."

The only way to capture the power of the bridges, he discovered, was to photograph them in a long and narrow format, much as Zola had done a century before. Richard used multiple cameras and lenses, working in color and black and white. "The bridges came alive for me," he said. "What got to me, really, was their beauty, their historic personalities, their character. They became the perfect artist's model, still and constantly vibrant, stretched out in perfect repose across the Seine."

Over the next several months, he walked from one end of Paris to the other, bingeing on bridge-hopping, "I photographed obsessively. Night and day."

The photos had to feel timeless, which to him meant devoid of traffic: "I didn't want signs of life. It had to be a hushed, sort of ideal world. I would have to wait in perpetuity not to have buses and cars, for nothing moving, for no people."

Eventually, Richard invited me to see his bridges. He uncovered dusty gray albums and boxes of panorama transparencies as well as small photographs and slides in packages bound with gray cloth ribbon that had not been untied for years.

"You'll get bored fast," he said.

"No, I won't," I replied. I didn't.

In the long panoramas, his "live models," as he called the bridges, appeared naked in metal and stone. The photographs had never been published as a collection, and I wanted to linger over each one so that I could appreciate and remember, but he flipped the pages quickly. He showed me footbridges, one hidden under a highway that had since been torn down, another spanning a canal. He showed me the underbelly of the Belle Époque Pont Alexandre III, with its magnificent crisscrossing and intricate braiding of trusses and girders, photographed from a tourist boat. "I must have traveled on the *bateaux-mouches* fifty times, maybe more," he said. He photographed the Pont des Arts footbridge,

which joins the Institut de France to the Louvre, with pointillistic fili-
gree in the foreground and a flowing haze behind.

Turning the pages, he stopped at an image of golden metal colon-
nades, a view of the viaduct for the No. 6 Métro line on the two-level
Pont de Bir-Hakeim. Soon the albums were closed, the boxes tied up
in ribbon again. He is certain his panoramas of the bridges will be
published one day. "It was so great photographing them," he said. "The
bridges are set, like everything else in Paris that miraculously doesn't
get torn down or moved somewhere else. The bridges seduce you with
the practical grace of their beauty. They don't move. And the Seine
underneath is in perpetual movement. Like time, like the weather, it
is never still, totally changeable, in a total state of flux. I wanted to
take pictures of the unmovable at one with the movable. The contrast
splashes my eye."

*A* bateau-mouche *boat filled with tourists on the Seine; the Pont des Arts and the Louvre can be seen in the distance.* GABRIELA SCIOLINO PLUMP.

*Jacky Galloy* (left), *one of Paris's* bouquinistes—*booksellers on the Seine—with a client on Quai des Grands-Augustins.* GABRIELA SCIOLINO PLUMP.

# NINETEEN

# Selling Books, Selling Dreams

*The Seine is the only river in
the world that runs between two
bookshelves.*

—British journalist and broadcaster
**KIRSTY LANG**

THE BOOKSTALL along the Quai des Grands-Augustins offered no Eiffel Tower key chains, as do so many stalls, no coasters with scenes of Montmartre, no poorly printed posters of cancan dancers. There were no place mats, pocket mirrors, or padlocks to hang on bridges.

There were only books.

This was the stall of one of the traditional *bouquinistes*, the booksellers who have plied their trade on the banks of the Seine for hundreds of years.

"Do you have any books about the Seine?" I asked.

"None at all" came the reply.

In defiance, I rifled through the seller's boxes.

"What's this?" I asked. I picked up a bottle-green leather book with the title *L'été à Paris* ("Summer in Paris") printed in shiny gold ink.

It was written by Jules Janin, who had been a prominent novelist and historian, and published in 1843. The engravings inside, with yellow-brown stains of age, included one that showed eight jousting teams competing in narrow boats on the Seine before a crowd of hundreds.

A chapter entitled "The Year 2440" was an elegy to *L'an 2440*, the utopian fantasy novel by Louis-Sébastien Mercier, the eighteenth-century writer considered to be the first street reporter in Paris. Since Mercier was the subject of my unfinished doctoral dissertation, I thought, *C'était le destin*—it was fate!

"So how much do you want for this book?" I asked.

"Forty euros," said the *bouquiniste*.

"Oh . . . forty euros . . ."

"Yes, forty euros. But if the book really interests you . . ."

That was the opening I needed. And he knew it.

"Would you say thirty euros? You see, it's fate that brought us together."

And then I told him my history with Mercier.

"Well, you've made your proposal, and with a big smile. I cannot refuse you. Thirty euros!"

I introduced myself, prompting him to follow suit.

"I'm Jacky Galloy," he said.

"What's your real name?" I asked.

"Jacky."

"C'mon, how did you get a name like Jacky?" I asked. "Were you a roulette player? Or a bartender in a cabaret? Or maybe a Corsican gangster?"

"Ah, do you want to hear a story?" he asked.

"*Bien sûr.*"

"It was 1940, and Germany had declared war on France. My parents were living in the Ardennes, and the Germans were coming. My mother was pregnant. She was only nineteen. My father was called up as a soldier. She was going to be all alone, and she wept."

Jacky stopped to catch his breath and regain his composure, then continued. "My father said, 'Don't worry. The war is going to last a maximum of one or two months because the Americans will come, and they will immediately push the Germans out. So we will call our son Jacky to thank the Americans.'

"My mother went south and got as far as Mâcon. The Germans occupied France. My father left for the war, and right away, he was taken prisoner by the Germans. So obviously he didn't come back until after I was born. And my mother was angry with the Americans because they didn't come. But she said, 'If I don't call my son Jacky, I am disobeying my husband.' And she couldn't do that."

Jacky has three children, seven grandchildren, and four great-grandchildren. A retired schoolteacher, he had dreamed of teaching literature and history but was relegated instead to instructing students—eleven to sixteen years old—in grammar and penmanship. In 2007, he and a friend filled out the paperwork to become *bouquinistes*. City Hall gave them a stall.

As we were talking, a middle-aged man stopped and picked up the book I had just bought but had not yet paid for.

"It's sold," said Jacky. "It was thirty euros, but madame insisted on paying forty for it. You see how nice she is?"

"Yes, but if you want it, I'll sell it to you for one hundred," I told him. The client picked up a volume of Proust instead.


THE *BOUQUINISTES* are the literary gatekeepers of Paris. They have survived four centuries of censorship, economic crises, and political unrest. They endure wind, heat, frost, noise, floods, and air pollution and tolerate idle tourists and stingy customers. They claim that their bookstalls along the quays of the Seine make up the biggest open-air bookstore in the world.

In the eighteenth century, Thomas Jefferson, an obsessive collector of artworks, furnishings, and books, searched through the *bouqui-nistes'* boxes for books on the United States, science, and architecture; he favored the Quai des Grands-Augustins, where Jacky now has his stall. Balzac called the bookstalls "catacombs of glory [that] have devoured many hours that belonged to the poets, to the philosophers, and to the men of science of Paris!" In his 1862 history of the Pont Neuf, Édouard Fournier wrote that this "famous bridge . . . was also a huge reading room." In the twentieth century, the American-born writer Julien Green gazed into the zinc-lined wooden cases and found "many windows through which to escape"; the novelist François Mauriac saw "a door for entering an enchanting world." Léon-Paul Fargue, the poet and essayist, celebrated the *bouquinistes* as Parisian heroes, calling them "the most delightful beings who contributed with elegance and discretion to the renown of intelligence that glori-fied Paris."

Before and during his presidency, François Mitterrand enjoyed strolling along the quays in search of literary treasures in the *bouqui-nistes'* stalls. Mitterrand wrote about his visits to the *bouquinistes* in letters to Anne Pingeot, the other woman in his life and with whom he had a daughter. In one letter, he described the joy of finding a rare, "deliciously rebound" book by the nineteenth-century poet and writer Gérard de Nerval; in another, he proposed a leisurely stroll, writing, "If the sun smiles on us while we walk, we will go to visit some good *bouquinistes.*"

In my early days in Paris, alone in a strange city, I spent long stretches of time strolling among the *bouquinistes.* I did not need to speak; the booksellers didn't have to know that I lacked the imperfect subjunctive in French. I lost myself in old books, prints, newspapers, and magazines.

One day I got up the nerve to begin a conversation in French with a *bouquiniste.* His wooden boxes overflowed with hundreds of exquisite leather-bound books with gold lettering, elaborate cover designs and engravings, and satin ribbon page markers. "Do you have a reprint of Louis-Sébastien Mercier's *Tableau de Paris?*" I asked in French.

"Mademoiselle," he replied, "why would you want a reprint when you can have the original?"

The twelve volumes had been published in the 1780s. Where would I find an original?

He pulled out a business card and wrote the name and address of a book dealer on the back of it, instructing me to mention his name and ask the dealer the same question.

I headed over that same day. The bookstore was in Saint-Germain-des-Prés, on the Left Bank. It was one of those places that looked too important for amateurs. A man in his sixties greeted me with a gaze that was neither warm nor cold. I asked about Mercier's *Tableau.*

He disappeared into a room hidden behind a curtain of moss-green velvet. Several minutes later, he emerged with a high stack of brown leather books: both *Tableau* and a later work of Mercier's, *Le nouveau Paris.* The pages had been rebound into nine volumes sometime in the late nineteenth century, but these first editions dated from between 1783 and 1793. When I opened the books, they smelled of old paper and dust. He asked for 1,750 francs—about $350. I said yes. He didn't take credit cards. I came back with cash the next day. I was too intimidated to bargain.

I went back to the *bouquiniste* to tell him what I had done. "*Pas mal,*" he said.

The volumes sit front and center on a desk in the foyer of my apartment for all to see. They are among my most prized possessions.

THE WORD *BOUQUINISTE* first appeared in print in a dictionary in 1752. It is derived from the word *bouquin,* which dates to 1459 and means "old book of little interest." The verb *bouquiner* means to read up and study and also to trawl the quays looking for books. The *bouquinistes* were born of religious censorship. In 1562, during the Protestant Reformation against Catholicism, the Catholic Church's Council of Trent created a list of banned books. France was gripped by the civil war between Huguenots and Catholics, and booksellers trafficked in Protestant pamphlets and *libelles*, or "little books"—illegal "libelous" pamphlets that slandered public officials.

To keep control over what the French were reading, in 1577 the king issued a royal decree that ordered booksellers to sell their merchandise from designated locations. When the Pont Neuf was built, booksellers set themselves up on the broad quays nearby, only to be shut down in 1628, reauthorized in 1640, then banned again in 1649. Books continued to be sold there unofficially until 1721, when Louis XV forbade bookselling on public walkways. Booksellers returned to the Pont Neuf under his grandson Louis XVI. During and shortly after the French Revolution, the *bouquinistes* salvaged books pillaged from the estates of the nobility, flooding the open market with rare first editions. During an ambitious renovation of the Pont Neuf, the booksellers began to be expelled in 1851; by 1854 they were gone.

Then the city of Paris began to regulate the *bouquinistes*. A decree in 1859 issued the first permits officially authorizing booksellers to sell their books along the quays. In 1891, they received permission to leave their books in place overnight; their boxes were enlarged and permanently fixed to the quays.

THERE WAS A TIME, on Sunday afternoons especially, when the *bouquinistes* facilitated romance. Searching for a rare or unusual book became part of the ritual of seduction. And "I think I'll visit the *bouquinistes*" was sometimes the cover husbands offered their wives when they went to visit their mistresses on Sunday afternoons. Fargue wrote about certain men who stopped there: "Elderly Parisians of no particular importance, dressed to the nines, gray trousers and spats, sideburns carefully combed, impeccable top hat, walking stick under the arm, imposing collar, flashy or delicate necktie under a well-proportioned collar, a flower in the buttonhole, a smile always in place on happy lips. They were well-cared-for, spoiled old gentlemen with private incomes; and while waiting to go off to their *rendezvous gallants* they would move in a trance of pleasure among astronomical maps, postage stamps, erotic prints, and first editions."

One of my favorite paintings of the *bouquinistes* hangs in the Musée Carnavalet: *Bouquiniste sur le Quai des Grands-Augustins* by Bernard Boutet de Monvel. A painter, sculptor, engraver, fashion illustrator, and interior decorator, Boutet de Monvel stayed in Paris during World War II, apparently oblivious to the Occupation. He devoted himself to painting the booksellers along the Seine's banks and continued to paint them after the war.

Boutet de Monvel's painting, completed in 1949, shows two men in topcoats who appear to be customers. One, a bearded, bespectacled figure wearing a hat, stands in profile as his companion bends over to look at something of interest. Already, at that time, more than books were for sale, as several groupings of prints hang from clips. The painting was one of Boutet de Monvel's last works; he died in a plane crash in the Azores the same year.

Each *bouquiniste* is allowed one stall with four boxes painted dark green (the same shade, "wagon green," as old railroad cars and park benches). Officially, three of the boxes must contain only books; the fourth can be devoted to other items, including prints, postcards, maps, posters, and stamps. The selling of "trinkets and other tourist objects" is supposed to be banned and result in the revocation of a license, but that doesn't happen.

There was a time when *bouquiniste* boxes were reserved for the war-wounded and fathers with large families. These days, the rules are different. Would-be *bouquinistes* must have experience with books and no criminal record. When a stall becomes vacant, a committee composed of representatives from the city government, the business world, and the book industry decides who should take it.

A *bouquiniste* pays no rent or taxes. Bookstore owners are banned from becoming *bouquinistes*. Subletting is forbidden. *Bouquinistes* should be present at least three days every week; on other days, employees can work the boxes. *Bouquinistes* can take no more than six weeks of consecutive vacation. The stalls, which must conform to rigid size standards, are limited to one per family.

These days, there are about 240 *bouquinistes*, and they operate stalls holding 300,000 books, spread along nearly two miles of riverfront. Some still specialize: in crime novels, or military history, or music, or antique maps that cost several hundred euros each that must be locked up or taken away for safekeeping at the end of the day. Cities such as Ottawa, Beijing, and Tokyo have copied Paris's open-air bookselling, but nowhere else do booksellers enjoy the magic and mystique of the Seine.

Yet the *bouquinistes* are suffering. A long, slow, inevitable decline began decades ago. The afternoon stroll along the Seine, when Frenchmen would come out to savor Paris and search for literary treasures, has gone out of fashion. People buy fewer books, and the books they do buy are cheaper and easier to find on the Internet. Now the customer of the Seine *bouquiniste* is more likely to be a souvenir-shopping foreign tourist who doesn't speak French.

In *Paris*, his classic book from 1975, the British-American art critic John Russell was already lamenting the decline. "The quays have lost much of their character in recent years," he wrote. "Many *bouquinistes* have given in to the mass market and now offer only prints, maps, and trumpery reproductions."

Still, Russell loved outdoor booksellers. He noted that in Paris they worked in "surroundings of extreme beauty" and offered "a public service in preserving an asylum of idleness in the very middle of the restless city."

The late Chanel designer Karl Lagerfeld would have agreed. For his 2018–19 haute couture show under the dome of the Grand Palais museum, he paid homage to the *bouquiniste*s, building an elaborate runway that featured miniature versions of the booksellers' wagon-green boxes linked to an imaginary quay of the Seine. He filled them with Chanel-related books, publicity materials, and magazines. He completed his set with streetlamps and park benches, installing a fifty-foot-tall image of the Institut de France as the centerpiece.

The models wore designs that matched the setting, including tweed jackets in shades of stone and concrete and silver-sequined minidresses with spaghetti straps. "Paris is about pale gray," said Lagerfeld.

I WENT BACK to see Jacky a few weeks after our first meeting. He pulled *Les Ponts de Paris*—"The Bridges of Paris"—from a backpack. It was a heavy coffee-table book of 240 pages, published in 1999 by Paris's City Hall. The price printed on the cover was 290 French francs (this was before the euro), or about fifty dollars. He had found it at the weekend book dealers' open-air flea market on the edge of Paris. He had paid ten euros, and that's what he wanted from me.

The cover was dreadful: a photograph of three bridges at night in garish colors. The sky and river were dyed rose; the bridges, a bright turquoise. It struck me as one of those mass-produced books destined for tourists. Then I opened it. The pages were printed on heavy, shiny, fine-quality paper. The book described the history of all of Paris's bridges and accompanied the text with reproductions of maps, paintings, engravings, and photographs.

"So often celebrated for their charm, the bridges of Paris punctuate the Seine with their diversity," Jean Tiberi, the mayor of Paris at the time, wrote in an introduction. "Each one, living witness to the history of the Capital, is both a technical feat and a work of art."

That sold me. I gave Jacky ten euros.

Jacky said he had something else for me. He produced a large white envelope containing prints of the *bouquinistes* on cheap beige poster board. The colors were muddy, the details blurred.

The painter, Tavik Frantisek Šimon, was a Czech artist living in Paris; the prints were copies of engravings he had done in the 1920s. One of them, on the Quai des Grands-Augustins, showed an elderly female bookseller, a sad look on her face as she read a newspaper.

"That's my stall!" said Jacky. "And that woman—she was my great-grandmother."

"You're joking," I said.

"Yes, I am. But it's a good story, no?"

I bought the prints, of course. On the back of each print was a stanza from "Nocturne Parisien," a poem written by Paul Verlaine in 1866, stark in its darkness:

> *You, Seine, you have nothing! Two quays, no more!*
> *A filthy, putrid quay spreading on either shore*
> *With dreary, musty books and idle crowds . . .*

In other stanzas, Verlaine calls the Seine "indolent," its waters "dismal," its bridges "lined with a nefarious mist." In another, the river becomes "an aged serpent . . . ever without pity." But one stanza is filled with light:

> *When sunset burns red splotches in a sky that hums,*
> *How blest for dreamers to emerge . . . to stare*
> *At Notre-Dame, dreaming in the cool peaceful air,*
> *Hearts and hair windswept . . .*

And that's why Jacky enjoys his book stand on the Seine. "My job gives me freedom to dream," he admitted. "Not like teaching, when you have strict hours. Not like a bookstore that you have to open at nine a.m. Of course, I have what I call empty days—when no one comes at all, when no one wants my books," he said. "That's when I feel completely useless."

To pass the time on those days, he likes to watch birds—kingfishers, herons, gulls, big double-crested cormorants, and numerous species of ducks. The river never bores him. "When I think of the Seine, I think of so many things. Poetry. Apollinaire. Power. And I keep myself going with the realization of being alive. I have no desire to sit in front of a television and eat peanuts."

*A team of the Brigade Fluviale, Paris's river police force, making its daily rounds on the Seine with the Musée d'Orsay in the background.* ALEXANDER HURST.

# TWENTY

# Guardians of the Peace

*The officers of the River Brigade belonged to a separate kingdom, a floating kingdom, and when they went up the river at night, they knew they were modern explorers, lucky enough to cast a virgin glance on the city. They knew Paris like no one else.*

—*Quai des enfers*, a 2010 police thriller by **INGRID ASTIER**

EVERY MORNING, a River Brigade team of four police officers covers a beat that is long, narrow, and wet. The Brigade Fluviale's mission is to patrol about 370 miles of waterways in and around Paris, including the Seine, its connecting canals and tributaries, and several small lakes. Paris owns the most important tourist river in the world, with eight million passengers boarding thousands of tour boats of varied sizes and shapes each year. The River Brigade is the first line of defense in a chain of law enforcement and lifesaving personnel. Its tasks range from the urgent to the ordinary: by night the river police might rescue somebody attempting suicide; by day they can find themselves disengaging a tree trunk from the hull of a houseboat. They enforce rules governing river life, handing out fines for swimming, speeding, and waterskiing. They are summoned when boats collide, suspicious packages are found, dead bodies surface. After their first response, firefighters, doctors, land police, and even electricians and plumbers pitch in.

"I am a boat pilot, a diver, a sonar operator and trainer, a judicial police officer, a team leader," said Brigadier Serge Denis, who was in his mid-forties and had been on the force for more than a decade. "The Brigade Fluviale is the Swiss Army knife of the river. We have a central blade but a lot of other tools, too." Denis was pleased with the image and laughed out loud. "Swiss Army knife," he said again. "That's the best way to describe us."

At seven o'clock one sunny morning in late June, I accompanied four "guardians of the peace," as the officers call themselves—Laurent, Fred, Tristan, and Fanny, one of the few female police divers—on a training and surveillance mission. They wore tight, custom-made wet-suit uniforms and had assigned roles: the captain gave the orders; the pilot drove the boat; the diver jumped into the water; and the rescuer administered first aid. At the start of the morning shift, the team members went through the daily ritual of news updates and maintenance checks.

We set out on the river in a sleek, black inflatable motorboat. First, the officers took turns swimming freestyle as part of their daily training. Then they strapped on diving gear and plunged deep into the river's darkness. Even though summer had officially started, the water was so cold that it numbed their heads and hands; twenty minutes was the longest any of them could bear to stay in. At one point, Tristan emerged clutching an object in his right hand like a trophy, a broad smile on his face. It was a twelve-inch metal statue of a man holding a dog.

Our moment of joyful discovery was shattered by an emergency announcement on the two-way radio. "Two men have taken a priest hostage . . . in a church . . . in Rouen!" said Fred. "With a knife!" Rouen was far from the team's area of operations in Paris—more than seventy miles away—but they needed to stand by in case they were called to respond.

In the next few minutes, more information came in. Two men wielding knives had taken several people hostage in Saint-Étienne-du-Rouvray Church, near Rouen. They had forced the eighty-five-year-old parish priest, Father Jacques Hamel, to his knees as he was saying Mass and had slit his throat. The horrified congregation had watched him die. Police officers then shot the killers dead.

At least one of the officers in our patrol had to be armed and ready. "We can't all be in our wet suits!" said Fanny. She stripped out of her wet suit, donned her police uniform, and strapped her handgun around her waist. "Above all, we are police officers," she said. "Our most important training in the service is shooting, not swimming."

One morning, when I went along on an emergency call for help from a tugboat owner near the Porte d'Ivry, in eastern Paris, we chopped through the waters of the Seine at fifty miles an hour. I had been warned not to wear a hat, but I had anyway, and it flew off. I gripped the steel back of the captain's perch as the wind whipped us. "Just like *Miami Vice*, no?" one of the brigadiers said.

Just about every member of the River Brigade has watched the reruns and is familiar with the ins and outs of *Miami Vice*, the 1980s American television series that celebrated police work from a perch on the water. Sonny (Don Johnson) and Rico (Philip Michael Thomas) played two cool alpha-male police detectives working undercover in Miami. Sonny lived on a sailboat with his pet alligator, Elvis, drove a Ferrari, and piloted a racing boat. He and Rico raced around Miami Beach in never-ending gun battles with drug traffickers, pimps, mafiosi, and serial home burglars. They changed clothes several times per episode. Sonny wore a three-day stubble, T-shirts under unstructured pastel Armani blazers, Ray-Ban sunglasses, white linen slacks, and slip-on, soft leather loafers without socks.

We reached our destination and tied the boat to a large iron ring cemented to the stone quay. Two police divers plunged in. They discovered that a piece of metal had jammed the tugboat's motor, and they pulled it free. An easy recovery.

TO BECOME A GUARDIAN of the peace on the river, candidates must be under the age of forty, have one year of service in the regular police force, be licensed boaters and excellent swimmers, know how to shoot a handgun, and have security clearances from the Ministry of the Interior. They must pass a series of verbal, written, physical, and psychological exams, and then undergo several months of specialized training, followed by tests in swimming, breath holding, rescue, diving, and first aid.

"We carefully examine their motives," said Sandrine Berjot, a career police officer who became commander of the Brigade Fluviale in 2012. "This is absolutely not a vacation club where you say, 'Isn't it nice that today we're in T-shirts sunning ourselves, and when it gets hot we'll jump into the river.' The psychologist will ask questions about death, because it is never easy to dive into a completely hostile environment in the middle of the night to search for a dead body."

Every graduating class is named after one of the bridges over the Seine; Serge's class was called Simone de Beauvoir. The ritual on graduation day is to jump from your bridge into the river.

THE SEINE IS a tranquil river, but its currents are unpredictable. The supporting pillars of bridges create invisible whirlpools that can send boats spinning and drag victims deep under the surface. The water temperature can rise to seventy-five degrees in summer and fall to freezing in winter. Fog can blind even the most experienced police diver. Pollution turns the water a murky brown. Algae blooms in the spring and summer, when the river can be tinted a sickly green.

Louis Lépine, the head of the Paris Police Prefecture at the turn of the last century, created the brigade in June 1900. Paris was hosting the Exposition Universelle, and most of the temporary structures built as national pavilions lined the banks of the river. The brigade did such an excellent job during the exposition (it saved twelve people from drowning and helped two hundred others to safety) that it became a permanent force. Within a few years, the brigade was trawling the bottom of the river in search of debris—and bodies.

The gateway to the River Brigade headquarters is hidden behind trees on the far side of the suburban commuter train tracks next to the Pont d'Austerlitz in the Fifth Arrondissement. To access it, you take a fork at the corner where the roadway meets the Quai Saint-Bernard and walk about a hundred feet down an access road until you reach a parking lot. Inside a metal gate is a narrow walkway leading to a floating police station.

These days, the brigade consists of several rotating teams with about a hundred personnel. Eighty of these employees are active-duty swimmers and divers, but even the maintenance and administrative workers are members of the police. Every year, they conduct some five thousand patrols and two hundred rescue missions. They also retrieve several dozen dead bodies.

A large two-story pontoon boat connected to three smaller pontoon boats was custom-designed to serve as the brigade's central command. The large boat has air-conditioning, a surveillance desk, a combined conference and dining room with long tables, a warren of offices, toilets, showers, lockers, and unobstructed views of the river. Food is important (this is France, after all), and the full-service kitchen is equipped to cook hot meals. A shelf holds mismatched cups, glasses, plates, and cutlery.

One of the smaller pontoon boats is a logistical base for surveillance cameras that monitor the river; another houses a repair shop and an underground storage facility; the third stores fuel. The brigade has sixteen boats, some of them moored outside Paris. The biggest is a seventy-two-foot-long towboat that carries a tall white crane capable of pulling up a car. The officers of the brigade know the rhythms and secrets of the river. There is a hidden spot between the Pont de l'Alma and the Passerelle Debilly, near the gold-painted Flame of Liberty, where, just as you turn the corner of the river going east, the Sacré-Coeur Basilica appears out of nowhere, high on its hill in Montmartre. The officers told me about a squatter who lives behind a door that opens into a small space in one of the stone quays near their headquarters and greets them every morning with a single *"Bonjour."*

One of the biggest threats comes not from criminals but from infection. Although the Seine's waters are getting cleaner, they are not yet clean enough for swimming. *E. coli,* an infection from fecal matter, is a risk; more serious is leptospirosis, a bacterial disease transmitted through rat urine. And the Seine is full of rats.

The officers of the brigade are armed with vaccinations—against typhus, tetanus, hepatitis, and yellow fever. They stay out of the water when they have open cuts or wounds and must shower off the river's dreck as soon as they return to headquarters.

The main pontoon boat shelters numerous species of fish, which live and spawn underneath it: perch, eels, carp, a variety of small shrimp. One morning when I visited, I leaned over the deck and looked deep into the water. A strong smell of seaweed and dead fish overpowered me. The visibility that day was good, and I could see down as far as five feet, where hundreds of tiny, fast-moving black fish swam.

In the same waters lives a well-fed, four-foot-long *silure,* a beast of the catfish family with a broad, flat head, beady eyes, and slimy skin that looks like dung and feels like rubber. The *silure* has poor eyesight, good hearing, and an ugly, ravenous mouth that opens round and wide to suck in fish, ducks, pigeons, water rats, and other prey. It can live to be fifty years old. The specimen under the police pontoon loves swimming back and forth in the muck at the bottom of the river. It makes an appearance near the surface about once a week.

"Does it have a name?" I asked Sébastien Bonneau, one of the senior officers. I thought it might be the brigade's mascot. He and his colleagues looked at me as if I were nuts.

"No—he eats all the ducks!" Bonneau said.

"So why don't you just get rid of him?"

"He's more at home here than we are."

The floor of the Seine is a massive garbage dump for objects big and small, a final resting place for rusty car chassis, busted air conditioners, old furniture, tree trunks, electrical wiring, slabs of drywall, beer bottle caps, cigarette butts. Once the brigade pulled up an entire zinc-topped bar from a café. When the crew discovers explosives or suspicious objects, it calls in a special team of bomb-dismantling experts. The black water and the unpredictable currents make it hard to find small but important objects for a criminal investigation—like a gun that may have been used in a robbery. Since 2009, the brigade has used American-made sonar devices to seek out submerged cars and bodies hidden from view.

Two heavy World War II–era German machine guns with the brand name "Rheinmetall" hang like trophies high on a wall of the brigade's main meeting room. A glass cabinet holds some of the best finds from the river's depths: other World War II relics, including grenades, shell casings, dog tags, and handcuffs; pistols in assorted sizes and shapes; a collection of sunglasses; a hunting knife in its leather case. The memorabilia also run to religious objects, such as crucifixes, a bronze statue of Saint Anthony of Padua, and a framed portrait of Jesus, as well as other ephemera: miniature Eiffel Towers, cigarette lighters, a metal hammer and sickle, a bust of Napoléon, an old sword, coins, a silver cup, a leather glove, a sculpture of a bird and a dog, a terra-cotta cherub, and keys that couples throw into the river after they lock their "love" padlocks to bridges.

In 2015, an officer diving near the Pont Neuf spotted a strange object. He dug around it and retrieved a *mascaron*, one of the carved stone masks with heads as big as two feet tall that decorate the bridge. This one, missing half of its nose and one ear, had fallen off. The brigade turned it over to the city of Paris and was rewarded with three replicas—which are now shown off to visitors as treasured possessions.

People release unwanted water pets into the river, even though it is illegal to do so. The brigade once pulled up a six-foot-long royal python. Royal pythons are native to sub-Saharan Africa, and their natural habitat is land—forest floors and grassy savannahs. But they can easily survive in water, and this one must have liked the Seine.

During one of my visits, two emergencies unfolded. A brigade team raced out to the Pont Marie to save a young man struggling in the river. A friend—either drunk or horsing around or both—had pushed him in. The man was saved, the friend arrested and charged with attempted murder. A second team rushed to the Pont de Tolbiac to rescue a fully clothed man in his forties who had jumped into the water in a suicide attempt. The call for help came too late. The man had been in the water for fifty minutes, his brain deprived of oxygen. The doctor on duty declared him dead.

The suicide weighed heavily on the team. "In France, life is difficult, complicated," said Fanny. "Some people deal with it better than others. Sometimes, when you throw yourself into the water, it is a cry for help. But sometimes people strap on a backpack to weigh themselves down, so they cannot come back to the surface."


FROM THEIR PERCH in the heart of Paris, the members of the brigade feel their spirits lift when they come close to their river. The light that can turn its surface warm green in summer and icy gray in winter holds them in awe. "At sunrise, the water has the look of calm, like a lake," said Berjot. "When you sail with the sun rising, you have the impression that Paris is yours. After ten a.m., the water begins to move a little. The boats take over for the rest of the day. Then it's nightfall, with super-beautiful colors, and an effervescence, always an effervescence. The spotlights of the tourist boats light up the buildings along the quays. And then, after one in the morning, everything turns off again."

"We are on the river and suddenly we are free, as if we are on a flying boat," Fanny said. "The veterans of the brigade, the ones who have been here for twenty, twenty-five years, never take it for granted when they pass the Eiffel Tower. It's much more than a job. We are guardians of the peace, and we are guardians of the river. We do not forget how lucky we are. *C'est magnifique.*"

Over time, I persuaded some of the police officers of the brigade to open a chest filled with official souvenirs of their profession. I bought a baseball cap with the Brigade Fluviale logo—chic in black and white—and bottles of Champagne with a Brigade Fluviale label. The souvenir I treasure most is an official River Brigade arm patch. It is round, with Velcro backing and an image of a golden sailboat with a plump sail sitting atop a river of dark blue. Commander Berjot gave it to me one day. It is the same design that she wears on her uniform. I keep it on my desk, as a reminder of the days I spent as an honored guest of the Paris River Brigade.

THE RIVER CAN NEVER BE completely trusted, even by those who know it best, as the brigade was reminded when tragedy struck one morning in January 2018. Amandine Giraud, a twenty-seven-year-old member of the brigade, disappeared in the waters near Notre-Dame during an optional training exercise. She had been on the force for sixteen months and had received her diving certificate only a month before.

Although the other members of the team were very experienced divers, they had underestimated the danger of diving that day. Because of storm flooding, the Seine's current churned wildly below the surface; the water was a chilling forty degrees. Giraud dove into an area of the Seine between the Petit Pont and the Pont Saint-Michel so treacherous that it is referred to as the "Himalayas" of the river in Paris.

When she signaled that she was in distress, the crew struggled to pull her back on board, only to be thwarted by the strong current. One crew member dove into the water yet failed to rescue her. The boat's supervisor ordered her life line to be cut, perhaps in the erroneous belief that she could save herself that way. But she disappeared.

Police and prosecutorial authorities opened investigations and reviews of procedures. A bargeman recovered her body at the end of April. The following month, she was promoted posthumously to the rank of captain and awarded the National Police Force Medal of Honor.

Outside the entrance to the Brigade Fluviale headquarters sits a small, decorative, blue-and-white wooden rowboat planted with flowers. Giraud's father added a black stone plaque in her memory that included her photo and the words "A dream much too short. I love you. Your Papa." Members of the brigade renamed the rowboat *Amandine* and painted her name on its side.

*The stone statue of the Zouave soldier at the base of the*
*Pont de l'Alma.* ELAINE SCIOLINO.

*A nineteenth-century engraving of Javert, the police
inspector in Victor Hugo's* Les Misérables, *as he is about
to throw himself off the parapet of Pont Notre-Dame.*

# TWENTY-ONE

# The Unknown Woman of the Seine

*For geographers, the Seine is a river; for engineers, it's a means of nature's communication; for the desperate, it's a resting place.*

—SAINT-JUIRS,

*La Seine à travers Paris,* 1890

THE SEINE IS A TEMPTING and a terrifying place to die.

For the desperate, it can be a means to end unbearable suffering. For murderers, it can be a secret repository for their victims. For the hapless, the unlucky, the drunken, or the drugged, it can be an accidental grave.

The Seine's danger is thrilling when it is exploited for entertainment in death-defying stunts. In 1882, Arsens Blondin, a Spanish acrobat, donned a sparkly silver jersey and tightroped back and forth on a 525-foot metal cable spanning the river between the Pont de l'Alma and the Pont des Invalides. Despite a torrential downpour, a huge crowd turned out to cheer him on. At the mid-point, Blondin stopped, perched a chair on the wire, and climbed onto it; a while later, he lay down on the cable. Blondin's real name was Antonio Federico Álvarez Calvo, but he had renamed himself after the French acrobat who was the first person to cross Niagara Falls on a tightrope. That man went by "Monsieur Charles Blondin"; his real name was Jean François Gravelet.

In 1909, Harry Houdini, the American magician and stunt performer, plunged into the Seine while handcuffed. Nervous policemen jumped in after him, thinking he needed saving (he didn't), and nearly drowned themselves.

The river is also a liquid graveyard. Although it is illegal to throw human ashes into the Seine, that does not prevent people from doing so. I have a friend who, along with her daughters and various friends and family members, deposited the ashes of her late husband into the water from the end of the Île Saint-Louis. "We knew we weren't supposed to do it, but that was his wish," she said. "We arrived with a jar of his ashes, and each of us threw in a handful. It was the middle of summer, and the place was covered with tourists who had no idea what we were doing. It turned out to be quite funny."

My friend said that when she dies, she wants her ashes to be thrown from the pea-green, lattice-worked Pont Mirabeau, the subject of one of France's most famous poems, "Le Pont Mirabeau" by Guillaume Apollinaire. She recited part of the poem aloud for me, a section about how love "goes by as water to the sea." The poem conveys a sense of calm, ending: "Let night come on bells end the day / The days go by me still I stay."


THE MOST FAMOUS PERSON to have died in the Seine has no identity at all. She is the Unknown Woman of the Seine—*L'Inconnue de la Seine*. In the late nineteenth century, the body of a young woman was fished out of the Seine in Paris. As was the custom in those days, her corpse was laid out on a block of ice and put on display in the Paris morgue, located behind Notre-Dame. Locals and tourists would come and peer through the windows to stare at the bodies, and many came to see her. L'Inconnue's face was so innocent that she might have been a teenager; her skin bore neither marks nor bruises, so she was presumed to have committed suicide. Her look so mesmerized the pathologist on duty that he summoned a *mouleur*—a molder—to preserve her face in a plaster death mask.

The mask was mass-produced and sold as a decorative object in the decades that followed. L'Inconnue became a muse for artists, poets, and writers, among them Pablo Picasso, Man Ray, Rainer Maria Rilke, and Vladimir Nabokov. Because so little was known about her, she served as a blank slate for their fantasies. Albert Camus, who hung a mask of L'Inconnue in his studio, called her a "drowned Mona Lisa." Filmmakers François Truffaut, Max Ophüls, and Alain Resnais evoked her image in film. In literature, L'Inconnue was imagined as an orphan who drowns herself in the Seine after her lover abandons her, a witch who destroys a young poet, and a seductress who witnesses a robbery and murder.

There is no report of L'Inconnue's death in the police archives, no record of what happened to her body after it arrived at the morgue, and no precise notation of the date when the mold was made. But she lives on. She became famous—as the model for a life-sized, first-aid mannequin used to teach cardiopulmonary resuscitation (CPR) called "Resusci Anne" or "CPR Annie" in the United States. Millions of people have learned CPR on reproductions of her, making her the world's most beloved and useful life-sized doll.

In the southern Paris suburb of Arcueil, L'Inconnue's memory is kept alive in a different way. At L'Atelier Lorenzi, a family-run workshop founded in 1871, artisans create plaster copies of figurines, busts, statues—and masks of L'Inconnue. A box on the second floor holds the atelier's most precious possession: a nineteenth-century, chestnut-brown plaster mold of a death mask that is said to be that of L'Inconnue. Copies of the mask hang in most rooms in the two-story, wood-beamed building, which was built as a relay postal station in the 1800s. The mask sells for about $150 in flat white plaster, $195 with a shiny glaze.

"You ask me if my great-grandfather made the mold himself, and I

don't know," said Laurent Lorenzi Forestier, who runs the family business. "You ask me how the morgue organized the casting of the mold,
and I don't know. What I do know is that we have a mold from that era."

L'Inconnue's face is serene. Her cheeks are round and full, her skin
smooth, her hair parted in the middle and pulled back behind her
neck. Her eyelashes give the impression that they are still wet. She
is pleasant-looking, not classically beautiful. The mystery of her half-
smile haunts. She seems happy in death or maybe only asleep; her eyes
look as if they might open at any time. Skeptics claim that the woman
depicted in the mask was not a drowning victim but a live model,
because her features are too perfect.

L'Inconnue continues to inspire. At a Bastille Day picnic near the
source of the Seine in deep Burgundy, I met a poet named Céline Wal-
ter. She had published a book of poetry entitled *L'Inconnue de la Seine*.
She was convinced that L'Inconnue had drowned herself after her heart
was broken. "To think that she didn't get the kiss she wanted and is
now the most kissed face in the world," Céline said. "It's so much more
beautiful, more romantic. She took beautiful revenge. Over time, she
gave me her voice, and I gave her mine. There was a sort of dialogue. I
grew fond of her. I got to know her."

THE SEINE CAN SERVE AS a communal burial ground. One of the
most disturbing images in French history comes from the 1572 St. Bar-
tholomew's Day Massacre, when Charles IX and his mother, Catherine de' Medici, ordered the assassinations of leading Protestants, and
Catholic mobs attacked. Over three days and three nights of violence,
thousands of bodies were thrown into the Seine. The river turned red
with blood.

In more recent history, during the final stages of Algeria's eight-
year war of independence, the Seine figured in the Paris Massacre of
1961. Maurice Papon, the chief of the Paris Police Prefecture, ordered
his officers to attack a mass protest of about twenty-five thousand Alge-

rians who were violating a curfew. The police were unforgiving. Some protesters were beaten to death in police stations. Others were tortured and killed in the nearby woods. Some were thrown into the Seine from the Pont Saint-Michel and left to drown. Graffiti painted on the bridge afterward read, "*Ici on noie les Algériens*" (Here we drown Algerians). The official death toll was three; in truth, perhaps as many as five hundred Algerians died. In 1998, Papon was convicted of crimes against humanity for his role—as an official in Bordeaux—in France's collaboration with the Nazis in World War II.

In 2001, on the fortieth anniversary of the massacre, Paris mayor Bertrand Delanoë hung a commemorative plaque on the Pont Saint-Michel. As the number of victims is in dispute, it reads, "In memory of the many Algerians killed during the bloody repression of the peaceful demonstration of 17 October 1961." The story of the tragedy is seldom taught in French schools.

Every year, dozens of corpses are pulled from the Seine, most of them suicides. In 1791, two years after the beginning of the French Revolution, suicide was decriminalized and lost some of its stigma. However torturous the decision to commit suicide may be, British historian Richard Cobb wrote in his 1978 book *Death in Paris* that the act itself became as simple as running an errand or making an everyday purchase. Using a mortuary archive from 1795–1801, he concluded that 75 percent of the people who committed suicide by drowning lived within a few minutes' walking distance of the Seine. Young women were most likely to choose suicide by drowning; men favored hanging.

In literature and film, the Seine has served as the default site when a character needs to disappear or be killed off. Émile Zola portrayed the river as an easy and discreet way to kill in *Thérèse Raquin*, a tawdry tale of adultery and murder. Thérèse cheats on her husband, Camille, taking his friend Laurent as her lover. The adulterous pair plot the husband's death. Laurent throws Camille overboard from a boat on the Seine. Laurent and Thérèse get married, but visions of the dead man push them into madness and suicide.

In Martin Scorsese's 2011 film *Hugo*, twelve-year-old Hugo Cabret is orphaned and must live with his alcoholic uncle Claude, who forces the boy to help him do his job winding the clocks at the Gare Montparnasse train station. In one scene, Claude disappears into the depths of the Seine. When, after many months, his body is found, it is unclear whether he was the victim of suicide, murder, or an accident, although the presence of his flask indicates that he was probably drunk. Hugo has continued to wind the clocks, so Claude had not been missed at work. But with Claude dead, the stationmaster wants to know who has been doing his job.

One of the darkest films involving the Seine is Francois Truffaut's *Jules and Jim* (1962), a tale of two friends who fall in love with the same woman. Catherine, played by Jeanne Moreau, is exciting but narcissistic. On a whim at one crucial moment, she jumps from the riverbank into the Seine then swims back to the quay. (Her body double was drunk at the time of filming, so Moreau played the scene herself.) The film ends tragically when Catherine, married to Jules, asks Jim to join her for a ride in her car. She tells Jules to "watch us carefully." She smiles sweetly at Jim, who is seated beside her, accelerates, and drives the car off a damaged bridge into the Seine, killing them both.

Perhaps no French writer has felt death on the Seine more acutely than Victor Hugo. Hugo loved the river. In the years after his 1831 opus *The Hunchback of Notre-Dame* made him rich and famous, he traveled around Normandy, sketching. But the Seine claimed his spirit.

The story of how the river came to torture Hugo is preserved in a three-story brick house—now a museum dedicated to Hugo—that faces the Seine in the town of Villequier, twenty-three miles west of Rouen. Roses fill the garden, and red and white wrought-iron chairs offer visitors a place to sit and read. Lazy cows graze on the hills, and apples grow in small orchards nearby, but there is neither a café nor a bakery in town. The house had belonged to Charles-Isidore Vacquerie, who appreciated the writings and beliefs of the much younger Hugo.

The two men became close friends, and the Hugo family came to visit in the summer. Vacquerie's son Charles and Hugo's daughter Léopoldine fell in love and married in February 1843; seven months later, the newlyweds were dead.

The Seine had not been tamed in Hugo's day. It was deeper, its currents more powerful. Silt formations moved silently, ominously, changing shape and forming mini-islands. The only way to travel along the river was by ferry or private boat. Sophie Schmidt, a guide at the museum, explained when I visited that Léopoldine and Charles went to consult their notary at nearby Caudebec-en-Caux on an exceptionally windy day.

"They went out on a small boat, and it was too light," she said. "It was a time when the Seine was much busier with more barges, and wider than it is today. The boat capsized. Charles came from a family of seamen. He was a good swimmer and knew the river well. But in those days, not many people knew how to swim, especially women. Léopoldine could not swim. She panicked. She was wearing a heavy dress. She sank deep into the river's depths. Charles dove in to try to save her. They both perished."

She was nineteen; he was twenty-six.

The furnishings in one of the bedrooms evoke their memory: their narrow bed, a piece of the veil worn by Léopoldine on her wedding day, a nightshirt that belonged to Charles. Her unadorned wedding dress hangs in an adjoining bedroom. The windows in both rooms look out onto the point in the river where they drowned.

"Hugo was on a walking tour in southwest France with his mistress when the accident happened," said Schmidt. "He learned about it only ten days later. He was in a café and he read about it in a newspaper. Léopoldine had already been buried. The Seine for Hugo meant death, a river that killed." A photocopy of the page about her death in the newspaper *Le Siècle* hangs on one wall.

Hugo poured his grief into poetry. In Villequier, he railed against the injustice of their deaths, and struggled to make peace with destiny:

*Anything good he owns, Fate takes away.*
*No gift was his, these days that disappear. . . .*
*The world is dark, O God! The set refrain*
*Is made of bitter tears as much as song.*

A wide riverfront path for strollers and bike riders extends five miles along the road outside the museum. It opens to a grassy park with weathered picnic tables. Its focal point is a stone statue of Hugo looking out to the river. His features are crudely chiseled; his face is grim. He is said to be searching for his daughter. Mercifully, large shady trees block his view of the water.

PERHAPS THE MOST IMPORTANT suicide in all modern French literature comes in Hugo's 1862 novel *Les Misérables*. It is the suicide of Javert, the troubled police inspector who doesn't even have a first name. Throughout the novel, Javert is gripped by an obsession: to punish and destroy the escaped convict Jean Valjean, who had been imprisoned for nineteen years for stealing a loaf of bread. But when Valjean saves Javert's life, Javert is faced with a moral dilemma: How can he arrest the man who saved him?

Unable to understand Valjean's act of generosity, Javert goes mad. In Paris, he approaches the edge of the Pont Notre-Dame and gazes down at the most treacherous part of the Seine. It is a suffocating, hemmed-in square of water bordered by two bridges and two quays, a stretch of the river that is "dreaded by mariners," Hugo writes. The water rolls in vast and terrible waves. Whirlpools loosen and tighten their grip like screws that never stop turning.

Javert is swallowed by the blackness of the night. When he reappears, he is ready for death: "Suddenly, he took off his hat and laid it on the edge of the quay," Hugo wrote. "A moment later a tall black form, which from the distance some belated pedestrian might have taken for a phantom, appeared standing on the parapet, bent toward the Seine, then sprang up and fell straight into the darkness; there was a dull splash; and the night alone was admitted to the secret convulsions of that obscure form which had disappeared under the water."

ALL IS NOT DARK. The Seine also has the power to keep people alive. Either its glittering beauty relieves them of their misery or its cold and sinister darkness is too terrifying to enter.

In 1900, the sculptor Augustus Saint-Gaudens was racked with stomach pain. A cancerous tumor was discovered in his lower intestine, and he fell into a deep depression. One day, he fled his Paris studio to kill himself. "I had definitely made up my mind to jump into the Seine," he told James Earle Fraser, his student and apprentice.

> I practically ran down the rue de Rennes toward the Seine, and when I looked up at the buildings they all seemed to have written across the top a huge word in black letters—"Death—Death—Death."
>
> I reached the river and went up on the bridge and as I looked over the water, I saw the Louvre in the bright sunlight and suddenly everything was beautiful to me. . . . Whether the running and the hurrying had changed my mental attitude, I can't say— possibly it might have been the beauty of the Louvre's architecture or the sparkling water of the Seine—whatever it was, suddenly the weight and blackness lifted from my mind and I was happy and found myself whistling.

Saint-Gaudens lived another seven years.

Novelists have captured the magnificent contradiction of the Seine as a place that lures you to death but then redeems itself and saves you from its darkness. In Balzac's *The Wild Ass's Skin*, the despairing Raphaël de Valentin, after gambling and losing the last of his money, prepares to take the fatal plunge from the Pont Royal one morning. "Bad time to drown," says an old woman dressed in rags, laughing at him. "The Seine—it's dirty and cold." He notices a rescue boat on duty and decides to wait until nightfall. But then he discovers a magical wish-granting parchment in a strange antiques shop on the Quai Voltaire. The urge to end his life vanishes.

In Jean-Paul Sartre's *The Age of Reason*, Mathieu Delarue, a professor of philosophy, is about to plunge from the Pont Neuf but at the last moment changes his mind. "That," he said, "will be for the next time."

Perhaps the fairy-tale architecture lining the quays works to counterbalance the sinister darkness of the water and the slime that can form on its surface. Is the river so beautiful that it cools the impulse to jump in? Or perhaps the Seine is a holder of the secrets and mysteries of life, as well as death, and many find salvation along its banks.

Le petit-pont, *an 1850 engraving by Charles Meryon with the
towers of Notre-Dame in the background.*

A PARIS.

M. DC XI.

*A map from 1611 depicting the city of Paris, centered around Île de la Cité.*
*To the right, three islands that will later become Île Saint-Louis.*

# TWENTY-TWO

# Island-Hopping

*The islands are like a pearl necklace*
*of nature decorating the river.*
*Each pearl has its own life, its*
*own identity. There are islands of*
*imagination that never existed and*
*islands that are no more.*

**—MILENA CHARBIT**, architect

LA SEINE MUSICALE, a modern performance center made of wood and glass, rises from the Seine like a sailboat with an egg-shaped hull. Its sail, an arc covered in solar panels, rotates around it on steel rails to follow the course of the sun.

Since it opened in 2017, this shining structure has begun to transform the Île Seguin, a twenty-eight-acre island west of the Paris city limits. It is the go-to place to experience some of the best global music and dance, to dine, shop, have a drink, walk through gardens, and take in the view from the roof. It is a crossroads for serious audiences and visitors passing through. "A boat on an island on a voyage of adventure" is how Olivier Haber, its chief executive officer, described it.

The Île Seguin is still unexplored terrain. A ten-minute walk from the end of a Métro line, it is not found on tourist maps. The Seine's two most famous islands, the Île Saint-Louis (about the same size as the Île Seguin) and the Île de la Cité (nearly twice as big) have always reigned over central Paris. The Seine is a river of islands, some reachable by bridges and many more only by boat. Centuries ago, there were more than three hundred, scattered from the source to the sea. Napoléon's grand public works projects to make the river more navigable swept away well over half of them, dredging some, joining some either to other islands or to the riverbanks. Today 117 Seine islands survive, forming an elongated archipelago of industry, culture, habitation, recreation, and refuge, full of sand and stone and stories.

The Île Seguin comes with a rich history, even if little known to Americans. Seven miles southwest of central Paris and five miles northeast of Versailles, the island was farmland until the eighteenth century, when Louis XV bought it for his daughters. From the early nineteenth century on, it housed leather tanneries, laundries, and riverside cabarets. In 1929, Louis Renault opened his first automobile factory on the island, and over time, Renault's operation became the largest factory in France. Renault raised the level of the island and erected two bridges to link the Right and Left Banks, facilitating access. The company also experimented in innovation—building its own electric power plant, testing sites (including an underground racetrack), and a docking operation big enough to ship finished cars.

During World War II, Renault produced trucks for the occupying Germans. The Allied forces bombed the site to force it to stop. After the Liberation, Louis Renault was accused of collaborating with the enemy; he died in prison in 1944, shortly before his trial was to start. After the war, the factory went back to making vehicles for the French; it was hit by serious labor strikes during the civil unrest in May 1968. Renault later moved manufacturing to sites outside Paris, and the factory closed in 1992. For years afterward it stood abandoned, a forlorn reminder of the Île Seguin's prosperous industrial past. Eventually it was demolished, and the site cleared of polluted soil and industrial residue that included ten thousand tons of iron.

In 2000, François-Henri Pinault, the chairman and chief executive of Kering, which owns luxury fashion brands including Gucci and
Saint Laurent, announced a plan to build a museum for his modern art
collection on the island. After five years of administrative delays, he
put it in Venice instead. "Île Seguin: I give up," he wrote in exaspera-
tion in *Le Monde*. A plan for a university campus went nowhere. Then,
in 2010, the regional government of Hauts-de-Seine bought a third of
the island for La Seine Musicale.

Now, from La Seine Musicale's rooftop, visitors can see panoramic
views: downstream, the Pont de Sèvres; upstream, Paris; to the side, on
the Right Bank, a clumsy office building designed by Jean Nouvel, a
General Electric plant, and a swath of the sleepy upper-middle-class
suburb of Boulogne-Billancourt. The Seine flows on both sides of the
site, creating unity between the indoor and outdoor spaces.

"The presence of water is inspiring, always," said Laurence Equil-
bey, the founder and artistic director of Insula, the orchestra in residence. "The water passes by, the river changes, and it is fantastic to
watch the movement and the reflection of light. You see the low hills
on the banks, the barges and the rowers on the river. You feel you are
in a less violent and more peaceful universe. It's beautiful to be on an
island, no?"


THE ARCHIPELAGO OF THE SEINE is nearly nonexistent at its
start, with only seven islands on the 230-mile route from the river's
source to Paris. They become denser on the west side of Paris, and
densest as the river approaches Rouen. The islands eliminated in
Napoléon's projects included all of those on the route from Rouen to
the sea. Today sandbars still come and go with the tide, creating pop-
up islands.

Over centuries, the Seine's currents claimed some now-vanished
islands and moved others, changing their shapes. The Île de Belcinac,
across from the town of Caudebec-en-Caux, for example, disappeared and

reappeared three times between the fourteenth and eighteenth centuries. The tiny Île des Ravageurs and the Île Robinson were added onto the town of Asnières-sur-Seine, west of Paris, in 1970. But Île des Ravageurs retains its identity as a destination for dog lovers: since 1899 it has been home to what locals proclaim is the first animal cemetery in the world. It holds the graves of more than forty thousand pets—dogs, of course, as well as other "domestic animals," including cats, horses, birds, rabbits, hamsters, and monkeys. One of the most famous graves is that of the French-born German shepherd Rin Tin Tin, who became known as the "Wonder Dog." Rescued in 1918 from a World War I battlefield by an American soldier from California, Rinty, as he was called, starred in more than two dozen Warner Bros. films. When he died in 1932, just shy of the age of fourteen, his body was sent back to his native France for burial.

The islands of the Seine have been used to house a maximum-security prison (Île Saint-Étienne), a theater (Île Louviers), a casino (Île aux Dames), a grand sports complex (Île de Puteaux), a model farm (Île de la Loge), and the station for a major dam and lock west of Paris invaded every year by Canada geese (Île de Chatou).

The flowing river makes its islands elongated and narrow. The smallest Seine island, the Île Paradis, on a bend in the river seven miles upstream of Rouen, is about the size of four tennis courts. The biggest, several miles farther on, is an amalgam of seven islands that were joined together—the Îles d'Harcourt, Bonport, Surgès, Launy, de Quatre Ages, du Courant, and aux Moines. About eight times bigger than Île de la Cité, this island lacks a new identity; instead, each of its component parts keeps its old name, like states in a union.

For many visitors to Paris, and even many Parisians, the most visited islands are the Île de la Cité and the smaller Île Saint-Louis. They are joined by a short bridge but are different from each other in nearly every way—history, function, architecture, and inhabitants.

The Île de la Cité is almond-shaped, three-quarters of a mile long, and just over a tenth of a mile wide, covering about fifty-four acres. Inhabited since pre-Roman times, it is still an important archaeological site. Its jewel is Notre-Dame Cathedral, which was built stone by stone from 1163 to 1345, triggering the construction of houses and churches, which attracted new inhabitants.

Under the square in front of Notre-Dame, a crypt open to the public holds vestiges of the city's ancient history, including large blocks of stone from the fortified fourth-century B.C. wall that once encircled the island, ancient gold and bronze coins, and the remains of fourth-century A.D. Gallo-Roman thermal baths. A piece of a quay from the first-century B.C. Gallo-Roman port on the island, along with amphoras and traces of a storage depot, bear witness to the robust trade on the river in that era.

In the eighteenth century, Paris city planners razed some of the medieval buildings to improve sanitation and ease congestion on the Île de la Cité. Then came Baron Haussmann and his radical transformation of the island in the nineteenth century. He destroyed a quaint but densely packed, dirty, and dangerous medieval legacy—a hundred houses, thirty streets and alleys, and several churches—on the Île de la Cité. The island's population shrank from fifteen thousand to five thousand.

On part of the cleared land, Haussmann built the new Hôtel-Dieu— a hospital and barracks that became the headquarters for the Prefecture of Police. Only about nine hundred people live on the island now, but thirteen million come every year to visit Notre-Dame. Partially hidden at the far edge of the garden behind Notre-Dame sits a memorial that honors the two hundred thousand "Martyrs of the Deportation," those who were sent to Nazi concentration camps during the Occupation and never returned. A staircase leads to a confined space with bars on the window. You can look through the bars and see the Seine; people along the Left Bank can see you, the prisoner, looking out at them.

The Île Saint-Louis was created in 1614, when the ditch between the Île aux Vaches and the Île Notre-Dame was filled in. A sandy, wet no-man's-land, it became one of the first laboratories for urban planning in France, thanks to the vision of Henri IV as implemented by his son Louis XIII. Over three decades, its circumference was diked, and elegant townhouses and mansions were built from pale local stone, not for the nobility but for the rich bourgeoisie. In a nod to modernity, some of the houses looked outward toward the Seine, rather than inward toward courtyards and interior streets. The streets were straight, wider than elsewhere in Paris, and, for the first time, plotted on a grid with a central straight road that spanned the island.

The Île Saint-Louis became arguably the most elegant address in central Paris in the mid-nineteenth century. The painter Paul Cézanne lived there, on the Quai d'Anjou facing the Right Bank. As a young dandy, Baudelaire lived at No. 22 Quai de Béthune facing the Left Bank. The Nobel-prize-winning physicist and chemist Marie Curie lived at No. 36 for twenty-two years. Years later, President Georges Pompidou and his wife, Claude, rented an apartment at No. 24; he died there in 1974. More recently, Jamel Debbouze, one of France's most popular humorists, and his wife moved to the only street that cuts through the length of the island.

Edmund White, the American writer, appreciated the Île Saint-Louis as a quiet refuge. In his novel *The Married Man*, one of the main characters, Austin, likes to come from a noisy bar or a talkative dinner party "on the mainland and cross the black, rapidly flowing Seine" to the Île Saint-Louis, "his poetic island, always five degrees cooler than the rest of Paris."

Crowds from all over the world descend on the Île Saint-Louis less for its peaceful vibe or elegant architecture than for its ice cream. They might wait in line for an hour at Berthillon for what some believe is the best ice cream in Paris. One of Berthillon's other great offerings is its tarte tatin, an upside-down caramelized apple tart served with crème fraiche; this dish was once—but is no longer—a staple of every respectable French bistro. It is a temptation too delicious to resist.

WEST OF THE CITY LIMITS is the Île de la Jatte, the setting for Georges Seurat's 1884 pointillist masterpiece, *A Sunday Afternoon on the Island of La Grande Jatte*. The painting depicts a crowded park on the Seine, full of activity. In the foreground a man and woman stand in profile, looking out at the river. She wears a long skirt with a large bustle and carries a black umbrella; he wears a top hat and a formal suit and holds a cigar. In the center, another woman takes the hand of a girl dressed in white. People lounge on the grass; a child scampers; a dog sniffs the ground. Sailboats, steamboats, and a fisherman's small boat line the river. A coxswain with a white parasol over her head travels with four rowers in a long, narrow shell.

The painting hangs in the Art Institute of Chicago; even if you've never seen it, you might still recognize it. Stephen Sondheim used it as inspiration for his musical *Sunday in the Park with George*; NBC's online store sold a poster where the characters from *The Office* pose in the same positions; Babar illustrator Laurent de Brunhoff mimicked it by turning its characters into elephants. In a *Sesame Street* version, Big Bird posed as the woman with the black umbrella; he replaced her bustle with his feathery ducklike tail. Visitors to the Île de la Jatte can take a two-and-a-half-mile tour around the island to see exactly where *Sunday Afternoon* and other important Impressionist works were painted, including two other Seurats, two Monets, and works by Van Gogh, Sisley, Albert Gleizes, and Alexandre Nozal.

The Île du Platais, where Émile Zola bought land and built a pavilion, is visible from his estate in Médan. Zola rowed his friends over to sunbathe, swim, and fish there. His boat, named *Nana* after the protagonist of one of his most successful novels, was a gift from Guy de Maupassant. "It was a very convivial life," his great-granddaughter Martine Le Blond-Zola told me when I visited one day. In the 1920s, the Île du Platais became a "naturist" recreation club, with bungalows and a large concrete swimming pool. Nudity was banned, but members wore minimal clothing—bathing trunks for men, outfits that resembled two-piece bathing suits for women, and this long before Louis Réard, a Frenchman, invented the bikini in 1946. Closed in 2002, the club remains abandoned.

The tiny Île aux Bernaches, fifteen miles west of Paris, was once the site of a giant water-pumping station that Louis XIV built for the

*The remnants of the Marly Machine on an island at Bougival. Louis XIV created the device to pump water five hundred feet uphill to supply the fountains of Versailles.* GABRIELA SCIOLINO PLUMP.

Marly Machine. The station, formally inaugurated by the king in 1684, contained fourteen wheels, thirty feet in diameter, and more than 250 pumps. It ran night and day, made a frightful racket, and emitted a horrible odor. Newer constructions replaced it, and the machines stopped turning in 1968. The Île aux Bernaches is not accessible today, but a brick administrative building is still there, choked with weeds and stringy plants. On the northern bank of the mainland, you can climb stairs up a hill alongside the chutes where the water ascended to the château.

MILENA CHARBIT, a young architect, is the preeminent expert on the Seine islands. She wrote her master's thesis on the subject and

developed it into a book and a museum exhibition that was shown at
the Pavillon de l'Arsenal, a cultural space perched over the Seine across
from the eastern end of the Île Saint-Louis. "No one was paying any
attention to the islands of the Seine," she told me when I toured the
exhibition and interviewed her there. "It was a little world that was
unknown, unexplored, and foreign."

Charbit pulled together images and documents from library collections in Paris, as well as archives from cities and towns all along the
Seine. To recall the era when the river was swimmable, she created
a life-sized black-and-white cardboard photo montage showing ten
champion swimmers from 1913 and 1914. The swimmers' faces were
arranged as cutouts; they could be popped out so that visitors could
insert their own into the holes and pose for pictures.

Every island tells its own story, Charbit said. Some disappeared,
absorbed into the mainland or larger islands during construction projects. The Île Louviers, which had once almost touched the Île Saint-
Louis and was used to stock wood, was joined to the Right Bank to
form what is now the Quartier Morland. The Île des Cygnes got its
name when Louis XIV populated it entirely with a special variety of
swans imported from Denmark. (The swan, considered pure and regal,
was the Sun King's favorite animal.) The island was little more than a
sliver of land separated from the Champ de Mars, on the Left Bank, by
a canal. In 1773, part of the canal was filled in; the island became part
of the Left Bank when the remainder was filled in to accommodate the
construction of the Pont d'Iéna in 1812.

Sixty miles upstream from Paris is the Île Olive, which was owned
by the mayor of the local commune in the 1880s, Dr. Sébastien Jean
Alexandre Olive. When he died, his widow bequeathed the island to
the nearby town, and it is now a wooded park with an arboretum and
a nature trail. It can be neither sold nor rented; no structures can be
erected, no refreshments sold.

The Île Saint-Denis occupies a bend in the river downstream from

Paris. A functioning town with its own mayor, it is home to both arti-sans whose work is connected to the river and warehouses for depart-ment stores like Printemps and Galeries Lafayette. The island is destined for fame—and perhaps fortune—as the site of the Paris Sum-mer Olympic Village in 2024.

Other islands are human creations. The Île aux Cygnes, a long, slen-der island near the Eiffel Tower, was created in 1827 and named in honor of the defunct Île des Cygnes. It served as a reinforcement for three new bridges and was part of a project to deepen the Seine. Wild plants like thistles, poppies, mallow, and bindweed crowd its walls, which slope steeply from the embankment to below the waterline. Bird species like mallard ducks, gray wagtails, short-toed tree creepers, and sometimes great crested grebes call the island home. A promenade run-ning the length of the island is lined with sixty tree species. At the island's western edge stands a quarter-size version of the Statue of Lib-erty surrounded by a clump of weeping willows that gives refuge to tiny, transparent freshwater shrimp.

Early one evening, I joined Charbit and other Seine experts on an invitation-only boat tour of the islands in and around Paris. Purple-gray rain clouds hovered above us as we boarded from the Quai de l'Hôtel de Ville. Armed with her microphone, Charbit took to the deck while we headed west, reaching as far as the Île Saint-Germain. Once a military camp, the island now contains businesses, residences, and a sculpture park, which features an eighty-foot-tall work by Jean Dubuf-fet that is considered one of his most important.

A few raindrops fell on the crowd, and then the sky burst open. We moved inside, close to the bar. When the boat turned to head back to central Paris, the sun pierced the clouds. As we passed the Eiffel Tour, a double rainbow appeared, as if on cue.

It was if we had entered what Proust called "the enchanted essence" of Monet's paintings. In writing about them, Proust singled out the ones "strewn with islands in those inert hours of the afternoon when the river is white and blue with clouds and sky."

# PART FOUR

# From City to Sea

*Auguste Renoir's painting* Luncheon of the Boating Party *(1881), depicting a scene on the balcony at the Maison Fournaise on the island of Chatou. Maison Fournaise is still a popular restaurant today.* THE PHILLIPS COLLECTION, WASHINGTON, D.C., USA. ACQUIRED 1923. / BRIDGEMAN IMAGES.

# TWENTY-THREE

# River of Light

*The Seine! I painted it all my life,
at all hours, in all seasons, from
Paris to the sea . . . I never tired of
it: it is for me always new. . . . I built
myself a studio in a boat. It was a
sort of quite large cabin: one could
sleep there. I lived there, with my
material, spying on the effects of the
light from one dusk to another.*

**—CLAUDE MONET**

AS THE SEINE LOOPS northwest out of Paris, through the prosperous suburbs of Île-de-France and into the farmland of Normandy, it glides into its ancient role as a roadway from Paris to the sea. Merchants, traders, adventurers, and invaders explored and exploited this final stretch of its route; even as it still functions as a commerical workhorse, boaters and tourists also travel it for pleasure. A century and a half ago, it carried bold painters into an artistic revolution.

The painters were entranced with the new idea of painting outdoors amid the chalk cliffs and woodlands of Normandy. The landscape that caressed the Seine's serpentine curves became an open-air studio, freeing the painters from the confines of their ateliers. The play of light on the river dared them to experiment. The weather, changing dramatically, whimsically, and without warning, required them to quicken their tempo and improvise. Their artistic adventures coincided with a technical discovery: the invention of zinc paint tubes. No longer did artists have to laboriously prepare colors by mixing pigments and oils in their studios. They could now easily work outside and, in doing so, learn about the light, the flow, the reflections, the colors of water.

"You go back in the history of art before the Impressionists, and water didn't move," my painter friend Richard Overstreet told me. "The great Venetian painters like Canaletto painted the canals of Venice and the sea and all of that, and the water—it's flat. It's a hard surface. The Impressionists, they thought about water. They thought about the Seine, how it moves and how it is lit. It's very hard to paint water; it's one of the hardest things to paint, because it's transient. But they did it."

Artists have depicted the Seine for centuries. Illustrated manuscripts from 1317 show everyday river scenes, like boats carrying wine, grain, and fish, alongside images of Saint Denis, the patron saint of France. On one page of *Les très riches heures du Duc de Berry*, a fifteenth-century collection of prayers for the canonical hours, the Seine flows past the Louvre as everyman's source of leisure, with small wooden boats moored at the river's edge and people strolling on its banks. In woodcuts from the same era, haulers and traders work the quays. Eighteenth-century pastoral paintings in the Musée Carnavalet show the Seine in Paris before its encasement in concrete and stone, with riverbanks easing into the river so fluidly that horses and cows wade in to drink and cool off. The museum also holds a series of large panoramic landscapes of the Seine by the eighteenth-century painter Nicolas-Jean-Baptiste Raguenet, who was so fascinated by daily life on the river that he captured it on canvas with the precision of a photographer. He documented both happy events, like a water jousting celebration, and tragedies, like the inferno at the city's oldest hospital in 1772, in which he filled the sky with violent orange and yellow flames.

Much later, the Seine transformed the style of the twentieth-century American painter Ellsworth Kelly, who arrived in Paris as a twenty-five-year-old student on the GI Bill after World War II. Transfixed by the patterns of light that scattered and spread across the river, in 1951 he painted *Seine*. It consisted of small black and white rectangles that incorporated chance into what became a geometric view of the movement of the river. And, of course, there was Impressionism.

Normandy offered a more cosmopolitan life than other French provinces, and as Paris became more crowded and industrial, the region became the city's artistic extension. The railroad, another innovation, made it easily reachable. The painters boarded the trains with their easels and paint tubes and followed the Seine westward, through towns and cities like Giverny and Rouen, until they reached the sea at Le Havre and Honfleur.

Eugène Boudin, born in Honfleur where the Seine meets the sea, was one of the first plein air landscape artists, and he succeeded in luring Claude Monet outdoors. "It was as if a veil were torn from my eyes," Monet wrote in a letter late in life. "I grasped what painting could be." In the beginning of the 1860s, a sort of artistic commune was created at La Ferme Saint Siméon, a country inn set in an apple orchard outside Honfleur. There, the close-knit trio of Monet, Boudin, and Johan Jongkind, as well as their friends Gustave Courbet, Charles-François Daubigny, Frédéric Bazille, James McNeill Whistler, and Adolphe-Félix Cals, met to drink and discuss their art. Below them was the great, nearly nine-mile-wide expanse of the Seine estuary. The hotel has been restored and largely preserved. Note to Monet lovers: his favorite room was No. 22.

Monet painted the Seine for the rest of his life, at any time of day or season of the year. While he was in Argenteuil, northwest of Paris, looking for a riverboat to convert into a floating studio, he met Gustave Caillebotte, a painter who was a boating fanatic—and rich enough to support his hobby. Together they found what became Monet's "studio boat," where he often worked, keeping many paintings going simultaneously. Once, when a journalist asked to see his studio, Monet gestured to the Seine and the rolling hills beyond it and replied, "This is my studio." He called his landscapes of water and their reflections "an obsession." The river both infuriated and liberated him.

Once the river almost lured Monet to his death. He struggled with depression and nearly committed suicide at the age of twenty-eight. "I was so upset yesterday that I had the stupidity to throw myself into the water," he wrote to fellow painter Frédéric Bazille in the summer of 1868. "Fortunately, no harm came of it." (Monet was a good swimmer.)

The river also brought Monet peace. It freed him to focus on color and light, to experiment with brushstrokes. He played with the water, dimpling it like peaks of meringue and flattening it like a mirror. In 1872, at Le Havre, Monet painted a sunrise in his new style and called it *Impression, soleil levant* ("Impression, Sunrise"). He included it in an exhibition of thirty artists' work in 1874, organized in retaliation against the Paris Salon, an annual showcase of academic art. The critic Louis Leroy mocked the title of Monet's painting, writing that the exhibition was full of "impressionists." Rather than taking offense, the group embraced their new identity. Impressionism was born.

As soon as the outdoors seduced him, Monet said he did not understand why artists would choose to shut themselves up in closed rooms. "To draw, yes; to paint, no," he wrote. In 1883, he moved to Giverny, a town in Île-de-France on the edge of Normandy, where the Epte River cuts through meadows and flows into the Seine. He bought a manor house, planted elaborate gardens, and dug a pond, which he filled with water lilies. He took his barge to a nearby river landing. Over the years, he expanded his fleet with two mahogany-hulled sculls and a rowing skiff with a high prow. In the summers of 1896 and 1897, he often left his house as early as three-thirty in the morning and went out on his studio boat to await the blue-gray-lavender light in the mists of dawn.

Monet's residence in Giverny is the Versailles of the Impressionist movement. The garden, with its changing seasonal blooms and lily ponds, wooden footbridge, climbing wisteria, and the house, just as it

was (well, almost) when Monet lived there—all raise this site high up
on the must-see list of any tourist with even the slightest interest in
Impressionist art. Because of Monet, this once-unknown village on the
slopes of the Seine is a place of pilgrimage for painters, private collec-
tors, museum curators, politicians, and tourists.

And like Versailles, it is overcrowded. Getting in and out of the long,
narrow house of rose-pink plaster can be a horror. There's usually a
wait to get into the house and gridlock in the narrow corridors. Not
one painting by Monet hangs on its walls; they are all reproductions.

But the house is worthy of a
visit, if only to see Monet's
spacious kitchen, decorated
in blue-and-white Rouen
tiles and hung with shiny
copper pots, and, in both the
kitchen and other rooms,
the Japanese engravings he
collected with such passion.

In the village, the rue
Claude Monet is lined with
galleries showing work by
local wannabe Monets and
small restaurants that post
multilingual menus outside.
Some are good, some are
bad. The most peaceful place
is the tiny cemetery where
Monet is buried. So pilgrims
still find Monet's spirit at
Giverny. It is the place where
he painted some of his most
famous works, including an
ambitious series of more than

*One of Henri Matisse's most famous paintings evoking
the Seine,* Studio, Quai Saint-Michel, *completed
in 1916. He painted it in his apartment studio
overlooking the Seine. Île de la Cité and the tip of
Notre-Dame Cathedral are visible in the background.*

twenty paintings entitled *Morning on the Seine*. He studied views along the river, painted them from his boat, then lined them up in his studio and finished them off together.

There are other ways to experience the world of the Impressionists. Several towns and islands west of Paris have "Impressionist" walks along the Seine. Visitors are guided to the exact spot where painters stood while they worked; plaques show reproductions of the famous paintings created there.

One Sunday morning Andy and I headed to Rueil-Malmaison, a town about a twenty-minute train ride northwest of Paris, for a boat tour devoted to the Impressionists. Across the river is the Île de Chatou, known as the Island of the Impressionists. We boarded the *Tivano*, a pleasure craft, and perched ourselves in comfortable metal armchairs in the front row. "I invite you to look at the density of green colors that we find in the paintings, and the light that projects on this greenery," our guide said. It wasn't the most exciting presentation, but for the older French crowd out for a Sunday afternoon outing on the river, it was good enough. She told us that Impressionist painters were visual journalists, because they documented the festivities and leisure activities of their era, particularly as they were enjoyed outside Paris. "Because this place was a bit difficult to access, it was also where the police could not come, so you can imagine some of the things that went on here," she said.

We passed the town of Bougival, a small but important urban center where the Impressionists and others—including Renoir, Sisley, Édouard Manet, Camille Pissarro, Cézanne, Bazille, Berthe Morisot, Derain, and Maurice de Vlaminck—gathered and painted. In summertime, the composer Georges Bizet lived there, too. "It is said that he committed suicide in the Seine because he was completely crushed by the negative reviews of *Carmen*," our guide related. "What is certain is that he swam in the Seine when it was much too cold and suffered a fatal heart attack afterward." (The truth is more complex. Bizet suffered from serious throat problems and was depressed after his opera *Carmen* failed. Feeling better one day in the spring of 1875, he went for a swim in the Seine. Racked by pain and a high fever the next day, he had two heart attacks and died. He was thirty-six.)

Renoir and Sisley felt such a strong connection to the river that in the summer of 1865, along with Sisley's brother Henry, they piloted a boat from Chatou all the way to Le Havre to meet Monet (Le Havre was his hometown) and watch a regatta. "I am taking my paint box in order to make sketches of the places I like. I think it will be charming," Renoir wrote to Bazille in asking him to come along. "There's nothing to keep you from leaving a place you don't like; nor anything to keep you from staying on in an enjoyable one." Renoir described the trip as "a long sea voyage in a sailing boat," even though they did not sail the entire way but had to be towed from Chatou to Rouen. There, they visited the cathedral. From Rouen on, they sailed toward Le Havre, passing steamboats, tugboats, and schooners, and marveling at the bustling industrial traffic along the way.

Well into the nineteenth century, navigation was difficult in this part of the Seine. The river twisted back on itself like a coiling snake. The current was fickle. Eventually a system of locks controlled the river flow. On our tour, the captain maneuvered our boat into a narrow lock, and we waited while the water level dropped.

We were only a few miles from Paris, but we had entered another world. Thick walls of trees and bushes alive with color—from deep green to pale gray—conjured thoughts of an Amazonian jungle. The water was perfectly still, reflecting the vegetation like a mirror. Swans swam alongside us. A man in an inflatable kayak rowed past. Families picnicked and fished. On the way back to the dock, we came upon the red brick and yellow stone façade and wrought-iron railings of La Maison Fournaise on the Île de Chatou. Awnings shielded the diners from the sun. It was here that Renoir painted *Luncheon of the Boating Party*.

THE STORY STARTED with Alphonse Fournaise, who came from a family of bargemen. In 1860, he created a recreational site to attract

the day-trippers coming by train to the countryside suburbs of Chatou, Argenteuil, Asnières, and Bougival. La Maison Fournaise became
a gathering place for Parisians of different classes and professions—
painters, writers, financiers, politicians, shopgirls. People came to rent
rowboats, swim in the river, enjoy a meal, and even stay the night.
The Fournaise family held on to the property until 1953, when the
building was sold and cut up into apartments. It soon turned shabby,
was abandoned, and attracted squatters. In 1979, the town of Chatou
bought it, renovating it one section at a time. It reopened as a restaurant eleven years later. After intense lobbying, Marie-Christine Davy,
president of the Association of the Friends of La Maison Fournaise,
persuaded local politicians to give the building landmark status.
These days, an outdoor wall shows off the building's importance with
the words "Maison Fournaise, Musée, Restaurant" painted in large
red and black letters. A small white sign leads to the "Renoir walk,"
a circuit that invites visitors to study the sites in Chatou painted by
the artist.

Renoir loved La Maison Fournaise. Thirty-three of his paintings show portraits of the Fournaise family or festive dining scenes
in the house. *Luncheon of the Boating Party*, painted between 1880
and 1881, included some of his closest friends, among them Aline
Charigot, a dressmaker who became his model and then his wife;
Charles Ephrussi, an art critic and collector; and Gustave Caillebotte,
the wealthy painter.

In 1923 Duncan Phillips, an American art collector, paid $125,000
for *Luncheon of the Boating Party*, calling it "one of the greatest paintings in the world." It is the most important work in the Phillips Collection in Washington, D.C., where it hangs. Parisian popular culture
has not forgotten it. It figured in the 2001 film *Amélie*, Jean-Pierre
Jeunet's love letter to a sweet, imaginary Paris. In the film, the lonely,
mischievous Amélie befriends her neighbor, an older, fragile artist
with a delicate countenance who never leaves his apartment. He is so

obsessed with *Luncheon of the Boating Party* that he paints it again and again, struggling to capture the inscrutable expression of a single character.

Inside the restaurant, a reproduction of *Luncheon* hangs in the main dining room. If you sit on the balcony and ignore the modern buildings on the other side of the river, you can imagine that you are near the spot where Renoir and his friends lunched, talked and laughed together on those distant Sunday afternoons that never seemed to end.

CAMILLE PISSARRO CALLED ROUEN "the most splendid landscape a painter could ever dream of" and painting is still crucial to life in the city. Every summer, Rouen celebrates its commitment to its artistic legacy with a speed-painting contest. The city's Musée des Beaux-Arts, one of the finest art museums in France, displays the winning work for a year.

One year, thirty professional and amateur painters lined up at seven in the morning at the *Pompon-Rouge*, a gray, white, and red barge transformed into a small art museum on the quay. They received blank canvases and were allowed to choose their own medium and style, as long as they painted a subject that evoked the Seine.

The artists staked out their territory along the river, with the bell towers of Rouen's churches on the Right Bank and tall industrial structures on the Left. Impressionism is all about painting quickly. The colors of the river and the sky in Normandy change with the sun, the mists, and the rain. Clouds and wind shift without warning. The skies were overcast and deep gray for much of the day. But the painters soldiered on.

The styles were as varied as the painters themselves. Some took inspiration from the Impressionists. One artist painted a chiaroscuro oil of the two yellow industrial cranes situated on the far side of the river, another a watercolor of grain silos shining silver despite the fickle sunlight that day, a third an orange-and-violet sunset with buildings in deep purple silhouette. The youngest participant, a nine-year-old girl, painted herself in a sailboat, an enormous yellow sun shining high in the sky, her hair blowing in the wind. Nearly fifty other adults and children contributed individual panels to a long group fresco that would be exhibited in Rouen's city hall. All made the 5 p.m. deadline, and their works were hung on the walls of the *Pompon-Rouge*.

"We had a great adventure of sharing today," Marie-Hélène Joyen-Conseil, an art therapist and painter, announced to the crowd gathered inside. "To produce a painting in ten hours, it was a challenge. Well done, given the gray skies."

The first-place winner was Michel Abdou, a seventy-two-year-old retired commercial artist. His painting, made in large brushstrokes in acrylics, showed the *Pompon-Rouge* parked on a peach-hued boardwalk flanked by trees. The barge seemed tiny next to a huge ship docked in the Seine. A couple strolled along a walkway, and a young man sat on a square boulder fixed in the water. In the 1970s, while working his day job, Abdou studied painting at night at the Le Crayon, Rouen's École des Beaux-Arts. He moved into decorative painting and, in 1992, full-time into figurative painting. He lamented the decline of interest in the art and craft of painting. "People today are saturated with images that come to them," he told me. "They are suffocated with television, the Internet, their iPhones. They forget that they can achieve things with their hands. They forget that painting is an art that has to be learned."

There was a lot of talk among the painters that day about the magic and lure of light. Some saw the play of sunlight on water and felt the urge to rush out and capture it on canvas. Some played cat and mouse with the light, watching as the deep gray sky turned clear blue and then, without warning, darkened again as mischievous white clouds blocked the sun. Some were entranced by the currents and colors of the water that shifted with the time of day.

"In Normandy, we must throw ourselves into our canvases to translate the essence of our emotions—before the sky changes!" said Joyen-Conseil. "The Seine has inspired us with its waves, its rumblings, its bridges, its tugs, its barges, its cranes. It waters our fields, our apple trees, cherry trees, whose flowering lights up our canvases. It's the life-blood of our region."

*A skeleton of a miniature model of* La Dauphine, *the boat that Giovanni da Verrazzano sailed from Rouen to New York in 1524.* ANDREW PLUMP.

# TWENTY-FOUR

# The Port That Rivaled Paris

*The horizon was defined by the curve of the river. It was flat as a mirror, with great insects skating on the tranquil water.*

**—GUSTAVE FLAUBERT,**
*Sentimental Education*

*It was the most exciting meal of my life.*
**—JULIA CHILD,** describing her lunch of raw oysters, *sole meunière*, a green salad with vinaigrette dressing, a Pouilly-Fumé wine, and *fromage blanc* at La Couronne in Rouen

THE SEINE CHANGES DRAMATICALLY at Rouen, emerging from one of its exaggerated loops deeper and wider—big enough, for the first time on its trip to the sea, to accommodate ocean-going ships. Traditionally, that made Rouen the port where goods were shipped on their way eastward toward Paris or westward toward international markets.

Passengers made the same transfer. For nineteenth-century American visitors seeing France for the first time, Rouen was a necessary stop on the way to Paris. In fact, it is only when you come to Rouen that you understand that Paris was not always the star of the Seine's commercial universe. Until the nineteenth century, Rouen was considered France's most important port, and even today, it is the number one port for cereal exports in Europe.

The Seine in Rouen spans three and a half miles. It begins at the eastern edge of the city at the tip of the Île Lacroix, the Seine's final island en route to the sea. It ends in the west amid three major shipping basins that receive both barges and container ships into and out of the city. The ships that come here keep getting bigger, which means that the riverbed must be continually dredged, deepened, and flattened to accommodate them. Rouen is also an increasingly popular cruise ship terminal not only because it is the closest ocean cruise port to Paris but also because of its proximity to port cities like London and Amsterdam. Rouen recovered from the destruction of World War II to become a sprawling industrial city. But its historic center remains intact, its timber-fronted houses and narrow cobbled streets lovingly preserved and restored. Visitors here step into a setting of Rouen's medieval heyday, when cargo ships arrived under sails to crowd the harbor and merchants in velvets and silks met on the quays. This was also the Rouen where the ashes of Joan of Arc were thrown into the Seine after her execution in the city's main square.

You cannot escape Joan of Arc in Rouen. The image of the cross-dressing teenage martyr who fought the English occupiers and helped restore the French throne six centuries ago pervades the port city. Her story, wrapped in myths, lives on. A fearless warrior, a free spirit, a great patriot, she still is considered by many French citizens (especially far-right politicians) to be the incarnation of France itself.

I first learned about Joan far away from the Seine, at Holy Angels Elementary School in Buffalo. She was one of the nuns' favorite martyrs, and they told the story of her life and her horrific death in Rouen in excruciating detail. The nuns taught us that we, too, could aspire to be martyred for the faith and go straight to heaven.

An illiterate girl from the country, Joan claimed to hear voices from heaven that ordered her to restore the French dauphin to his throne. She led a siege against the English at Orléans and paved the way for him to be crowned King Charles VII at Reims. After a string of military defeats, she was captured by Burgundians and ransomed off to the English. She was imprisoned and put on trial in Rouen in 1431 for a series of crimes, including witchcraft, dressing like a man, and heresy. She was convicted, sentenced to death, tied to a stake in the place du Vieux Marché, the central market square, and set on fire. She was nineteen.

To prevent a cult of martyrdom, Joan's judges were determined to leave no trace of her body. The executioner scooped her ashes from the foot of the pyre into sacks and poured them from a bridge into the Seine. According to some versions of this story, her heart refused to burn, so it was dumped, along with her ashes, into the river.

Many historians believe that Joan's ashes were thrown from the bridge that was then called Pont Mathilde, now Pont Boieldieu, in the center of Rouen. A color engraving by artist-writer Émile Deshays in his 1911 book about Joan captured the kinetic scene. Two men in red cast the ashes off the bridge as a small crowd gathers behind them. The ashes fly out of their sacks and form a thick, dark cloud

*A stone plaque in Rouen that marks the approximate place where Joan of Arc's ashes are claimed to have been thrown into the Seine after she was burned at the stake.*
IRIS SAMUELS.

in a bright, peach-colored sky. Today, a humble stone plaque marks the spot. "Near here on Wednesday, May 30, 1431, after torture at the Old Market, the ashes of Joan of Arc were thrown from the top of the old Pont Mathilde," it reads.

Every city, town, and church of any worth in France has a statue or painting dedicated to Joan, but Rouen celebrates her memory with more enthusiasm than most. She has given her name to a street, a square, a café, a restaurant, a cocktail, a market stall, a bridge, a parking lot, a real estate agency, a hotel, and a wine cave. Her image graces labels for French mineral water, liqueur, and cheese. Boutiques sell *les larmes de Jeanne d'Arc*—Joan of Arc's tears—a rich confection of grilled almonds covered with crispy nougat and chocolate and rolled in unsweetened cocoa.

A walk through the old city center of Rouen takes visitors past various monuments and landmarks evoking Joan, including the Tower of Joan of Arc where soldiers may have threatened her with torture, and the modern Joan of Arc Church, built in 1979. Then there is the Historial Jeanne d'Arc, a multimedia space opened in 2015 that is part theatre, part museum. Created in the fifteenth-century Archbishop's Palace, where Joan was tried in 1431, the Historial projects 3-D film dramatizations of Joan's life onto the pale stone walls, including testimony from accusers at her trial and a wall of fierce, crackling orange flames that carried her to her death.


IN THE LONG HISTORY of Rouen, Joan can seem recent. Romans settled in Rouen in antiquity, as they did in Paris, drawn by its natural harbor in a bend in the river. The city's Musée des Antiquités, housed in a former convent, displays Roman-era objects found throughout Normandy. The highlight is a room devoted to a mosaic taken from the dining room floor of a third-or fourth-century villa, discovered in a garden in Lillebonne, west of Rouen, in 1870. The mosaic, approximately nineteen by nineteen feet in size, was broken into pieces, sold and resold, restored both badly and beautifully over the years, and, in the end, preserved for posterity. It depicts a stag hunt in a wooded landscape evoking the Norman forest, a sacrifice to the goddess Diana, and a circular central panel showing a lustful young man pursuing a woman, naked except for a veil draped over the tops of her legs. Was she a nymph? Was he the god Apollo? Would she escape?

IN THE NINTH CENTURY, the Vikings sailed up the Seine to invade and plunder. Its wide estuary, slow current, and ready access to the North Sea and the English Channel made it an easy pathway inland. After decades of war and destruction, in 911, King Charles the Simple of France capitulated. He exchanged the land that is now Normandy and his daughter's hand in marriage to the Viking chief Rollo for peace and protection. Rollo became the first Duke of Normandy, settled in, and made Rouen his capital. The Vikings assimilated into the local population and converted to Christianity.

William the Conqueror, Rollo's direct descendant, is best known in history as the Norman military leader who amassed a flotilla of boats and conquered England in 1066. He was also an able ruler of Normandy who built close ties with the church and traveled extensively around his region, collecting taxes, administering charters, and holding court in Rouen. More than a century later, in 1189, one of his descendants, Richard the Lionheart, would be invested as Duke of Normandy at Château Gaillard, the fortress he built high on a hill in Normandy. (Richard was crowned king of England in Westminster Abbey later that year.) In the 1400s, their descendants still laid claim to Normandy and had expanded English control over territory in France, including Paris during the Hundred Years' War (1337–1453). It was in resisting them that Joan of Arc played her heroic role.

Joan's story played out in the shadow of Rouen's cathedral, the same one that inspired Emma Willard, the nineteenth-century American educator, to write that when she saw it, her "mind was smitten with a feeling of sublimity almost too intense for mortality." More than double the size of Notre-Dame, it can still overpower first-time visitors with its grace and grandeur. Its latticed cast-iron spire, the tallest in France, punctures the skyline.

When Monet visited Rouen in the 1890s, the cathedral unsettled him. "I had a night filled with nightmares: the cathedral was falling down on me, it appeared either blue, pink, or yellow," he wrote. He planted himself in the square facing its western façade, compelled by some feverish devotion to paint it over and over. The façade alone mesmerized him; he never set foot inside.

Monet had learned all about the movement of light by painting the Seine, but the Rouen Cathedral challenged him anew. The light changed so often that at one point he was working on fourteen canvases simultaneously; by the end of his project, he had painted the cathedral façade more than thirty times. "What Monet painted was not the cathedral, but the light bouncing off the cathedral," wrote art historian and Monet specialist Douglas Skeggs.

Proust appreciated Monet's genius. In his most famous work, *In Search of Lost Time*, he fantasized about whether a writer could achieve what Monet had done with his paintings of the cathedral of Rouen and the waterlilies of Giverny. "Imagine today a writer to whom the idea would occur to treat twenty times under different lights the same theme, and who would have the sensation of creating something profound, subtle, powerful, overwhelming, original, startling like the fifty cathedrals or forty water-lily ponds of Monet," he wrote. But in an unfinished essay published after his death, Proust suggested that after experiencing the beauty of physical sites through Monet's eye, the reality of visiting them may disappoint. "It is of the ideal that we are enamored," he wrote.


IN THE AFTERMATH of World War II, the port in Rouen revived its commercial and industrial activities, rendering the river largely inaccessible to the public. Then, in the late 1980s, Rouen launched a sweeping urban-renewal plan that continues today, razing decrepit warehouses along the Right Bank and later creating pedestrian walkways and bicycle paths. The main walkway in Rouen is wider than those along the Seine in Paris, and it is largely uninterrupted by bridges or stairs. Though not as scenic as the gilded paths in Paris, this longer, straighter river walk gives joggers and bikers more freedom. Restaurants, tourist boats, a health club, and a maritime museum line the waterfront. People picnic on the banks of the Seine and on the Île Lacroix. The tourist site Panorama XXL features a giant rotunda with huge circular 3-D paintings of Rouen in Joan of Arc's day. The historic center of the city boasts new boutique hotels, including one named the Gustave Flaubert Literary Hotel.

Flaubert was born in Rouen in 1821 and spent much of his early life there, but he never loved the city. The *Rouennais* don't care. Entering the hotel is like entering his world. The ground floor is devoted to Normandy and the world of *Madame Bovary*, the second floor to *Sentimental Education*. Guest rooms are associated with characters from his novels or with his friends, including Maupassant and George Sand. A library holds five hundred works, some of them first editions of Flaubert's novels. The hotel's calling card—which doubles as a bookmark—features details of Flaubert-inspired paintings by a local artist and quotations from the writer's works. A soundtrack of his favorite opera arias and sonata movements plays in the public spaces.

A neighborhood and a bridge are named after Flaubert. The ten-room Flaubert museum holds the room where he was born and the small hospital where his father worked as a surgeon. His grave can be visited, along with that of artist Marcel Duchamp, in the Cimetière Monumental de Rouen.

Despite his dislike for Rouen, Flaubert drew strength from the Seine. From 1844, when he was in his early twenties, until his death when he was fifty-eight, he lived with his mother and his niece in a large eighteenth-century country house at Croisset, four miles outside Rouen. He wrote his major novels in a ground-floor study overlooking the river. At night he would walk from the house along a towpath bordered with linden trees on the riverbanks, a spot he called his *gueuloir* (shouting parlor). A perfectionist of style, he loudly recited the passages he had written to judge their musicality. The house has been torn down; the only remnant is a garden pavilion that has been turned into a small museum with some of his personal possessions, including an armchair, an inkwell, goose quills, a writing case, photographs, and portraits.

I DISCOVERED ANOTHER CHARACTER of Rouen's history, and the Seine's: Giovanni da Verrazzano, the Italian explorer from Florence who discovered New York. In the first part of the sixteenth century, King François I sought new trade routes, sources of wealth, and an expansion of his empire in the New World. Verrazzano, who had settled in France years before, was part of his team.

In Rouen, Verrazzano Frenchified his name to Jean de Verrazane, raised money from rich Italian merchants based in Lyon, trained a crew of Norman sailors, and prepared his armadas. In 1524, he set out for the New World, sailing out to sea, via the Seine, with four ships loaded with cannons, lifeboats, scientific equipment, and provisions. Two ships were lost in a storm, and a third was forced to return to France. But the fourth, *La Dauphine*, carrying Verrazzano and a crew of fifty men, landed at Cape Fear, in the Carolinas, after fifty days at sea. Verrazzano became the first European to explore and chart the Atlantic coast of North America between the Carolinas and Newfoundland, discovering New York Bay and the southern tip of Manhattan along the way.

"Verrazane was a Rouennais of Italian origin who traveled to the New World and fell in love with the place," said Jacques Tanguy, an amateur local historian whose passion is burnishing the explorer's reputation. "At the mouth of a river, he discovered New York." Verrazzano called the area "New Angoulême," Tanguy said, in honor of François I's former title as Count of Angoulême.

In 1609, the English explorer Henry Hudson, working for the Dutch, got credit for discovering New York, largely because he traveled the region more extensively—including the river that would bear his name. It was not until the Italian Historical Society of America mounted a successful campaign in the mid-twentieth century that Verrazzano's achievement as the discoverer of New York was formally recognized.

These days, just about everybody living in New York City knows the name Verrazzano. It's the name of the double-decker suspension bridge that spans the strait between Brooklyn and Staten Island, the gateway to New York Harbor. The New York City Marathon starts at its Staten Island end. All day during every workweek, news about the flow of traffic on the bridge blares on local radio and television stations. But Verrazzano got only a bridge named after him; Henry Hudson got a 315-mile river. Adding to the humiliation for Verrazzano's legacy, the official name of the bridge used an incorrect spelling of his name for decades. Late in 2018, the state of New York added the missing z to his name to official signs. When Rouen built a new lift bridge over the Seine in 2008, Tanguy lobbied hard to have it named after Verrazzano, just like the one in New York, but Flaubert won the contest.

In Rouen, Verrazzano is celebrated at the Maritime, Fluvial, and Harbor Museum, on the right bank of the river. In a giant workshop stands a partially built small replica of *La Dauphine*, the ship Verrazzano sailed to the New World. In the sixteenth century, ship blueprints did not exist, so a team of amateur historians and master carpenters consulted archives and maritime historians to replicate the ship. They found examples of sixteenth-century graffiti on walls in the Seine Valley and referred to historical contracts to deduce the number of sailors and the quantity of food on board, which helped them define the ship's proportions.

Volunteer carpenters are working in oak and pine, the same woods used in Verrazzano's time, to create a lightweight vessel. The goal is to build a full-sized replica that can sail from Rouen to New York in 2024, five hundred years after Verrazzano's exploration.

Other exhibits feature barge and trawler motors, the skeleton of a fin whale, and two hundred miniature models of the most famous boats of the twentieth century. The museum also has a reproduction of the interior of the submarine *Nautilus*, built by Robert Fulton. Robert Fulton? The American inventor? I knew that he had tested his steam engine on the Seine in Paris in 1803—"a water chariot moved by fire," the French called it. Napoléon was not impressed, dismissing it as nothing "but a child's toy." It turns out, however, that Fulton had earlier experimented with the world's first working submarine in Rouen. The French government twice rejected his request for funding, but in 1800 the *Nautilus* was built in a Rouen shipyard and launched on the Seine. It descended twenty-five feet for seventeen minutes.

Like so much of French history, the story of Verrazzano is a subject of lively debate. Guy Pessiot, a writer, editor, and publisher who has devoted much of his life to Rouen's history, questions whether Verrazzano really set sail from Rouen. "There could be chicanery here," he says, even though he promotes the museum's work and Tanguy is one of his closest friends. "We know for sure where Verrazzano got his money, but some historians disagree that Rouen was his place of departure."

As an American whose four grandparents emigrated from Sicily to the United States, I'm on the side of Rouen's believers in Verrazzano.


ROUEN COMMEMORATES another famous explorer born there in the seventeenth century, René-Robert Cavelier, Sieur de La Salle. The first time I went to Rouen long ago, I told my hosts I had never heard of him. On a later trip, I connected the dots and figured out that René-Robert Cavelier, Sieur de La Salle, was the explorer Americans know as Robert de La Salle. La Salle was the Frenchman who explored the Gulf of Mexico and traveled down the Mississippi, claiming the entire river basin for France.

This was the same La Salle who, with his crew and the Italian soldier of fortune Henri de Tonti, built a fort in 1679 at the mouth of the Niagara River on Lake Ontario. Today it is the site of Fort Niagara. La Salle struck up a friendship with the Seneca Indians above Niagara Falls. They gave him permission to construct the first commercial sailing vessel on Lake Erie and taught him how to make long overland trips on foot and in snowy weather.

Growing up in Buffalo, I often went to LaSalle Park, a few blocks from where I lived. I jogged from LaSalle Park to city hall and back on the one-mile track built along my first river, the Niagara, at the point where it begins at Lake Erie. Years and another continent later, during a cruise of the Seine, I found myself once again in Rouen, in front of the La Salle plaque. The French guide called him by his full name, and given the blank look on the Americans' faces, I assumed that none of them recognized it.

"May I intervene?" I asked and informed the group that this was "our" La Salle.

"I've been a teacher and a principal altogether for thirty-six years, and I never heard of Cavelier," said Joanna from Charleston. "But I know La Salle!"


GUY PESSIOT OWNS the world's most comprehensive private collection of old photos of Rouen. His home in the historical center overflows with books, engravings, maps, and prints of the city. Officially retired, he serves as the city's adviser in charge of tourism and heritage and is its biggest cheerleader. On one visit, Guy said I had to see a view of the river from a hill above the city—much different from any perspective in Paris. I risked missing my train back to Paris, but he insisted. We drove up a winding road to Saint Catherine's Hill and looked out over the chalky cliffs. Below us were the spires and belfries of churches on the right bank of the river. The Seine snaked on its course, and tiny ripples lit up in silver in the late afternoon light.

I thought of Flaubert and how he experienced the sensuality of the Seine when he swam in it, like "a thousand liquid nipples traveling over the body."

"It's a three-star panoramic view, no?" Pessiot said. "I've done the Danube and the Rhine. But the Seine is much more beautiful."

And so it was.

CAUDEBEC-en-CAUX. - Le Mascaret

*An early twentieth-century postcard of* le mascaret, *the tidal wave that appeared at Caudebec-en-Caux four times a year. The wave was a popular tourist attraction until the early 1960s, when the Seine was dredged and the river tamed.*

# TWENTY-FIVE

# Tsunami on the Seine

*One immense wave rolled on*
*majestically foaming from bank to*
*bank, leaving everything in uproar*
*in its train, while all before was*
*perfectly calm.*
—JEAN-BAPTISTE-BALTHAZAR SAUVAN,
*Picturesque Tour of the Seine,*
*from Paris to the Sea*, 1821

THE WAVE ROSE AND ROARED, then disappeared. *Le mascaret,*
as the wave was called, began at the Seine estuary when the tides of
spring rose high. Salt water rushed upstream at up to fifteen miles
per hour, funneling into the narrow channel of the freshwater river.
Four times a year, for centuries, the *mascaret* appeared from nowhere at
Caudebec-en-Caux, in northern Normandy. After rushing at its greatest height—up to thirteen feet tall—it slowed, diminishing to ripples
by the time it reached Rouen, to the east.

The oldest account of the *mascaret*, known by geographers as a tidal
bore, is in the ninth-century Latin chronicles of the Abbey of Saint-

Wandrille. The wave slowed the longboats of the Vikings and helped Caudebec defend itself against their raids. Even as late as the nineteenth century, the *mascaret* could wreak havoc with river commerce, one study revealing that between 1789 and 1850, more than two hundred ships disappeared in its fury. With the advent of the railroad, the *mascaret* also became a huge tourist attraction. Its timing was predictable, occurring when tides were at their highest near the equinoxes, allowing sightseers all the way from Paris to schedule trips to see it. Then, in the early 1960s, the river was dredged; dams, locks, and a canal tamed the wave forever.

I learned about the *mascaret* the first time I visited Caudebec-en-Caux, in 2016, for the inauguration of MuséoSeine, a museum devoted to the history, commerce, culture, geography, and personalities of the river from Paris to the sea. I was writing an article on the museum for the *New York Times*, and for Caudebec, a town of two thousand inhabitants, the combination of the opening and the international press coverage made the whole affair big news. Andy and I got the celebrity treatment; the local newspaper took our photograph, and luminaries turned out to welcome us.

The MuséoSeine sits so close to the water that you almost expect its basement to flood when it rains too hard. "We want to be in direct conversation with the Seine, to have both visual and human connections with the river," said Jean-Claude Weiss, a regional official. "So we are putting our feet in the water."

A short footbridge connects the museum to the only surviving *gribane*, a late nineteenth-century sailboat, floating on the water and anchored to the shore. Its flat bottom helped it glide over sandbars; its wide deck was efficient for transporting blocks of stone used to dike the river. The *gribane* had been turned into a houseboat, and after much negotiation was finally sold to the museum. From its deck, we could see stark differences between the Seine's two banks. The right bank, where we stood, was lined with high cliffs and unusual vegetation, including the region's signature "tadpole trees"—with big heads and narrow trunks. On the flat terrain across the river were corn and wheat fields and the forest of Brotonne, which often flooded before the river was diked.

As if on cue to greet us, a red-and-white 480-foot oil tanker named *Songa Breeze* lumbered by. We waved and the captain, perched high on the tanker's bridge, waved back.

The name Caudebec originated with the Vikings. In their language, *bec* meant stream and *caud* came from *cald*, or cold. The town grew up around two streams flowing from the hills into the Seine. In the Middle Ages, the plentiful fresh water fueled the development of a prosperous tannery industry. The river also facilitated the export of local merchandise, especially the wide-brimmed *chapeau de Caudebec*—the Caudebec hat, which came into fashion in the sixteenth-century. Made from lamb's wool, camel hair, and ostrich feathers, it was felted and waterproofed, and may even have been worn by Louis XIV at Versailles.

BEFORE WORLD WAR II, Caudebec's medieval town center had wood-timbered houses and dark, narrow streets. In 1940, the advancing German army used incendiary bombs to prevent residents from fleeing across the Seine. The bombs hit cars clustered at the docks, and the town was set on fire. The town burned for three days; 80 percent of its buildings were destroyed.

After the war there was little money to rebuild, and residents had to settle for structures lacking so much charm and originality they were called "the barracks." But the city is proud of what survived and is now a routine stop for tens of thousands of passengers on Seine river cruises. "We have to take care of these visitors," said Mayor Bastien Coriton. "We can't just sell them Calvados and camembert. We have to show them our city, to put our treasures on display." He insisted on giving us a tour.

City hall was the first stop. Built from sturdy brick along the river, it survived the bombing. We continued along a half-mile-long riverside promenade. In the town center, Coriton took us to the most spectacular survivor of the 1940 fire, the Notre-Dame de Caudebec-en-Caux

Church, built in the Flamboyant Gothic style in the fifteenth and sixteenth centuries. We stood outside and admired the hundreds of sculpted human figures decorating its western portal. "When Henri IV came here, he said this was the most beautiful chapel in his realm," Coriton told us. He tried to push open the heavy doors, but they were locked. He smiled; as mayor, he had the keys to the church in his pocket. "It's one of the perks of the job," he said. Inside, he pointed out the massive pillars on each side of the nave, the stained-glass windows that had been taken from an abbey, and the Renaissance organ with a magical trumpet sound, restored to its full glory in 2007. He spoke with pride about raising €400,000 to replace the bell tower.

As we resumed our tour of the town, we saw other vestiges of the city's history as a thriving regional capital: the House of the Knights Templar, a medieval prison, and pieces of fortification walls. One of the only timbered houses still standing is a royal administrative dwelling built in 1516; during the German attack, the church shielded the house from the fire. The French couple who had bought the house a few years earlier invited us in. They were restoring it, painstakingly, because the house was *classée*—landmarked—so there were strict rules about what they could do. They showed us the uneven glass panes, the intricate seventeenth-century woodwork, and crude graffiti of fish and ships that seamen had etched into the stone wall of a cobblestoned entryway, sometimes as thanks to the Virgin Mary for a safe return, sometimes as a wish for the next voyage to go well. "We wanted the house for its history, despite all its problems," Yann Rousselet, the husband, said. "We live with the constraints—like the wind that whips through in the winter, because we can't put in double-glazed windows. Can you imagine taking care of this place?"

"You'd have to be crazy to do it," his wife, Johanna, added. "And we are crazy."

For Mayor Coriton, the house represents a piece of the town's lost history. "When you come here, you really have the feel of what Caudebec was like before the war," he said.

We returned to the MuséoSeine to tour the museum, with artifacts dating from the paleolithic era to modern times. A giant ancient iron anchor discovered in nearby Aizier was proof of the first-century maritime trade that had brought goods from as far as the Mediterranean; a third-century copper statuette of Mercury, the god of commerce and travel, most likely belonged to a merchant who'd carried it to sea as a good-luck charm. Three-dimensional hologram videos showed professional actors playing historical figures: a ninth-century monk described the horrible scenes of fire and pillaging by the Vikings; a sixteenth-century hatmaker talked about the famous Caudebec hat. A detailed aerial photo of the river from Paris to Le Havre, with all of its loops and curves, stretched across one long wall. It showed where the river had been dramatically wider before it was diked, and where land masses replaced what was once underwater.

Downstairs, a boat like the one that Victor Hugo's daughter and son-in-law had been traveling in before they drowned hung from the ceiling. An old-fashioned blue-striped beach tent and a display of old swimsuits got us talking about swimming in the Seine. "In the 1920s and 1930s in Caudebec, there was a beach club with changing rooms and a diving board," said Mayor Coriton. "Right up until the war. My grandmother learned to swim in the Seine."

"I knew a monk who swam in the Seine every week," Nathalie Demunck, another official, chimed in. "And he never got sick."

We approached a digital apparatus with a multiple-choice Seine quiz, where players could compete to be the first to choose the right answers. I nagged Andy to play, just as our kids would have done. We faced off on either side of a flat screen and selected a game of eighteen questions in French.

What is a tidal bore? (A funneling of sea water back into a river at high tide.)

What causes shipwrecks? (Before levees were built, sandbanks and shoals did.)

How old is the Seine? (Three million years old.)

What is the length of the Seine? (777 kilometers.)

Why does the estuary from Honfleur extend a hundred miles east to the commune of Poses? (The tide is felt until the Poses dam; the dam stops the tide from going any farther.)

How many rivers longer than fifty kilometers flow into the Seine? (Fourteen.)

What fish can be found in the estuary? (Eel, stickleback, flounder, bass.)

Has the Seine ever frozen over? (Often.)

BACK ON THE MAIN LEVEL of the MuséoSeine, we watched a short film about Jean-Marc Vintrin, a *pilote*, or river pilot. In the film, the Seine looks calm, but danger lurks beneath its surface and along its banks. Sandbars shift without notice; silt builds up; chains of islands create barriers; sharp curves present visual delights and navigational nightmares.

All large ships that travel between Rouen and Le Havre must hire registered Seine *pilotes* to do the steering. The film showed Vintrin at the port of Rouen at six-fifteen a.m. meeting a cargo ship that had been loaded with two thousand tons of grain for delivery to Lisbon; he would get it safely to Le Havre.

Afterward, I contacted Vintrin, and we rendezvoused in Rouen. He and his first mate, David Robert, invited me for a ride on *Lady Mary*, a three-hundred-foot freighter registered in Antigua, which was carrying fertilizer to Germany. They strapped me into a red life jacket and helped me climb up a long metal gangplank with rope bannisters to the vessel's high bridge. A slim man dressed in tight jeans and wrap-around sunglasses introduced himself as Alex, the captain. He was Russian and oversaw a Russian and Ukrainian crew.

The wind blew the strong smell of gasoline into the cabin as we set off toward Caudebec-en-Caux. The water was still and safe enough for us to move the conversation "*du coq à l'âne*"—"from the cock to the donkey," or from one subject to another. The common language was grammatically broken but navigationally correct English. Alex, who had spent much of his professional life in rough English ports, asked me to join him for a cup of tea.

We talked about the threat of terrorism, the troubled euro, the frequency of strikes in France, and the doping scandal in the Tour de France. And, of course, about the river, which was the color not of dark khaki, the way it often is Paris, but of translucent sea glass. This was a well-traveled, predictable course, not a high-seas adventure of discovery. But Vintrin reveled in its routine. "It's not like being a sea captain, where you're on the water for months," he said. "We can have a nap in the afternoon. We can see our kids growing up."

Then he launched into a running commentary of the sites we passed, starting with Val-de-la-Haye, a village a few miles west of Rouen. A monument there commemorates the transfer of Napoléon's ashes to the boat that carried them to their final resting place in Paris. He pointed out châteaus, eighteenth-century manor houses, and wooden church steeples with twisted bell towers. We passed the ruins of a feudal château perched high on a hill; it was named after Robert the Devil, a legendary figure who may or may not have been the father of William the Conqueror. We moved along a narrow stretch of the Seine, with high chalk cliffs used by paragliders and a landscape as dense and green as the tropics. Suddenly Vintrin snapped to attention. He eased the ship into a slow, sharp curve. "A sand bar," he said. "You can't see it, but I know it's there."

GPS has taken much of the guesswork out of steering. Paradoxically, climate change has eliminated the blocks and "pancakes" of ice that made the river impassable in winter. Nevertheless, a *pilote*'s familiarity with every bend and mood of the river is essential. The work is more stressful when the weather is bad. The fog blinds and suffocates, and the wind whips the rain against the bridge.

We passed the twelfth-century Saint-Georges de Boscherville abbey, now open to visitors, and small farms, where cows and sheep grazed in green meadows. High on a hill to our right was a white rocky outcrop that indeed looked like a giant armchair. "Do you know the story of Gargantua's chair?" Vintrin asked. He explainted that Gargantua was a creation of sixteenth-century writer François Rabelais and, of course, the origin of the word "gargantuan." According to legend, the giant stopped at this place and made a stone armchair for himself. These days, the cliffs are ideal perches for paragliding.

As we moved on, we spotted a small beach with kayaks bobbing in the waves. "It's gravel, only a gravel beach," said Vintrin, in a tone that sounded like an apology. Even though it was not a beach of fine sand like those on the Atlantic, a small sailing club made its home there.

Captain Alex reveled in the scenery and the good weather. "In Norway, you're in the middle of nowhere, no neighbors around you for miles, and no sunshine," he said. "In western Scotland, it's like a moonscape! A few castles on the rocks, stones, and the sea. Nothing else. Here, it's different. People pay a fortune to travel like this. I like to say, 'I travel on a cruise ship, just a different kind of cruise ship.'"

We arrived at the port of Caudebec and said good-bye to Alex, who would spend the night on board with his crew and continue his journey with another *pilote*. Vintrin climbed down a ladder attached to the outside of the barge. As a pilot cutter passed at high speed, he leapt in at just the right moment. Then it was my turn. I climbed down the ladder and got ready to jump. *What if I fell into the river?* I knew I had to aim just right. The cutter sped by, but I was too scared to move. When it circled around a second time, I threw myself forward and fell into Vintrin's arms.

We had a good day on the river, a day that belonged to the sun and turned the river's surface into shards of shimmering light. "Compared to other rivers I have worked on—the Elbe, the Amazon, the Loire, the Gironde—the Seine is narrow and shallow," Vintrin said as we walked along the deck. He never had to contend with the *mascaret*, tamed long before his career began. But the river, with its powerful tides and hidden obstacles, has set many more subtle traps. "The biggest risk is routine," Vintrin said. "I might say to myself, 'Oh, today there is nothing to see, nothing to do.' But that's not true. There is always something to watch out for."

Inside the MuséoSeine, I had noticed a virtual-reality Timescope with a rotating viewfinder outfitted with a 3-D lens. You point it at the river and move back in time. You see the great tidal wave as it appears from nowhere to suddenly overwhelm the banks. You hear the roar of the wave and the shouts and cries of the spectators as they run from the rising, foaming rush of water.

In that moment, the *mascaret* lives.

*An image of Moulin de Pierre, a thirteenth-century windmill in Normandy constructed by the monks at the abbey of Jumièges.* ANDREW PLUMP.

# TWENTY-SIX

# Windmills and War

> *Dusk sifted over the Seine valley . . .*
> *and the day's last light faded from*
> *the chalk cliffs . . . where antiaircraft*
> *gunners strained for the drone of*
> *approaching bombers."*
>
> **—RICK ATKINSON,**
> *The Guns at Last Light*

THE ROMANESQUE ARCHES and fragmented stone walls stood naked and gray in a drizzly fog early on a January morning. High on a hill at a bend in the Seine near Rouen is the Abbey of Jumièges, what Victor Hugo described as "the most beautiful ruins in France."

Philippe Jean, an amateur historian and volunteer guide, sat in the heated staff kitchen to escape the cold. "The weather is sad today, the soul a little melancholy," he said.

He made strong coffee and told the story of Jumièges and the other Norman monasteries. The Seine Valley from Rouen to the sea was once the domain of monks. They organized and financed the construction of their own harbors and ports, collected taxes from the local farmers, sold the right to fish, and managed commerce through a centralized string of abbeys built along the river. Jumièges, a grand Benedictine abbey founded in the seventh century by Saint Philibert, was the most powerful of them all.

With control of the river valley, a place of fertile land and forests filled with wild game, the monks were rich—until the Vikings raided, plundered, torched, and destroyed abbeys and towns. Afterward, Jumièges was rebuilt on a grander scale, and William the Conqueror consecrated it in 1067. It became a great center of religion and learning, and a haven where the local poor could find food and shelter. But there was more trouble ahead. During the sixteenth-century Wars of Religion, Huguenots looted the abbey. Two hundred years later, the French Revolution doomed it forever. The contents of its library were sent to Rouen, and much of the stone of its buildings was sold and carted away. Later, the ruins bore silent witness, first to German and later to Allied armies sweeping through this part of France during World War II.

Outside, Jean stopped at a round bronze marker that said "3D" and opened a program on his iPad. He pointed its camera at what once was the long nave of the Notre-Dame Church, the best-preserved part of the abbey complex. Suddenly we were back centuries in time, looking at a three-dimensional, 360-degree panoramic projection of Jumièges at the height of its power and glory. The iPad projection transformed the gray stones of the nave into a grand, sunlit hall of soaring 150-foot towers, eighty-foot walls, Gothic and Romanesque arches, a wood-beamed ceiling, even a roof. The choir appeared as it had looked in the Gothic period. More sites and eras came alive on the screen: Saint Peter's Church in the ninth century, the sixteenth-century cloister with fine carvings and frescoes, the gardens, and the large eighteenth-century dormitory where the monks slept.

"The ruins invite the viewer to imagine," Jean said. "We are in a place halfway between dream and reality. We are not just spectators. We are also actors, because each of us sees it, each of us feels it in a personal way. Here we are in a total work of art."

The glow of Jean's words lingered as I headed ten miles north to the Abbey of Saint-Wandrille. Much of its history mirrors that of Jumièges, but it is a remarkably alive place that still functions as an abbey and is home to thirty Benedictine monks. The rule of the Benedictines is prayer, work, and silence. Monks at Saint-Wandrille restore oil paintings, old books, and gold-leaf frames; make beer, honey, and furniture wax. They sing and record Gregorian chants and write books. A gift shop sells an array of the abbey's own publications and products as well as those of other abbeys, including herbal remedies, jams, spiced cakes, and bonbons.

Some of the monks are designated talkers, authorized to deal with the public. And so it happened one Saturday that I met Brother Magnier, a stout, sixty-something monk with a brush cut; he was dressed in a long black robe and black sandals and socks. His responsibilities include giving tours of the abbey's public spaces: the chapel, cloisters, refectory, and gardens.

Brother Magnier gathered several dozen mostly French visitors into a great hall with folding chairs and regaled them with stories. One was about a seventh-century hermit and holy man named Milon who, for twenty-five years, lived in a huge cave nearby, along the Seine. "The Seine was still wild and snaked between the wetlands and the rocky coastline," said Brother Magnier. "Milon blew his horn whenever there was a heavy fog to alert the boats and help them avoid accidents." Brother Magnier had a wry sense of humor. When a visitor asked about the abbey's beer production, he replied, "Ah, if people asked as many questions about God as they did about beer, religion would be growing in full effervescence!"

THE SEINE VALLEY is crowded with ancient ruins, Romanesque churches, villages that inspired the Impressionists, nature parks, local museums, and reminders of its last great cataclysm, World War II. The valley has a rural feel. It is home to rare species of water plants as well as farm cattle and fields of sugar beets, corn, wheat, flax, and rapeseed. You can find white limestone cliffs speckled with black flint and quaint houses. This rustic quality can be sneakily chic; if, at sophisticated dinner parties in Paris, you mention that you have a thatched-roof cottage in Normandy, many people are impressed.

Several dozen châteaus of various sizes and degrees of grandeur rise from the valley, many of them visible from the river, including the ruins of Château Gaillard, the military fortress of genius and hubris built by Richard the Lionheart on a limestone cliff above the town of Les Andelys. Normandy is also filled with *bocages normands*, areas of farmland and fields characterized by high, dense hedges that date back centuries and make it difficult to cross the countryside. After D-Day, as advancing American troops moved inland, these hedgerows created dangerous, costly obstacles. The Americans were unable to see, shoot, or move through them, and the ousting of the Germans from Normandy turned into what has gone down in history as "hedge warfare."

The Seine Valley is not on the must-visit list of many American tourists; most of them see it as merely a highway from Paris to the World War II beaches of Normandy. Even in the high season, you can have the back roads here to yourself. On one drive, I happened by chance on the Moulin de Pierre at Hauville, a restored windmill built in the thirteenth century by the monks at Jumièges. Except for the young caretaker at the entrance, I was alone. Birds, dozens of birds of many species, cackled and swept low around us, like Hitchcock's menacing flocks.

"Have you ever seen *The Birds*?" I asked the caretaker.

The reference didn't register.

"The movie? Alfred Hitchcock?"

"Ah, yes," he said, and laughed. "Okay, if you don't return in twenty minutes, I'll come and get you."

Inside, the windmill smelled of damp wood and dust. As I climbed a steep, curving staircase to the top, my mind flashed on an earlier Hitchcock movie, the 1940 spy thriller *Foreign Correspondent*, with its most famous scene: the blades of an abandoned windmill reversing direction as a signal for the enemy plane to land. Joel McCrea played the dashing American foreign correspondent, whose trench coat got caught in the mechanism of the windmill, nearly pulling him in.

I made my way down, unscathed.

From there, Jean-Pierre Girod, a regional councilor who knows all the back roads, took over. We drove through forests, marshes, peat bogs, and meadows, stopping at a farm dating back to the sixteenth century that raises white-bibbed Duclair ducks. He sprinkled his running dialogue with odd bits of information: how the region has eighty species of bees and more than 270 species of birds, including area rarities like the Eurasian bittern, the white spoonbill, and the black-tailed godwit. "People come from all over the world to watch them," he said.

We cut through a park with the unwieldy name of Regional Natural Park of the Meanders of the Norman Seine. It blankets part of the river valley between Rouen and Le Havre, and its trails include the *route des fruits*—a thirty-nine-mile trail of fruit-producing trees. (Normandy has been planted with ten million apple trees.) We passed overgrown fields scarred with enormous craters, which Girod explained were made by World War II bombs. The craters had never been cleared out, he said, and might still contain live bombs.

THE AUGUST '44 MUSEUM, near Rouen, a warren of connected rooms in a stone-walled stable, is a repository for World War II artifacts. It offers glimpses into the daily lives of soldiers who fought and died in the Allies' bloody march to Paris from the Normandy beaches.

Nicolas Navarro, a self-taught historian in his thirties, has poured his soul into the modest museum. It sits to the side of the centuries-old Château du Taillis, which Nicolas's parents bought in 1998, and which he is renovating, stone by stone. In 2016 he received a prize as France's Young Restorer of a Historic Monument.

His primary passion, however, is the museum, the goal of which is to present the last stage of the war in France in all its complexity. The familiar story line skips from D-Day, the Allied landing on Normandy beaches on June 6, 1944, to the liberation of Paris. What often gets lost is the account of the fierce battles in Normandy and the Seine Valley after the Allies landed.

The Seine, much wider as it approaches the sea than it is in Paris, was a strategic barrier that bedeviled both sides. After D-Day, it took nearly three more months of warfare and the loss of hundreds of thousands of lives for the Allies to push east and triumphantly enter Paris on August 25, 1944. "I tell visitors the fight only began on the beaches," said Nicolas. "I explain that afterward, there was terrible combat, terrible suffering."

Four years earlier, in 1940, the Germans had been the invaders. They destroyed bridges as they attacked and occupied Rouen. The area around the city's cathedral burned for forty-eight hours, because the Germans stopped local firemen from getting near the fiery site. Monique Rannaud, who lived in Rouen during the war and was ninety when I met her, shared her story of life during these years.

Monique was thirteen when the war started. She and her mother watched warplanes flying overhead. Since each plane had a cross painted underneath it, her mother thought they were Canadian planes. She was wrong. The Germans were coming. "The first bomb fell on the house next door to ours," Monique told me. "The Germans blew up the bridges. Many people were killed. We went to the banks of the Seine afterward, my mother and I, and we saw dead bodies in the river. My mother wept."

At the time, Monique did not cry. "I was only thirteen," she said. "I didn't understand."

Daily life during the war years was hard, she recalled, with little to eat. But more traumatic was the memory of those bodies floating on the Seine. "I was scarred by it," she said, her voice low and flat.

It would take several years before the Seine stopped reminding her of the war. She was eighteen when the fighting ended; peacetime meant joy and relaxation, activities like canoeing on the Seine. She became a star rower and signed up to compete in the national championship of France, on a route that would take her along the Seine past the Eiffel Tower. The competition paid off unexpectedly. Before the war, Monique had met a boy named Pierre. He had lived in Rouen, though they'd lost contact after he moved away. Somehow, Pierre learned that she would be rowing in the canoeing competition and traveled to the river to find her.

"We got married five years later," she said. "I really love the Seine."

BEFORE D-DAY, the Allies bombed the Seine's bridges and ferries to make it difficult for German tanks and big guns to get to the Normandy beaches before the Allied landing. After D-Day, the Allies took turns bombing parts of Rouen, aiming to dislodge the German occupiers. Allied bombers knocked out the city's bridges. Most of the left bank, including the Saint-André tower and the rue des Charrettes, a street that Flaubert wrote about in *Madame Bovary*, was destroyed. Much of the old city caught fire. The soaring cathedral, the Palais de Justice, and the Gothic Church of Saint-Maclou were damaged but saved from destruction. In 1944 alone, twenty-seven hundred civilians in Rouen were killed.

The Seine divides Normandy into eastern and western sections, and after D-Day, Hitler at first prevented his army's retreat from the western bank. Soon the German troops were under such fierce attack, however, that they had no choice but to cross the river and head east, toward Germany. Since the bridges had been destroyed, they struggled to cram onto ferries. Many soldiers were trapped on the banks and died waiting for ferry boats that never came to their rescue. The Seine thereafter became a barrier to the Allies, blocking them in their push eastward. General Eisenhower decided that all of his forces—American, British, Canadian, and Free French—had to cross. But without its bridges, the Seine was a formidable obstacle.

"A marvelous natural barrier," Navarro explained as he pointed out photographs of the destruction.

The solution was to build both fixed and floating bridges, sometimes under enemy fire. The most famous were the British Baileys, easy to assemble piece by piece from prefabricated parts. Forty soldiers could build a sixty-foot, single-lane bridge in three to four hours and a three-hundred-foot, two-lane bridge in thirty-six hours. With the German retreat, the Allied forces moved east toward Paris, while Canadian infantry soldiers cleared out the remaining enemy positions around Rouen. Paris was liberated on August 25, Rouen five days later. By the time the fighting ended, Normandy had become the repository of artifacts from the battles.

Navarro began collecting World War II memorabilia as a teenager. Over the years, he amassed thousands of objects: maps, bayonets, binoculars, goggles, gas canisters, and mess kits. Pocket knives, sewing kits, razors, and shaving brushes. Dog tags and faded photographs of wives and sweethearts. Playing cards, empty Lucky Strike and Chesterfield cigarette packs, coins, and postage stamps. A shortwave radio that a friend's parents had used to tune in broadcasts of the Free French forces from London. "I still find empty cartridges on the banks of the Seine with my kids," Navarro said.

Some objects in Navarro's collection are large, like the wing of a British Lancaster bomber. Some are small, like the clickers Allied paratroopers used to signal each other. He displays metal helmets pierced with bullet holes and uniforms on resin mannequins. One room of the museum concentrates on the Germans, others on the Allies. In one tableau, a German soldier stands, grim-faced, behind an enormous machine gun and belts of ammunition, as if ready to fire. In another, soldiers are smoking. In still another, the body of a dead soldier lies on a stretcher under a camouflage blanket. Outside the museum sits a small French naval boat found at the bottom of the Seine in 2013. It resembles a sculpture of twisted metal.

By the end of the war, much of the Seine Valley, the highway to

Paris, would have to be rebuilt. Yet Paris, that city of light divided into two banks by the Seine, was spared.

HITLER ADMIRED PARIS, though he spent very little time there. But that is not the reason his armies left it intact. One of the most famous photographs of the Nazi Occupation shows the dictator at the place du Trocadéro early one Sunday morning in June 1940, the day after France and Germany signed their armistice. A master propagandist, Hitler had brought his personal photographer with him. Hitler's architect Albert Speer stands to his left; his favorite sculptor, Arno Breker, to his right. They are posed against the backdrop of the Eiffel Tower, on the other side of the river. Hitler and his aides are center stage, rendered in stark black and white, the background of Paris in pale shades of gray.

In their memoirs years later, Speer and Hermann Giesler, another of Hitler's architects, told their versions of that two-and-a-half-hour visit to Paris. Hitler sat in the front seat of a six-wheeled Mercedes convertible next to the chauffeur for a predawn tour of the city: past the Opéra and the Madeleine, down the rue Royale and through the place de la Concorde, up the Champs-Élysées to the Arc de Triomphe. Hitler stood for a long time at Napoléon's tomb in the Invalides. He inspected the Panthéon and looked out over Paris from the Sacré-Coeur Basilica. "Paris has always fascinated me," he said at one point during the visit. "Now the gates stand open."

At that moment in 1940, the world knew little of Hitler's ultimate ambitions for France. In the plane, before leaving Paris's airspace, he ordered his pilot to circle the city several times. He and his party looked down on Paris and the steely-gray curve of the Seine arching through it.

Hitler toyed with the idea of destroying Paris, then declared it unnecessary, preferring to redesign and aggrandize Berlin. "When we are finished with Berlin, Paris will only be a shadow," he said. "So why should we destroy it?"

He would change his mind again.

Near the war's end, Hitler decided that if the Allies took Paris, it would be a city in ruins. He ordered the destruction of its bridges and monuments, including the Opéra, the Eiffel Tower, and the Louvre; he hoped to leave tens of thousands of people dead. The British intercepted and decrypted Hitler's communiqué of August 23, 1944, addressed to General Dietrich von Choltitz, the German commander of Greater Paris, which gave the order: "The Seine bridges are to be prepared for blowing up. Never, or at any rate only as a heap of rubble, must Paris fall into the hands of the enemy."

In his 1951 memoirs, von Choltitz told the story. On the day Paris was liberated, he surrendered—without following Hitler's orders to destroy the city. He wrote that he saved Paris because of his love of the city and his conviction that Hitler had gone mad. Some of von Choltitz's writing has been called into question over the years, but Hitler's plan to destroy Paris makes for great reading. It has been the stuff of novels, movies, and myths.

Larry Collins and Dominique Lapierre spun the story into *Is Paris Burning?*, their best-selling account of the final days of the Nazi Occupation and the liberation of the city. Then came the film of the same name in 1966, directed by René Clément, with a screenplay by Gore Vidal, Francis Ford Coppola, and others. Some critics called it messy in its structure, flat in its storytelling, and thin in its veracity. As far as we know, Hitler did not, as the film claims in its last scene, get on the telephone to von Choltitz and scream over and over, "*Brennt Paris?*"— "Is Paris burning?"

The movie is shot almost entirely in black and white, seamlessly weaving in documentary footage. The cast reads like a who's who of American and French cinema: Alain Delon, Leslie Caron, Charles Boyer, Simone Signoret, Yves Montand, Jean-Louis Trintignant, and Michael Lonsdale on the French side; Anthony Perkins, Orson Welles, Glenn Ford, Kirk Douglas, Robert Stack, and E. G. Marshall on the American.

In 2014 came another version, the French-German film *Diplomacy*, adapted from a play produced three years before. It tells the story of von Choltitz's soul-searching and ultimate decision during a night of verbal jousting with a Swedish diplomat named Raoul Nordling. The diplomatic persuasiveness of Nordling sealed von Choltitz's decision to disobey Hitler. The conversations are fictional, but the general story line is accurate.

The final scene of the film takes viewers along a calm Seine bathed in diamond-white light. The camera passes under the Pont de Bir-Hakeim, the Eiffel Tower visible on the right. The pillars of the Pont Alexandre III gleam golden in the sun. The Seine reigns triumphant.

*A modern sculpture on the beach in Le Havre where the Seine meets the sea. The artwork was built in 2017 as part of a temporary installation to commemorate the five hundredth anniversary of the city's founding.* ANDREW PLUMP.

TWENTY-SEVEN

# No End to the Seine?

*Is the destiny of the Seine to water
Paris, or to flow to the sea?*
—FRANÇOIS MITTERRAND, journal entry
the day after losing the presidential election to
Valéry Giscard d'Estaing in 1974

THE CITIES OF LE HAVRE AND HONFLEUR are worlds apart, but each can claim to be the end of the Seine.

Le Havre, at the northwest tip, is an industrial giant and France's most important seaport. It boasts that every year, a billion bottles of French wine and spirits move from here to the rest of the world, making Le Havre the biggest global port for the transport of wine and spirits. The Seine here functions as a workhorse, moving cargo through its main channel and smaller canals on the southern rim of the city.

In the days when American tourists began crossing the ocean en masse, Le Havre was their point of entry into the Old World. The French Line, which offered luxury cruise service, pampered rich Americans with fancy suites and fine French cuisine on a direct New York–Le Havre route. Conversely, continental Europe once went through Le Havre to reach America. Even though it is on the English Channel, Le Havre, the door that opened to the sea, earned the nickname "Cité Océane"— Ocean City.

In World War II, Allied bombings leveled Le Havre. The city was rebuilt in concrete and derided as ugly. Although it is only 120 miles from Paris, I avoided it for years. It wasn't until my curiosity for every mile of the Seine took me there in 2017 that I realized I had not understood the city. On the other side of the water is Honfleur, where the river has the quaint, intimate feel of the past. When the French head to the end of the Seine for a vacation, they choose Honfleur, not Le Havre. Honfleur has 10,000 inhabitants but receives 3.5 million tourists annually; Le Havre, with a population of 180,000 attracts only 50,000.

Travel guides often refer to Honfleur as one of the prettiest towns in France. Spared in the war, the city looks much as it did when it seduced the Impressionists with its winding cobbled lanes, its half-timbered townhouses, and an inner harbor for pleasure boats. Even the untrained amateur is inspired to pick up a paintbrush. It's also an offbeat gastronomic mecca. Local specialties include *bulots* (chewy sea snails) and *tête de veau* (calf's head). Sea breezes blow into the estuary and change the atmosphere throughout the day, making Honfleur a city of painted skies. I woke one morning to find the sky blazing a strong orange. I drank in the clear light during the day. At nine that evening, the sky was striped with yellows and grays. An hour later it softened to deep rose, the horizon black.

Alas, Honfleur's picture perfection can be a nightmare to maneuver, especially in the historic center of town in summer. Tourists spill out from the sidewalks onto the streets, blocking cars from passing. Vendors peddling ice cream and waffles clog the inner harbor. But then, if you walk away from the center to the end of the estuary, where the river meets the sea, and turn a corner, you find yourself at a sandy public beach that stretches for four miles. Families swim and play in the water; it's the English Channel, not really the Seine, but it's awfully close.

*Pleasure boats at the inner harbor of Honfleur at the
tip of the estuary of the Seine.* ANDREW PLUMP.

The best view of the Seine estuary is found atop Mont-Joli, outside
Honfleur. To get there, I climbed snaking paths that grew steeper, passing private villas and farms with grazing cows. At the overlook, from a
worn wooden bench inscribed with the names of hikers, I could see the
river and Le Havre in the distance. The gondolas of the white Ferris
wheel in the center of Honfleur gleamed silver in the sun. Church bells
and cries of seagulls pierced the silence. A bit farther on was the house
where the deposed Louis-Philippe, who had reigned as the "bourgeois
king," and his wife, Marie-Amélie, slept as they secretly fled France en
route to England in 1848.

The day I viewed the estuary from Mont-Joli, I was on the way
to Lillebonne, a town of 9,000 people twenty-three miles east of Le
Havre. Lillebonne—Juliobona in ancient times—had been an impor-

tant Gallo-Roman port and administrative, military, communications, and commercial center. The Romans took over what are now the regions of Normandy and Brittany in 51 B.C., soon after they occupied Lutetia on the Île de la Cité. The Seine was much wider than it is today, and Juliobona was built as a sophisticated port in a valley on the estuary. Over time, the town declined as Rouen grew into a much more important port. Now that the Seine has narrowed and receded, the town sits three miles from the water.

A small, modern museum contains curiosities from Lillebonne's Gallo-Roman past, among them inlaid red pottery mass-produced far away in Millau, to the south, a rare blown-glass dolphin found in the tomb of a young man, and practical objects of daily life: glass flacons for oil and perfume, a *strigile* (a cleansing implement used in the baths to scrape off dead skin), keys, tools, jewelry, safety pins, tear catchers, and a terra-cotta baby's pacifier. Lillebonne declined in the third century and forever lost its status as a political powerhouse. In modern times, it had trouble hanging on to its most precious archaeological treasures. A well-preserved six-foot bronze statue of Apollo discovered in 1823 near its amphitheater, for example, is considered the largest bronze of a god to have survived from ancient Gaul. It was scooped up by the Louvre.

In the city center, Vincenzo Mutarelli, the Italian-born chief archaeologist in Lillebonne, was waiting to show me around. We climbed to the top of a hill and could see the Seine below in the distance. Then we descended the rue des Bains Romains—the Street of Roman Baths— where in Gallo-Roman times, private establishments had offered cold, lukewarm, and hot baths, fed by spring water that came down the valley via an aqueduct.

At the bottom of the road was a manicured lawn with the vestiges of a Gallo-Roman amphitheater for gladiator combat and animal killings and a smaller adjoining theater for performances of both tragedies and comedies. Built in the first century and later expanded, the amphitheater was a third the size of the Gallo-Roman Arènes de Lutèce in Paris and seated about five thousand spectators.

Discovered in 1764, the amphitheater has been only partially excavated, and the vestiges of the theater have been buried under a paved
roadway. Other ruins were destroyed. Mutarelli waged a lonely battle
to uncover the secrets of the site, stone by stone. Even though it had
begun to rain hard during our walk, he pushed ahead with the determination of a soldier going into battle, leading me among stones that
had once been part of the amphitheater's façade and wall. "Here were
the entrances," he said, pointing to huge boulders piled helter-skelter
on the grass. "Here was the wall. I did all this myself." His dream was
to restore the entire site one day. "Archaeologists have stars in their
eyes when they think of the possibilities," he said. He acknowledged
that his was a lonely crusade, without the necessary funds, staff, or
technical support, but he had vowed to continue. "I am all alone, all
alone," he said that day. "But there are so many more treasures to find."

When, at the end of 2018, at the age of sixty-five, Mutarelli retired,
he criticized the country's lack of political will to excavate, preserve,
and showcase its archaeological sites. "Archaeology counts for nothing
in France," he told an interviewer. "It is a discipline ten times more
prestigious in Italy, Spain, or England, even though ancient French
heritage is at least as rich."

He reminded me of Antoine Hoareau, the self-taught historian of
the sources of the Seine, who longed to develop the ancient temple site
of the goddess Sequana.

GETTING FROM LE HAVRE to Honfleur isn't easy. You drive east
for eight miles. Then a six-mile stretch south takes you on a straight
road and over the Pont de Normandie. You head west for two more
miles into Honfleur's city center. All in all, the journey takes slightly
more than half an hour. The barrier between Honfleur and Le Havre,
however, is more than the physical distance across the mouth of the
Seine. No matter that the Pont de Normandie, a butterfly of a bridge
completed in 1995, is a feat of engineering and a work of art. With a

span more than half a mile long between its two pillars—and a total
length exceeding that of the Champs-Élysées—it is one of the longest
cable-stayed bridges in the world, invulnerable to fierce winds and tall
enough to allow modern cargo and passenger vessels to pass underneath. All the same, the *Honfleurais*—inhabitants of Honfleur—are
oriented in the other direction, southwest toward Caen or Deauville.
For them, there is little of interest across the bridge.

"When you live in Honfleur, you don't say you are 'going to Le
Havre,'" remarked Frédéric Lefebvre, a curator at the Eugène Boudin
Museum in Honfleur. "You say you are 'going to the other side of the
water.' It's unknown territory. It feels like an adventure, like you have
to make an effort."

"Do you go to Le Havre often?" I asked.

"Ah, sincerely, no!" Lefebvre said. "I grew up at a time when it was
unimaginable. Before the Pont de Normandie was built, you had to
drive east for thirty miles, cross the bridge to Tancarville, and drive
west to Le Havre. And Le Havre is perceived as a city without a soul."

Lefebvre's critique was unfair, but it is an opinion widely held
among Honfleurians. I understood it better when we crossed the Pont
de Normandie from Honfleur, then drove over the Grand Canal on the
viaduct of Le Havre. Huge cranes stood at attention on one side of us,
smokestacks on the other. Even as we headed east through the outskirts
of Le Havre, we passed one industrial installation after another.

Le Havre is trying hard to burnish its image. In 2017, the city celebrated the five-hundredth anniversary of its founding with an out-
pouring of scholarly tomes, photo collections, travel guides, and even
coloring books about the city. There were months of festivities. It was a
moment to join in the celebrations.

I knew that Le Havre was a city on the sea, but I assumed it was a
river city as well. I expected to find riverfront cafés and restaurants,
houseboats, barges, and tourist boats, maybe even a tree-lined path for
bicyclists and joggers. Imagine my surprise when I arrived and learned
that you can't see the Seine from the center of Le Havre. Instead of cut-

ting through the city, as it does in Paris and Rouen, the Seine—a wide estuary here, rather than a narrow river—touches only a small part of Le Havre's southern flank, almost missing the city completely.

ALONG WITH OTHER JOURNALISTS, I was invited to interview Vincent Ganivet, an artist who had painted thirty-six shipping containers in bright colors and built them into a hundred-foot construction of two arches. It looked like a Lego project for giants. "Were you inspired by the Seine?" I asked him.

"I was inspired by big containers," he said flatly.

Over lunch, Sophie Guillaume-Petit, a Le Havre native and the co-author of a book of five hundred anecdotes about the city, answered my questions about how the river figures in the minds of the city's inhabitants.

"You don't have the Seine here, not at all," she replied. "This is not like Paris or Rouen, where the Seine cuts right through. You don't see it. You don't feel it."

I remembered Napoléon's famous quote that Le Havre, Rouen, and Paris were part of the same town on Main Street—the Seine. And I found a line in Le Havre's full-color, 172-page press package calling the Seine "the spine that unites Paris and Le Havre." I was confused.

I called on Luc Lemonnier, Le Havre's deputy mayor. I had met him a few months earlier, when he came to Paris to promote the much-publicized competition Réinventer la Seine, where I had entered my proposal for a Sequana statue.

"The Seine is not a water route for us," he said. "The port is what matters. We're on the port."

"So how can you be part of a project to reinvent the Seine?" I asked.

"The idea of reinventing the Seine is to construct partnerships, to reestablish a new rapport with water," he replied. "When we talk of reinventing the Seine, it's a small piece of our relationship with water."

I became more confused.

Like Lemonnier, people in town talk about *le port* and *la mer* (the sea), but never *la rivière* or *le fleuve*. It's as if the river didn't exist.

Finally, I found a Seine enthusiast: Annette Haudiquet, the director of the Musée d'Art Moderne André Malraux. But it was an imagined river that excited her. The museum boasts the second-largest collection of Impressionist art in France (after the Musée d'Orsay) and some of the world's most famous Impressionist and Fauvist paintings of the Seine. Monet, Raoul Dufy, Boudin, and Georges Braque began their artistic careers in Le Havre.

She showed me Monet's 1878 painting *The Seine at Vétheuil*, with its symmetrical reflection of trees and bushes in the still waters of a golden-lit late summer morning. Haudiquet said that in the summer of that year, Monet, who grew up in Le Havre, was too poor to stay in Paris, so he moved his family forty miles northwest of the capital to the village of Vétheuil.

We viewed Albert Marquet's *Quai des Grands-Augustins*, where fog shrouds the quays and monuments of Paris in muted grays, and the river shines like a dark silver mirror. Then we studied Jean-Baptiste Arnaud Guillaumin's *The Seine at Samois*, a rendering of the river in shades of sugar-sweet lavender, blue, and pink. Haudiquet was mesmerized by the natural phenomenon created by the clash of river and sea waters in the Seine estuary. "This meeting of two different bodies of water, this mixture of the sweet and salty, it produces a unique light," she said. "I find it fascinating."

Under the water of the estuary, the tide erodes and reshapes the river bottom, creating a huge fluctuating accumulation of sediment called a mud plug. When the tides rise, the mud mass moves east, upstream; when the tides fall, it moves back toward the sea. The closer to the mouth of the estuary, the deeper brown it gets. The mud color is deceiving—the mass carries nutrients that feed the estuary's ecosystem and bacteria that filter pollutants.

WHEN FRANÇOIS I, a Renaissance man, created the port of Le Havre in 1517, a habitable city was an afterthought. His priority was to create *"un havre"*—a harbor—that would serve as both a defensive military site to protect France from invaders and a commercial port to open Paris to the world.

Militarily, the Seine was vulnerable, an opening into French territory from the sea used, as I had learned before, by invading Vikings in the ninth century, as a route to Paris, and by English troops as a landing site in the Hundred Years' War. However, as a transport route, the Seine was also shallow and unreliable. Its existing international ports of Harfleur, on the north bank of the river, and Honfleur, on the southern side of the estuary, were continually silting up.

The site chosen for Le Havre was an expanse of marshlands and mudflats riven with creeks. François I had to call in port-building experts to help drain the land. Several months after the king decided to build a port, he was persuaded to create a city to go with it.

Trade exploded over time. Wealthy merchants built monumental homes in the coastal suburb of Sainte-Adresse, above Le Havre. The city itself became a showpiece of architectural grace and elegance. The nineteenth-century poet Casimir Delavigne, who was born in Le Havre and lived upriver in Les Andelys, had a soft spot for his hometown, saying that "after Constantinople, there is nothing so beautiful."

In August 1944, the British encircled Le Havre and demanded that its German occupiers surrender. When they refused, the Allies rained bombs on the city and its inhabitants for seven days. By the time Le Havre was liberated on September 12, 2,000 civilians had been killed, 80,000 left homeless, and more than 80 percent of the city destroyed. At the ruined port, 350 ships lay on the bottom of the sea. The *Havrais* still ask why the English felt compelled to destroy their city after it was clear the war was over.

When Julia Child and her husband, Paul, crossed the Atlantic to move to Paris in 1948—three years after the war's end and long before her cooking made her famous—their ship arrived at Le Havre. A crane pulled their sky-blue station wagon from the ship's hold and deposited it on the dock, and they set out along the Seine toward Paris. "We could see giant cranes, piles of brick, bombed-out empty spaces, and rusting half-sunk hulks left over from the war," Child wrote in her memoirs.

The French architect Auguste Perret, working with a tight budget and a short deadline, oversaw the master plan for the city's reconstruction. He used liquid stone—precast concrete—to build identical modular frames, a rectangular grid system of streets, and wide sidewalks. The buildings on the 150 residential blocks were all the same height.

From 1965 to 1995, Le Havre was run by Communist mayors and became the largest bastion of the Communist Party of France. Some French people branded it Stalingrad-on-the-Sea. In his 1994 memoir *The Secret Life of the Seine*, Mort Rosenblum called it "the ugliest city in France, possibly the world. . . . A gray Stalinist tower dominates a ragged skyline of boxy apartments and office blocks, factory stacks, port cranes, and silos, all jumbled together with no space to breathe."

Le Havre's five hundredth anniversary celebration was an *opération séduction*. The city proclaimed itself a living museum of modern architecture, erecting several large-scale public art projects around town. It played host to the last leg of a tall ships race, welcoming thirty of the largest sailing ships in the world.

As part of a press trip for the kickoff weekend, we toured a model 1950s high-ceilinged apartment in a Perret building featuring period furniture and design. At first glance, all the buildings looked alike; then we discovered that the concrete came in different shades—creamy beige, gray, taupe, khaki, terra-cotta, ochre—and that the geometric columns and beams were finished with varying patterns and textures of concrete. City officials pointed out that in 2005, Le Havre was the first example of French modern architecture to achieve UNESCO World Heritage status. The city is a model of urban experimentation and reconstruction, they said, studied in architecture schools the world over. Indeed, Perret's geometrical architecture has aged well, and 1950s design is now chic. Saint Joseph's Church, completed in 1957, three years after Perret's death, soars to 350 feet and resembles a small-scale New York City skyscraper. Concrete columns rise to angled buttresses and an octagonal cupola. The steeple is lined with stained glass, and reflections from the colored panels dance on the walls.

In the center of town, we visited Le Volcan, a partially underground complex designed by the Brazilian architect Oscar Niemeyer. It consists of a volcano-shaped theater and a smaller crater converted into a library. At an inner dock area of part of the port, we saw Jean Nouvel's Les Bains des Docks, a white-on-white swimming complex and spa with eleven swimming pools; inspired by the ancient Roman baths, it is covered in thirty-two million tiny mosaic tiles. Nearby is the Docks Vauban, with a cinema, restaurants, and high-end boutiques.

At the Port Center, French singer-songwriter Catherine Ringer appeared with an air of mysterious detachment, her hair in a waist-length braid. She is famous in France as part of a pop-rock duo whose song "Marcia Baïla" was a *tube de l'été*—a summer hit—in 1984. When it is played at parties, the song still inspires French people to jump out of their seats and dance. Ringer seemed bored and was abrupt in fielding questions from journalists. A radio reporter asked if she could capture the spirit of Le Havre in a few words. Suddenly she burst into a song, "Au fil du Havre," an ode of love she had composed with a local musician. "It's at the end of the world under the edge of the cliffs, / Where the Seine makes love to the sea," she sang, her voice low and strong.

"Voilà," she said, smiling for the first time. "Other questions?"

The journalists applauded and cheered.

BENOÎT DUTEURTRE IS A NOVELIST who grew up in Le Havre and hosts a weekly radio broadcast on France Musique called *Étonnez-moi, Benoît!*—"Surprise me, Benoît!" His 2001 novel *Le voyage en France* won the prestigious Médicis Prize. We arranged to meet at his Paris apartment, which is filled with old books, engravings, and maps, including many of Le Havre.

"When you live in Le Havre, sure, it's near the Seine, but you don't think of the Seine," he said. "You think of the sea."

He recalled childhood visits on the luxury steamships heading to New York, the feeling of adventure. "We had the right to board the boats, so parents brought their children. We imagined going to the United States."

Maupassant, André Gide, Sartre, Balzac, and Zola wrote about Le Havre and inspired the young Benoît. "I fell under their spell," he said. "And I might not have become a writer—at least not the same kind of writer—without such a magnificent and powerful setting."

When Duteurtre was growing up in Le Havre in the 1960s, he encountered the Seine on Sunday pilgrimages with his family to the Abbey of Saint-Wandrille. Duteurtre's father had trained to become a monk before he chose marriage and had gotten to know the monks who lived and worked there. The family would drive from Le Havre, passing the industrial port along the estuary of the Seine, with its huge tankers and refineries.

Duteurtre described the Seine estuary as being like a large wedge that cuts Normandy in two: "For people on either side, there is the world where one lives and the world one calls 'on the other side of the water.'" The other side of the water . . . that was exactly what Frédéric Lefebvre, the museum administrator in Honfleur, had called the divide.

Duteurtre gave me a copy of *Le voyage en France*, after first inscribing his name with a fountain pen. When I got home late that afternoon, I read what he had written.

"To Elaine, the novel that takes the Seine from Paris to Le Havre, and that crosses the ocean from Le Havre to New York."

Perhaps the Seine really does come to Le Havre.

# PART FIVE

# River of Dreams

*Salsa dancers in the Tino Rossi, an open-air square and garden along the Seine in Paris's Fifth Arrondissement. From late spring to early fall, people gather nightly for dancing.* BÉRENGÈRE SIM.

# TWENTY-EIGHT

# Reinventing the River

*Citizens ... today we are inviting you to invent our shared future together.*
—MISSION STATEMENT of Reinvent the Seine for Paris, Rouen, and Le Havre

SEQUANA LOST.

My proposal to build a statue of the ancient river goddess failed to win over the judges in the contest named Réinventer la Seine.

Reinvent the Seine of Le Havre sent the first rejection. "Madame Sciolino, you were so kind to submit a proposal," it read. "We want to thank you for the quality of your proposal and your contribution to the emergence of an identity for the Seine axis. The members of the jury were impressed with the quality of your work.... Please accept, Madame, our most sincere salutations."

A similar rejection followed from Rouen. The city of Paris didn't even bother to write. I learned of the Paris rejection when I ran into Jean-Louis Missika, the deputy mayor in charge of the Reinvent the

Seine project, at a cocktail reception at City Hall. "Madame, your proposal was flawed," he said. "You had no way to pay for it."

"Monsieur, I'm American, and raising money is never a problem
for Americans," I said. "Sequana—the Gallo-Roman Joan of Arc, Lady
of Lourdes, and Marianne all wrapped into one. It's just what France
needs right now." Missika was unswayed. He gave me one of those half-
smiles French bureaucrats are so good at.

Reinvent the Seine's goal was to come up with new possibilities for
living on the water and along the banks of the Seine in Paris, Rouen,
and Le Havre. Sequana had been the healing goddess of an empire,
presiding from an ancient temple at the source of the Seine. I had
hoped to create a grand replica of the two-thousand-year-old Gallo-
Roman bronze statue of her standing in a duck-billed boat, the repre-
sentation that had so captivated me when I'd first seen it in a museum.
I'd envisioned her rising as proud and tall as the quarter-scale Statue
of Liberty that stands on an island in the Seine. I was sure she had the
symbolic power to reconquer the river.

Several months later, the juries announced twenty winners: thirteen for sites in Paris, five in Le Havre, and two in Rouen. None of
the winning projects was strictly cultural or artistic; all involved making a profit. Among the winners in Paris were a floating art center
with a library, bar, shared work areas, performance space, and workshops; a round-the-clock electronic cabaret for music, theater, dance,
art, light shows, and dining; a craft brewery based on land and water;
programs in public parking lots to educate people about the environment and transportation; a floating bakery that will deliver goods in
small, electric-powered boats; and a sports center with a swimming
pool that could eventually be filled with Seine water if the river ever
gets clean enough.

THE REINVENTION of the Seine didn't begin with this contest and
wouldn't end with it. Since the 1980s, authorities in Paris have found

new uses for the river and its banks, as the industrial and commercial Seine gave way to the recreational Seine. In 1983, the Port de l'Arsenal, once a commercial storage facility near the place de la Bastille, became a marina with a footpath and a garden. In 1992, a grand urban-renewal project replaced the André Citroën automobile plant in western Paris, with a modern park adjacent to what was then called the Quai de Javel. In 2012, the early-twentieth-century Austerlitz warehouses became the Cité de la Mode et du Design cultural center, with its popular night-clubs NUBA and Wanderlust.

Environmental concerns in Paris led to initiatives that banned car traffic and encouraged walking and biking. It hadn't always been that way. In 1967, Georges Pompidou, as prime minister, built an eight-mile-long expressway on the Right Bank. It was considered the height of modernity, a symbol of the public will to open the riverbanks to

*Storage silos at the port of Paris located in Gennevilliers.*
© HAROPA—PORTS DE PARIS TERRE D'IMAGES.

automobile traffic, and the fulfillment of Pompidou's promise that Paris could be crossed by car from one end to the other in fifteen minutes. "Paris must adapt to the car," Pompidou said. Eventually, more than thirty-five thousand vehicles used the expressway every day.

Then, in 2002, Mayor Bertrand Delanoë began to liberate the river from car traffic along part of its lower banks. In 2013, he closed nearly a mile and a half of road on the Left Bank and opened Les Berges, a riverside walk with floating gardens, restaurants, and playgrounds. In 2016, Anne Hidalgo, his successor, permanently banned all cars, trucks, and motorcycles from the most important stretch of the Right Bank expressway in central Paris. She called it "the reconquest of the Right Bank of the Seine." The city spent about €9 million to rebuild the route for pedestrians and cyclists, install wooden walkways, and plant trees and shrubs. On the Left Bank, the city constructed small installations for sunbathing and exercise, a botanical garden and museum space, and a picnic area in front of the Musée d'Orsay.

Creating the no-car areas was part of a larger campaign to curb a worsening pollution crisis in Paris. Cars manufactured before 1997 were banned from Paris streets except on weekends and weekday evenings. That rendered our elegant 1995 Audi 6, with fewer than fifty thousand miles and garaged throughout its life, hopelessly out-of-date. I was sad to see it go.

Taxi drivers, commuters, merchants, restaurant owners, and booksellers along the river hated the carless Seine initiative. But City Hall stood firm. In 2018, Hidalgo promoted her crusade with the unveiling of a plaque near the place du Châtelet that celebrated UNESCO's decision almost thirty years before to declare the Paris riverbanks a World Heritage cultural site. She used the words of a warrior. The "liberated banks," she said, "symbolize my battle for Paris."

Art projects helped integrate the Seine physically and symbolically into the heart of Paris. Stéphane Thidet's 2018 exhibition *Détournement* ("Diversion") diverted water from the river near the Pont au Change through a pinewood roller coaster of braces and sluices and through the Conciergerie court building. The passage of the Seine's waters across what had been the seat of power in the Middle Ages and the prison where Marie-Antoinette spent her last weeks during the French Revolution felt like a symbolic nourishing of the foundations of France's past.

The river's reinvention became an ongoing activity. The Grand Palais complex of galleries and exhibition spaces launched a renovation that is expected to cost hundreds of millions of euros. It will feature a pedestrian street with ticket offices and restaurants linking the Champs-Élysées to the Seine. Mayor Hidalgo devised a plan to build three new pedestrian and bicycling bridges over the Seine away from well-trodden tourist areas. The bridges would be lined with gardens, cafés, shops, and small businesses, reviving the feel of centuries ago, when bridges were destinations, not just pathways to the other side of the river.

There are plans to develop alternative transportation options along the river. *La Seine à Vélo*—The Seine by Bike—envisions the construction of a continuous 250-mile bike path along the river between Paris and the sea. On the river itself, the minister of finance already gets around Paris quickly via a speedboat docked in front of his ministry in Bercy; and the city of Paris is experimenting with taxi boat service for the general public.

The river is reinventing itself most dramatically at night. Thanks to the work of City Hall's lighting engineers over the years and, more recently, to evening recreational and entertainment initiatives, the riverbanks have become destinations for strolling, drinking, concertgoing, dancing, and even fine dining.

In September 2018, Alain Ducasse, the chef with the most Michelin stars in the world, embarked on a new culinary adventure; he launched a floating gastronomic restaurant on the Seine. After five years and a $12.6 million investment, the one-hundred-seat Ducasse sur Seine began transporting diners from its berth on the Right Bank across from the Eiffel Tower in a loop upstream and downstream. The custom-made glass-and-iron structure, which runs solely on electric power, features state-of-the-art kitchens larger than those of many restaurants on land. The silverware is engraved with the emblem of the boat; the carpet and chairs in the main dining room are printed with partial maps of Paris streets and the Seine. Other Seine river boats offer meals, some elegant and expensive, but only Ducasse sur Seine prepares all the dishes from start to finish on-site. "The first time I came to Paris, when I was eighteen, one of the first things I did was to take a boat ride on the Seine," he recalled. "Seeing Paris from the water—well, I had the most dazzling architecture of the world before me. It was like an electric shock to my system."

REINVENTION CAN MEAN a new way of experiencing what you already know. City dwellers have long congregated at the Tino Rossi garden along the river at the Left Bank's Fifth Arrondissement, strolling past the modern sculptures and picnicking on the patches of green. Increasingly, they fill the open-air space with dance.

Every night from late spring to early fall, the three small stone and concrete amphitheaters that touch the river host impromptu dance-a-thons that go on until midnight. One is reserved for tango, another for the traditional *musette*, performed to accordion and violin. In between is salsa.

Is there anything more romantic than dancing along the banks of the Seine on the solstice, June 21, when the day never seems to end and light is at its peak? On one recent summer solstice night, it was ninety-nine degrees even as the sun was setting. Most Parisians do not have air-conditioning, and it seemed as if the entire city had descended onto the riverbanks for some relief. Indeed, when the river is embraced in light from its banks and the passing boats, it shimmers in points of silver and fools you into thinking it is cooler outside. I arrived with Bérengère, intrepid journalist by day, salsa queen by night. She's nearly six feet tall; when she walks onto the dance floor, heads turn.

A dozen dancers were showing off their moves. The women were *reinas*—queens. One, middle-aged and full-figured, was dressed in capris and a sheer white blouse; she made her entrance onto the dance floor alone. Her face announced her confidence. Another, younger, was dressed in a flashy green-and-blue Hawaiian shirt, tight jeans, and black Nike sneakers; she knew precisely how to follow her more experienced partner, when to strut and twirl and dip. Then, she spun from partner to partner, as a stream of *salseros*—men who dance salsa— waited their turn.

As the night went on, the dance floor became so crowded that couples could not avoid touching each other as they moved. It is common *politesse* in Paris to avoid making physical contact on the street, or in the Métro. If you accidentally bump into someone, you are expected to say *pardon*. Here, personal space melted away. Barriers fell. Whether young or old, black or white, ingenue or expert, French or foreigner, French speaker or Spanish speaker—everyone enjoyed equal status. Cuban salsa, with its syncopated rhythm and constant twirling, shared time with bachata, with its three back-and-forth steps and a tap. Tourists passing on the big *bateaux-mouches* stood on the deck and cheered the dancers.

The master of salsa on the Seine is Serge Heller. He is the ultimate DJ, choosing music according to the vibes he feels from the floor. If you arrive before the amphitheater opens to the public at seven, he will teach you the basic moves. Both enthusiastic and patient, he grabs reluctant beginners by the hand and guides their bodies into the steps.

Serge is elusive about his age, but I'd guess that he is in his sixties. When he dances, he becomes a young man again. He heads to the dance floor and salsas through the crowd alone. His jeans are tight on his slim hips, his shirt unbuttoned at the top. A woman approaches. He takes her into his arms, and they move together. "I have never said no when a woman asks me to dance," he told me. "We are here to please women." At the end of the evening, a hat is passed to take up a collection for him.

I had never danced salsa in my life, and tonight was not the time to start. Who would want to dance with me, anyway? Swept away by the romance of the music, I longed to glide through space in the arms of the perfect partner. As if on cue, my husband arrived. Andy is an enthusiast on the dance floor, even if he is self-taught and undisciplined. I fell in love with him the first time we danced.

I suggested an alternative to salsa. A DJ was playing American swing and old-fashioned rock and roll on an open terrace nearby. That I could dance to. And there, on the banks of the Seine, we danced.

*Fluctuart, a floating art museum, which opened in 2019, on the
Right Bank of the Seine.* © FLUCTUART.

*A quarter-scale replica of the Statue of Liberty on Île aux Cygnes, with the Eiffel Tower in the background. Paris's Lady Liberty was a gift from American expatriates in France to commemorate the one hundredth anniversary of the French Revolution.* ELAINE SCIOLINO.

# TWENTY-NINE

# The Joy of Life

*The river will have flowed through*
*my life as an instinctive force*
*informs a man's destiny.*
**—JULIEN GREEN,** *Paris*

THE BRAND-NEW luxury cruise liner had just set off on its Seine River journey from Paris toward the sea when we were summoned to the upper deck. The setting sun was painting the sky pink and orange. With no notice, the ship—which had been built 33 feet shorter than the standard 443 feet just so that it could be compact enough to turn around in the river—swung into a sharp 180-degree turn and stopped short. Before us on our right was the Eiffel Tower. Straight ahead, at the westernmost tip of the narrow artificial island known as the Île aux Cygnes, stood a much smaller structure: a quarter-scale replica of the Statue of Liberty.

The Eiffel Tower defines Paris, and the Statue of Liberty is America's best-known icon. Even though Paris's Statue of Liberty is so much smaller than New York's, before us was a celebration of Americanness in Paris.

My fellow passengers were a well-traveled, cruise-loving crowd of seventy Americans, twenty-three Australians, six Canadians, two South Africans, and one Japanese. Some of them had been visiting

Paris for decades. Some had been reluctant to come to Paris this time, perceiving the city as a target for terrorists.

None of them seemed to know the story of how a Liberty replica came to rest in the middle of the river.

In the 1880s, a French sculptor, Frédéric-Auguste Bartholdi, designed the original Statue of Liberty as a gift to the United States with funding from a group of French individuals. One of Bartholdi's chief engineers was none other than Gustave Eiffel, who tested on Lady Liberty some of the techniques he later used on the tower that bears his name. In 1885, the statue was transported in pieces by train from Paris to Rouen and from there by boat along the Seine to Le Havre, then across the ocean to its perch in New York Harbor.

Four years later, Paris inaugurated both the Eiffel Tower and the miniature replica of the Statue. The tower, Eiffel's wrought-iron masterpiece, was built as a temporary structure for the Exposition Universelle of 1889; the replica of the Statue of Liberty was a gift from the American community of Paris to commemorate the centennial of the French Revolution. Initially, she faced east, toward the Eiffel Tower and the Élysée Palace, but in 1937, in a gesture of Franco-American friendship, she was turned to face west, toward the United States.

Many of us had never seen Paris from this glorious perspective. And the two mismatched structures fit elegantly into an iPhone photo frame, which empowered even the most photographically challenged in our group. We crowded at the front of the deck and snapped the postcard-perfect image. "I've never seen anything so beautiful," said Joanna, a retired schoolteacher from South Carolina.

The cruise of the SS *Joie de Vivre*—"Joy of Life"—was off to a great start.

I have never been a cruise lover. But I'd wanted to see the Seine from this vantage point. To travel along a river as the light changes the perspective is to savor slowness, to absorb and reflect as you move toward your destination.

The views of the banks from the river are gentle and peaceful but not fairy-tale wondrous like those from the Rhine, where castles with turrets seem to pop out from every hill. That may explain why the trip planners emphasized the destinations rather than the journey. We traveled much of the time at night, so that I watched the lights of the boat reflecting on the water from my posh top-deck cabin with floor-to-ceiling windows. The river flowed beneath us, as black as a Soulages painting. We spent many daylight hours on excursions ashore. Uniworld knew its clientele. The majority of the passengers had been on at least one of its other river cruises—the Rhine, the Danube, the Rhône—and they were satisfied with the approach.

We embarked from the Quai de Grenelle, on the western edge of Paris, entering the ship via a red-carpeted gangplank that led us into a two-story, white marble atrium. A Murano chandelier in green and gold glass worthy of Versailles hung from the ceiling. Uniworld had decorated the ship's interior with Dutch paneling and cabinets of polished walnut, French and English fabrics, marble-lined bathrooms, period advertising posters, nineteenth-century aquatints, and solid bronze Italian fixtures custom-made to look old. Our cruise featured all we could eat of the farm-to-table cuisine, an open bar, a French captain, and a Dutch chef. The general manager, sommelier, yoga instructor—masseuse, and crew were Romanian.

Uniworld wanted us to feel that we were having a French experience, and so the decks had been named after novelists Victor Hugo, Jules Verne, and Honoré de Balzac. We enjoyed sit-down multicourse dinners in the formal Le Pigalle restaurant and casual fare in Le Bistrot, where red-and-white checked cloths covered the tables and loudspeakers played recorded accordion music. The guests expected old-fashioned fare like onion soup, escargots in parsley-garlic butter, frogs' legs, country pâté, fish soup, cheese platters, and pear sorbet, and they got it. A fizzy white French wine was served in Champagne flutes. French cabaret singers serenaded us. One of the Romanian hostesses taught the guests—in her musical accent—to say *"Bonjour," "Voilà, voilà," "Ooh, la, la,"* and *"Oui, oui, oui."*

———

OVER SEVEN DAYS and nights on the river, we covered 186 miles, traveled through six locks, passed seventy-six islands, went under more than seventy bridges, and were joined by fifteen rivers. In Caudebec-en-Caux we left the ship and rode thirty-six miles by bus to meet the sea at Honfleur; the port docking facilities there were not large enough to accommodate our craft.

We did not travel through the heart of Paris. A ship of this design is too high to pass safely under many of its bridges; there would have to be a separate trip on a *bateau-mouche* to admire Paris from the river. We journeyed under the Pont Mirabeau as we left the city limits, and residential areas gradually morphed into industrial Paris. On our left, the giant Lafarge cement factory loomed through rows of trees on the Quai André Citroën. We reached the highway bridge over the Boulevard Périphérique and left Paris behind. There the river sharply swung south, made a hairpin turn north, and began looping its way westward.

The countryside provided a respite from the overstimulation of Paris. Jean-Baptiste-Balthazar Sauvan captured that lazy feeling in his 1821 travel book *Picturesque Tour of the Seine, from Paris to the Sea*. The tourist, he wrote, is "fatigued with admiration" for the structures lining the river in Paris and finds the countryside visually restful. "The eye," he explained, "needs the repose afforded by the scenery of nature."

For most of our route, the Seine remained narrow, its banks flat. Even though I was on the water, I felt a connection with both sides, as if I were traveling along a narrow highway, witnessing the everyday life of towns and countryside by day and the twinkling of lights at night. We passed the wealthy suburbs lining the Seine west of Paris, like Saint-Cloud, where my two daughters attended the American School of Paris; Neuilly, where the *New York Times*' Paris bureau was briefly located; Argenteuil, where my younger daughter's French soccer team sometimes played; Chatou, where I had gone rowing in a century-old boat with the Sequana Association; and Saint-Germain-en-Laye, where I often took guests to visit France's national archaeological museum in a centuries-old château.

We reveled in rural riverbanks lined with limestone and flint cliffs, green marshes, gardens, and fields of grain. In some places, the landscapes recall what the Impressionists captured when they painted outdoors near the river—Monet from a studio boat, Cézanne and Caillebotte from an island where Zola owned land near the house where he wrote. We saw the house on the Seine where Bizet wrote *Carmen* and, farther on, past Rouen, the place where Flaubert swam. Châteaus peeked out from behind the trees, more like austere eighteenth-century manor houses, not fantasy palaces with towers and turrets like those on the Rhine.

In other places, the working river greeted us with factories, storage facilities, oil refineries, and grain silos. The banks have been rebuilt so many times that often they resemble the walls of manmade canals, defined by concrete and stone.

Our daytime excursions took us away from the river, to the château at Versailles, Monet's house and gardens at Giverny, the Bayeux Tapestry, the Normandy beaches of the D-Day landings. In Rouen, I walked again across the bridge from which Joan of Arc's ashes were thrown into the Seine and revisited the maritime museum to see the miniature skeleton of Verrazzano's boat. We hiked on a gravel road up a hill and toured the ruins of the once impregnable fortress of Château Gaillard.

Along the way, a French guide named Dominique compressed centuries of history into short lectures, livening them up with tales of leaders and warriors: Charles the Simple, Geoffrey the Handsome, William the Conqueror, Richard the Lionheart.

I had chosen to go solo on this trip, and I found myself surprisingly lonely. One evening at dinner, I spoke about my service at the *New York Times,* and suddenly, I was an outsider. My fellow passengers included many Trump supporters convinced that journalists were enemies of the people who wrote fake news. One man left the table when he learned of my professional affiliation. I sometimes joined the Canadians or the Australians, but they tended to cluster among themselves. For the first time in my life, I understood what it's like to be a woman of a certain age traveling alone.

Then I met Julie. Julie was Australian, in her early fifties; she wore glasses, loose clothing, and no makeup. During mealtimes, she preferred listening to her fellow passengers' anecdotes to telling her own stories. She had little in common with the big-city Australians, who were older and worldlier. She had never gone abroad as an adult, taken a cruise, ridden a subway, or vacationed on her own. She had never tasted frogs' legs or escargots.

During long conversations, we shared our life stories. Julie grew up in the suburbs of Hobart in the small island state of Tasmania. She

*The* SS Joie de Vivre *luxury cruise liner navigating one of the many curves in the Seine.* UNIWORLD BOUTIQUE RIVER CRUISE COLLECTION.

became a single mother at seventeen; married a man who turned violent and abused alcohol and drugs; divorced him, then married a man
fourteen years her senior. They raised their blended family of five children together, and they now have two grandchildren. She went back
to school for advanced degrees, ran a homeless shelter for men, learned
how to ride a motorcycle, began to paint. These days, she rides a bike
several miles to her job as a school administrator. Her most recent project was taking up beekeeping in her urban food garden.

Julie had saved money for her dream trip: a seven-week tour of
Europe that included a cruise along the Seine, a trip she'd had to keep
on hold for decades. "I went straight from being a teenager to managing a growing family," she said. "I couldn't travel abroad while my
parents needed me in their twilight years. I never got to be me. It was
a huge thing to finally be doing something for myself."

Julie suffered from both a crippling fear of flying and motion sick-
ness; the flight from Australia to Europe came via Abu Dhabi and
required twenty-two hours in the air. To ease her terror, she plunked
down $12,000 for a round-trip, first-class plane ticket. Her anxiety
about getting sick on the hour-long bus ride to Honfleur was so intense
that she planned to stay behind on the boat—until I negotiated a front-
row seat for her on the bus.

Julie and I decided that on the last morning we would watch the sun
as it rose over the Seine. As the cruise was coming to an end, the ship
docked at the same quay on the far western end of the Left Bank where
we had begun seven days before. It was an unromantic industrial part
of Paris, with graffiti-scarred factories and nondescript modern apartment blocks.

There is something satisfying about getting up early in Paris before
sunrise. Most Parisians are still asleep, and the river feels as if it's
yours. I arrived on the upper deck well before dawn in a fleece-lined
rain jacket with a hood, long underwear, and sweatpants. Still, there
was no escaping the cold, damp Paris night. The only people on deck
were members of the crew; they smoked and drank espressos, oblivi-

ous to my presence as they gathered behind a "Staff Only" partition
before their six a.m. shift began. They were listening to an all-jazz
radio station playing the sentimental-sweet "Bada-bada-da-bada-bada-
da" theme song from *A Man and a Woman*, the Claude Lelouch film
that decades ago had won the Academy Award for best foreign film.

Julie arrived, smiling. The deck chairs were wet from a hard rain.
We wiped two of them dry, covered them with towels, wrapped ourselves in blankets, and waited.

The Seine was still, as if in a deep sleep, unperturbed by the boats
passing by. We stayed silent in the haunting blue darkness and watched
as the streetlights' reflections burned bright gold on the water, then
faded to mists of silver as the early light crept in. Gray-pink clouds
rested on the horizon as the sky turned a pale translucent blue.

The Eiffel Tower appeared above the treetops, hazy in the morning
light. Closer to us stood a row of apartment buildings, some of their
windows framing warm yellow light. In front was a barge loaded with
lines of brown containers. A few hundred yards away, we could see the
Pont Mirabeau, and as we walked to the ship's stern, the Pont du Garigliano. Beyond the Pont Mirabeau, the dark silhouette of the Statue of
Liberty announced her presence.

I thought of a print of the Seine at dawn that hangs in our Paris
apartment. It is a blurry two-by-three-foot image that Karl Lagerfeld,
Chanel's creative director until his death in 2019, sent me to ring in the
year 2009. I had interviewed him for *Newsweek* in the late 1970s, on my
first assignment as a foreign correspondent: Paris Fashion Week. We
met again in 2009, and I told him that his patience with a rookie had
touched me. Shortly afterwards, his print arrived with a note written
in silver ink on the black mat. "Happy 2009 . . . 30 years later. Very sincerely yours, Karl." The image shows a swath of the river shimmering
in silver-blue, the sky a paler hue, the dark outline of a statue on the Pont
du Carrousel in the foreground, the Pont des Arts behind. It captures the
mood of the river at dawn, when Paris, full of possibility, is awakening.

Julie and I took photos of the transformation as Paris moved from night to day. We settled back into our deck chairs and talked. Julie was heading to Bordeaux for another eight-day river cruise; I was going home to my Paris apartment, where my dining room table was piled high with dozens of books and thousands of files on Paris and the Seine. She invited me to visit her in her home in Tasmania, on the other side of the world. I told her I would love to come, though I didn't think I'd get there anytime soon. But *on ne sait jamais*—you never know.

We sat only a short distance from the Pont de l'Alma, the bridge I had crossed every day, walking home from work as a young, restless, newly divorced, and very green foreign correspondent. As Julie and I said our goodbyes, I thought about how my process of self-discovery had started on that bridge over the river, and it still hadn't ended.

I had come to Paris to find happiness and freedom. It was in Paris— not in Tokyo or London or Hong Kong—that I had deposited my dreams. It was Paris that carried me along and stayed with me. I had healed in Paris after a failed marriage, traveled as a foreign correspondent from Paris to faraway places, and had fallen in and out of love in Paris. Years later, I shared a life with my husband and two daughters in Paris.

The river that created Paris is not long. But it has carried me to new worlds and seduced me with its history, culture, and beauty. I have watched the seasons from its banks and bridges: the pink, cone-shaped blossoms of the horse chestnut trees in April; the long, hot July days that refuse to end before ten p.m.; the fickleness of October, when the weather changes half a dozen times in as many hours; the damp, gray, short days of December.

Julien Green, in *The Strange River*, a novel of sadness and loss published in French in 1932, gives a human voice to the Seine. "I am the road running through Paris," says the river. "I have carried off many images since you were a child and reflected many clouds. I am changeable, but as people are. . . . We have something in common, you everlasting passersby and I, the fleeing water, which is that we never go back: your time is my space."

The ancient Greek philosopher Heraclitus, who lived in the sixth and fifth centuries B.C., put it slightly differently: "You can never step in the same river twice, for it is not the same river and you are not same person."

That is the secret of the Seine. It is forever changing—widening, deepening, reflecting, twisting, shriveling from too little rain, overflowing its banks. But it always moves forward.

As, I hope, do I.

*Container ship moving past Caudebec-en-Caux on the Seine.* ELAINE SCIOLINO.

*Paris firefighters on the* Île de France, *a floating fire station that filtered and pumped water from the Seine to help extinguish the fire at Notre-Dame Cathedral on April 15, 2019.* Brigade de Sapeurs-Pompiers de Paris—Bureau Communication.

# Afterword

*The water of the Seine saved
Notre-Dame.*
—GENERAL JEAN-CLAUDE GALLET,
commandant of the firefighting
brigade of Paris

ON APRIL 15, 2019, the day of the great Notre-Dame fire, crowds lined the bridges and the banks across the Seine, watching in sorrow and disbelief as flames devoured the cathedral's roof and columns of thick, dark smoke shot into the sky. Some people prayed. Some wept. Some were close enough to be assaulted by embers and ash. Except for the crackling of the flames, the area around Notre-Dame and along the river was cloaked in eerie silence.

Little noticed was a firefighting boat docked along the riverbank beneath the cathedral. Its powerful motors furiously pumped water from the depths of the river into hoses connected to mobile fire stations on land. After the fire was extinguished, hours later, the Brigade de Sapeurs-Pompiers de Paris, the city's firefighting force, estimated that half the water used in the operation had come from the Seine.

"We had before us two elements of nature, fire and water," said three-star general Jean-Claude Gallet, commander of the firefighters brigade of Paris, the first rescue service in Europe. "The fire had the face of a demon with a mind of its own. Every time we went after it, it found another attack route on its path of destruction, as if it understood our desperation.

"Then, right in front of us, we had the Seine. It was as if the Seine were human. The Seine was an ally, but more than an ally. She was a serene, tranquil force supporting us against the chaos of the flames. It all sounds a bit mystical, but the Seine came to our rescue."

And so it was that the Seine, the life-giver of Paris, saved the monument that sits at the city's historic and geographic heart: Notre-Dame.

Earlier that day, Paris had been enjoying one of those rare bright April afternoons made famous in song. Sunlight streamed from a cloud-flecked blue sky, transforming the Seine's waters into glittering shards. *Bateaux-mouches* cruised past the city's architectural treasures with insouciance. As the afternoon was ending, *bouquinistes* along the quays began to pack up their old books and souvenirs and close their stalls for the day. Tourists competed with commuters for space on the sidewalks and in cafés, as rush hour merged with happy hour.

It was the Monday of Holy Week, and inside Notre-Dame, clerics and lay workers prepared for days of services that would culminate in Easter Sunday. Many more sightseers and worshippers than usual were gathered in the cathedral's cool, cavernous interior, after having waited an hour or more to enter.

Out of sight, the fire was smoldering in the high reaches of the cathedral's attic, a frame of medieval oak tree trunks nicknamed "the forest" that supported the lead-covered roof. The fire was so silent and cunning that when the internal fire alarm sounded, at six-eighteen p.m., a guard found nothing. As a precaution, however, church officials cut short the evening Mass, ordered the visitors to leave, and locked the doors. Within half an hour, flames roared from the rafters for all to see, transforming the 850-year-old stone structure into a blazing inferno.

By eight p.m., most of the roof and the attic had collapsed. The delicate nineteenth-century spire, built with 500 tons of oak and covered in 250 tons of lead, was too weak to stand. It had proudly soared 305 feet high over the transept; now it snapped in two and crashed to the ground.

With thirteen million visitors a year, Notre-Dame was the most visited monument in Paris; it attracted more people than even Saint Peter's Basilica. The world watched in disbelief and mourned as this unique symbol of Paris, a masterpiece of medieval architecture, faced destruction. "Like all of my fellow citizens, I am sad to see this part of us burn tonight," President Emmanuel Macron wrote on Twitter, as if the tragedy were universal. Later, Monsignor Patrick Chauvet, the rector of the cathedral, said, "Notre-Dame is a home, and I feel in my heart that everyone feels at home here."

THE SAPEURS-POMPIERS DE PARIS is not a civilian force but part of the French armed forces and, therefore, trained to respond to crises with military discipline and precision. At one dramatic moment, even after a steady water supply on land and from the river was secure, General Gallet feared a chain reaction. After the spire fell, it crashed into the nave. High winds and pockets of hot gases caused the fire to spread quickly inside the cathedral, weakening the stone vaulting above the nave and reaching the northern bell tower. If the tower collapsed, the weight of the eight bronze bells within it would pull down the southern bell tower as well. In a closed-door meeting with Macron and his closest ministers, Gallet announced that the cathedral was on the verge of destruction. "I told them that it was a question of minutes," he said. "I told them we had half an hour—no longer—before the cathedral would fall into ruin."

The motto of the Sapeurs-Pompiers is "Save or perish." Gallet had served in several war zones, including a two-year stint in Afghanistan. He immediately thought of the collapse of the twin towers of the World Trade Center on September 11, 2001, and the bold decision by the New York City Fire Department to send its firefighters into the towering inferno to rescue people trapped inside. Gallet and his operational commander, General Jean-Marie Gontier, ordered twenty-five firefighters into the bowels of the burning cathedral. They would either save the northern tower from within or face certain death. "Mr. President, if you want to see the towers of Notre-Dame standing tomorrow, there is no other solution," Gallet said.

The firefighters mounted the north tower with handheld hoses. They sprayed water into the air and onto the stone walls to cool them down from the inside. Through the openings in the tower's walls, the operational command on the ground could see the lamps mounted on the sides of the firefighters' helmets. "Fireflies," Gallet called them. "It was surreal," he said. "In the background, there were flames sixty-five feet high, and then you saw the line of firefighters progressing, very calmly, and the fireflies of their helmet lamps." The firefighters managed to ascend the stairs, steadily cooling the internal temperatures degree by degree. It was enough to prevent the collapse of the north tower.

SINCE ITS CREATION, Notre-Dame has been more than just a structure of chiseled limestone. With the Seine as its mirror and protector, the cathedral serves as the geographical, spiritual, and cultural heart of France. The site is officially recognized as the center of France, the starting point for any voyage of discovery. In 1769, Louis XV issued a royal decree ordering all distances in France to be calculated from a designated point in the parvis, the open forecourt in front of the cathedral. (The word "parvis" takes its name from the Latin word for paradise.) The triangular square marking the spot came to be known as *point zéro*. In 1924, it became the point of reference to calculate the mileage of highways in France, and an octagonal brass compass was set into the cobblestones, a visible reminder of the centrality of the cathedral in the country's life.

The site of Notre-Dame has been a holy place since antiquity. A Druid shrine and then a pagan temple dedicated to Jupiter, the chief of the Roman gods, are believed to have stood on this very spot. Further, a Frankish church dedicated to the first Christian martyr, Saint Stephen; a Merovingian basilica; and Carolingian and Romanesque cathedrals. Perhaps that explains why Notre-Dame holds within its walls a profound spirituality, even for nonbelievers.

The parvis—although six times smaller in the Middle Ages than it is today—was for centuries the *maison commune* (the meeting place) of the French people: "Serfs were set free there, mysteries played, and banquets given," wrote Jacques Hillairet, the twentieth-century historian of Paris. "The poor and the hunted could always find asylum. Night and day, anyone who went on a long journey could put his valuables in Notre-Dame. Contracts were drawn up there, and oddities put on exhibition."

The cathedral has served as the setting for momentous events in French history. In 1431, during the Hundred Years' War, Henry VI of England was crowned king of France to assert English claims to the French throne. In 1804, Napoléon Bonaparte crowned himself emperor. In 1909, Pope Pius X beatified Joan of Arc in her first step toward sainthood.

Louis XIII and Anne of Austria, his queen, built a new altar for the chapel of the Virgin to mark three miraculous cures that occurred in the cathedral in 1626; Marie-Antoinette came to Notre-Dame to give thanks for the birth of a son in 1781, after eleven years of marriage to Louis XVI.

In 1944, on the day after Paris was liberated from the Nazis, General Charles de Gaulle marched with his troops down the Champs-Élysées and across the Seine to celebrate with a Mass in Notre-Dame, just as a Mass at the cathedral had marked the end of World War I. As he entered the cathedral, snipers began shooting, first onto the parvis, then into the cathedral itself; de Gaulle ignored the commotion and took his seat.

When Socialist president Francois Mitterrand, an agnostic, died in 1996, more than sixty world leaders and thirteen hundred other dignitaries gathered in Notre-Dame to mourn him. Cuba's Fidel Castro came in civilian dress, while Palestinian chief Yasser Arafat wore a uniform and his signature keffiyeh.

NOTRE-DAME, with the Seine protecting, showcasing, and coursing around it, has lived many lives and undergone many transformations. It took almost two hundred years—from 1163 to 1345—to build the cathedral, the result an amalgam of Gothic architectural styles. Over the centuries that followed, it survived desecrations and renovations. In the sixteenth century, Huguenot Protestants vandalized statues they regarded as sacrilegious. A century later, Louis XIV raised the altar so that it looked like a stage, covered its columns in marble and gilded bronze, ripped out some stained-glass windows, and added statues, including one of himself and another of his father, Louis XIII. In the eighteenth century, when the spire went wobbly, church authorities pulled it down.

The most violent destruction occurred during the anticlerical frenzy following France's 1789 revolution, which transformed Notre-Dame into a Temple of Reason in the service of the new secular republic. Revolutionaries pulled the stone heads of Old Testament figures off the façade, having mistakenly assumed that they were French kings; even depictions of the Three Magi were destroyed. The cathedral was so badly damaged that by the end of the eighteenth century, extremists were calling for it to be demolished and its stone to be sold as construction material.

Victor Hugo's 1831 epic novel, *The Hunchback of Notre-Dame*, ignited a national awakening. For Hugo, the cathedral was "a vast symphony in stone, the colossal handwork of a man and a people" that had suffered "innumerable degradations and mutilations . . . both by the ravages of time and the hand of man." In 1845, Eugène Emmanuel Viollet-le-Duc, a young architect in his early thirties, in partnership with his friend and fellow architect Jean-Baptiste Lassus, was put in charge of the restoration of Notre-Dame, a project that would take more than twenty years. He re-created stained-glass windows, restored the western façade, replaced sculptures destroyed during the revolution, rebuilt the sacristy, designed the gargoyles on the rooftops, and, most memorably, created the delicate lead-covered wooden spire, the one that collapsed in the great fire of 2019.

On the day of the blaze, the cathedral was a structure in varying stages of decay, encased in a web of scaffolding. Decorative balustrades and gargoyles that evacuated rainwater had fallen. Flying buttresses, blackened from car emissions, were crumbling. Some limestone sculptures were so fragile that they turned to dust when touched. The ambitious renovation project was underfunded and moving slowly.

As planning for the current restoration of the cathedral begins, Viollet-le-Duc's vision for Notre-Dame rings true today. "In a project of this sort, one cannot proceed with enough prudence and discretion," he wrote in the early stage of his work. "A restoration can do more harm to a monument than the ravages of the centuries and the fury of rioters."

Even now, after the great fire, the best way to view the cathedral is to embrace its historic complexity—by navigating around it from the Seine. The cathedral's medieval symmetrical façade, with its twin bell towers and hundreds of figures sculpted in stone, enjoys an unobstructed view from the parvis. The cathedral's southern flank stretches along the river and can be seen in all its magnificence from the Quai de Montebello, on the Left Bank.

The back side of Notre-Dame, the nineteenth-century creation of Viollet-le-Duc, is less celebrated by the populace but shows its splendor at night, the flat, dark silhouette of the cathedral's flying buttresses visible through the trees. I found, like many others, a special place and time in which to make this view my own: the middle of the Pont de la Tournelle, just before dawn. Facing west, I watch as the sky moves from blue-black to deep blue velvet to soft gray, then light blue. The delicate architectural details of the back of Notre-Dame gradually reveal themselves, until finally, the early morning sun adorns them in warm orange hues.

ON APRIL 15, 2019, as urgent calls poured into the headquarters of the Paris police and the Sapeurs-Pompiers, the first reaction was disbelief. "There was stupefaction, total stupefaction," said Captain Damien Quilhot, deputy commander of the Brigade Fluviale, the police force on the Seine. "Notre-Dame is the building we see every day from our patrol boats on the river. It was not possible that one day it could disappear."

When it was obvious that the fire was real, the Sapeurs-Pompiers faced a threat of unimaginable proportions. In 2018, Paris firefighters had conducted two practice exercises to evacuate Notre-Dame and rescue its treasures in the event of a fire. The firefighters knew the cathedral's corridors, staircases, and hidden corners, as well as the locations of its relics and artwork. Once the flames were visible, the firefighters, together with the Paris police, cut off all land and water access around the cathedral. They turned the parvis into a command center, ringing the forecourt with dozens of giant fire trucks. They frantically pumped water high up onto the cathedral's roof, with the help of aerial drones that pinpointed the sources of the flames and measured the heat intensity with thermal imaging.

But nothing had prepared them for a fire of this magnitude. Both the water supply and the water pressure from the fire hydrants on land were much too weak to extinguish the fire. Not only that, but a break in the steady water flow could have caused the hoses to explode. "The fire on the roof was the equivalent of five hundred apartments or twenty tanker trucks burning," said General Gallet. "We absolutely had to have another water source."

That source was the Seine. Two fire brigade boats equipped with special pumping equipment sped to the lower bank of the river near Notre-Dame. *Colonel Paulin*, a small fireboat, was permanently anchored in front of the Monnaie de Paris, the French Mint, on the Quai de Conti, just across the river; it arrived within minutes of the first emergency alert. But it was designed to put out fires in private boats and cars, and its pumping capacity was much too weak.

The *Île-de-France*, an older but much more powerful floating fire station, was moored seven miles upstream at Joinville-le-Pont on the Marne River, which makes a giant loop before it joins the Seine. The thirty-six-foot-long vessel chopped through the water at record speed, passed through a lock, and arrived about thirty minutes later. As soon as it docked at the riverbank beneath the cathedral, firefighters on land attached four huge hoses to it. The boat's two turbo-diesel motors began pumping and filtering water from the depths of the Seine, with the same force of a giant fire truck. The *Île-de-France* pumped nonstop until the flames were extinguished in the early hours of the morning. About five hundred firefighters had participated in the effort. None died; one was slightly injured.

When the world awoke the next morning, the stone structure of Notre-Dame was standing tall. Its twin belfry towers on either side of the façade were intact. The multicolored rose windows, the great organ, the thirteen-ton bell with the perfect F-sharp timbre, and the cathedral's other bells had survived. The crown of thorns said to have been worn by Jesus at the Crucifixion, a tunic worn by the sainted crusader Louis IX in the thirteenth century, and major art, religious, and cultural artifacts had been removed to safety. Investigators would need time to assess the extent of damage to the structure, but it had not fallen.

IN THE MIDDLE AGES, the Seine contributed to the creation of Notre-Dame. Barges on the river and oxcarts on land brought thousands of tons of stone and other construction materials from faraway places in France to the building site. On the night of the great fire, the river was the cathedral's salvation.

In a conversation at the Sapeurs-Pompiers headquarters in northwest Paris, General Gallet acknowledged his special affinity for the Seine. A giant color photograph of the river after sunset, with bridges lighted and Notre-Dame and the Eiffel Tower anchoring the background, covers a wall of his office. He led me to a glass case containing ornamental firefighters' helmets in shiny silver adorned with the seal of Paris: a boat floating on the waves of the Seine, along with the city's motto, *Fluctuat nec mergitur*—"She is tossed on the waves but does not sink." Now there was even more reason to venerate the river.

"The water of the Seine is inexhaustible," he said. "We could pump as much water as we needed. In the drama of that night, the cathedral and the river were connected; they were one.

"The water of the Seine saved Notre-Dame."

France is officially a secular country, but Lieutenant-Colonel Gabriel Plus, the spokesman for the Sapeurs-Pompiers, talked of miracles: "One miracle is that there was no gas explosion; another miracle is that no one died, no one was seriously injured."

I grew up Catholic, and I would never dare to contradict those who believe that God answered their prayers in saving Notre-Dame from the flames. But I have also come to believe in the spiritual as well as the physical power of the Seine. I often tell the story of how even before the ancient Romans arrived and conquered Gaul, its source had been the site of a temple and a place of pilgrimage dedicated to Sequana, a healing goddess. Sequana was the original name of the Seine, and her waters were said to contain the power to make miracles. Pilgrims came from hundreds of miles away to pray, be healed, give thanks, and deposit offerings in her waters.

Notre-Dame will be rebuilt, different perhaps, but its primal place in French life and its symbolic meaning for the world will remain intact. It will be reborn as a vibrant place of music, ritual, and prayer for believers and a beautiful museum for all.

The holy waters of the river that once bore the name Sequana saved the greatest cathedral in the world. I want to believe that the spirit of the goddess Sequana herself lives on.

# Acknowledgments

EVERY TIME I WRITE a book, one of the first questions I get asked is "What made you decide to write it?"

In this case, the idea came during a long conversation with a friend several years ago. He asked me what had given me joy and comfort when I first moved to Paris as a young journalist so many years ago.

"The Seine," I replied.

I decided the time had finally come to explore a river I loved but knew only superficially. During much of my time living in France, I wandered along only part of its eight-mile stretch in Paris. In writing this book, I traveled from the source of the Seine in deep Burgundy, to the estuary where its waters meet the sea, and to cities, towns, tributaries, islands, ports, and bridges in between. The result is a deeply personal book shaped by my impressions of life on the river. I have told the stories that resonated with me and shared encounters with people whose lives touched me.

I get by in my book-writing life with a lot of help from a lot of friends. I treasure our conversations—our *partage*, that elusive concept that means "sharing," and one of my favorite words in the French language. Paul Golob asked the question that set me on this journey. Barbara Ireland, a former *New York Times* editor and friend who can do just about anything with the written word, helped me structure, shape, and polish the manuscript, over and over. Joyce Seltzer, a former senior editor at Harvard University Press, whom I've known and loved since graduate school, weighed in with brilliant ideas along the way. Bertrand Vannier, a fellow journalist and friend since we covered Iran's 1979 revolution together, read the manuscript with his keen French analytical eye, as he has done before. My former *Newsweek* colleague Steve Strasser and my former Princeton student Rachel Stone also read and critiqued the manuscript. My art historian friend Lin Widmann helped with crucial, last-minute copyediting. Jean-Claude Ribaut contributed his vast knowledge of French history, gastronomy, architecture, and culture. Elizabeth Stribling, president of the French Heritage Society, joined me in my adventures along the way. Once again, Amy and Peter Bernstein offered sound strategic advice.

Gary Zuercher shared his luminous black-and-white photographs of the bridges of Paris at night, collected in his 2015 book *The Glow of Paris*. Mort Rosenblum welcomed me to his floating home on the Seine. Pascal Blondeau, the photographer and performance artist, wrote a song for me—all about the joys and sorrows of the river. He has promised to sing it one day.

I'm also indebted to other friends: Stephen Heyman, Stephen Barclay, Richard Overstreet, Paris Huxley, Donna Smith Vinter, Sanaë Lemoine, Darius Khondji, Susan Fraker, Julia Husson, Andrew Joscelyne, Carol Giacomo, Guy Savoy, Maureen Dowd, Bernette Baer Plump, Marie-Christine Vannier, Susan Benner, Yves-André Istel, and Kathleen Begala, all rock-solid pillars of support.

Despite the burden of their scholarly research and teaching schedules, Professor David Bell of Princeton University and Professor Elisabeth Ladenson of Columbia University meticulously read the manuscript. David shared his wisdom about centuries of French history, and Elisabeth filled in gaps and told me stories about nineteenth-century French literature.

I take joy in surrounding myself with young people, and I learn so much from them. I discovered long ago that putting a hot, multicourse lunch on the kitchen table every weekday at one p.m. is a strategic way to get a conversation going about French habits and customs. Bérengère Sim, a gifted young journalist, worked by my side for more than a year. We bonded with river captains and river police, toured locks and water treatment facilities, and went swimming in the Seine. Laura Kennedy, a talented researcher and probably the most positive person I've ever met, brought joy to the office every day. Sophie Stuber, as a graduate student at Sciences Po, picked up where Laura left off, bringing the editing process to closure. Joanna Beaufoy shared her deep knowledge of French literature and music, recording songs of the Seine for me. David Broad of Left of Frame Pictures documented life on the Seine in video and photographs.

Heather Milke, Iris Samuels, Anna Windemuth, Nora Gosselin, Assia Labbas, Alice Stockwell, Maëlys Bablon, Elizabeth Rosen, Nellie Peyton, Olivia Grochmal, Alex Hurst, Felix Hoffmann, and Jamie Lee Jones joined the team at various stages, carrying out both routine and arcane research assignments. We ate well, too.

This is the second time I have had the good fortune to be published by W. W. Norton & Company. Jill Bialosky, my editor and an accomplished poet and author in her own right, immediately embraced the idea for a multifaceted book about Paris and France, as she did for *The Only Street in Paris*. Meredith McGinnis, director of marketing; Louise Brockett, director of publicity; Elizabeth Shreve, the founder and managing partner of Shreve Williams Public Relations; and Jill worked together to make the book a success. Drew Elizabeth Weitman, Jill's assistant, pushed the editorial process toward completion. Beth Steidle oversaw production, and Ingsu Liu art directed the cover. Once again, Bonnie Thompson was a rigorous copy editor who eliminated errors and imprecisions and handled the manuscript with care.

Andrew Wylie, a force of nature and my literary agent, and Jeffrey Posternak, his deputy, were active and patient partners through the ups and downs that go with creating a book. Andrew seldom sleeps, never wastes time on meals, and always responds to emails and calls in record time. Jeff—always good-natured, always fair-minded—can get just about anything done. We've been working together for more than twenty years, and they've always come through.

Princeton University hosted me for the second time as a Ferris Professor of Journalism in the humanities council, this time in 2017, which gave me access to the tremendous resources of the university and its libraries. A special thanks to Kathleen Crown, Joe Stephens, Margo Bresnen, and Princeton's army of librarians.

Thanks to Dena Kaye, journalist and philanthropist, I received a generous grant from the Danny Kaye and Sylvia Fine Kaye Foundation to fund reproduction rights for photographic and artistic images. Artist Carol Gillott, creator of the *ParisBreakfast* blog, designed a delightful illustrated map of the river. The gifted publicist Dee Dee Debartlo organized a coast-to-coast book tour with fifty events..

I'm deeply grateful to the people who live on, work on, study, and love the Seine; they taught me so much. Allow me to name a few: Marie Landron, director of the MuséoSeine and a living encyclopedia of the river, patiently answered questions—both serious and frivolous— about the Seine's history. Guy Pessiot, a scholar and a storyteller, and his friend Jacques Tanguy shared their bottomless knowledge of Rouen and showed me around town. Sandrine Berjot, commandant of the Paris Brigade Fluviale, and her team welcomed me several times to police headquarters on the river. Sophie Casadebaig, director of the Musée Archéologique de Dijon, allowed the priceless ancient Sequana bronze statue to be taken out of its protective case for the first time in decades so I could photograph it. Antoine Hoareau taught me all about the source of the Seine in deep Burgundy. Juliette Jestaz, curator of prints and manuscripts at the Bibliothèque Historique de la Ville de Paris, located obscure historical documents about the Seine with passion and determination. Nicolas Le Goff, author of two books on the little-known corners of Paris, took me on a tour of some of the city's hidden treasures. Miguel Biard and Arlette Renau, his mother, broke with tradition by inviting me, a landlubber, into the little-understood world of barge life.

After the great Notre-Dame fire of April 15, 2019, General Jean-Claude Gallet, commander of the firefighting brigade of Paris, and Lieutenant Colonel Gabriel Plus, the brigade's chief spokesman, welcomed me to their headquarters. As the book was going to print, they told me the dramatic story of how the fire spread quickly and finally was extinguished, revealing new details and correcting errors along the way.

Some writers need to get away from family to work. I need constant contact with mine. My older daughter Alessandra Plump, who was born with a generous spirit and a sense of humor, kept me laughing. My younger daughter Gabriela Plump was my visual inspiration; she photographed the river over and over, in all its sparkling light, in summer, winter, morning, and night, and painstakingly edited photos afterwards. My mother-in-law Sondra Brown offered love and hospitality during my stays in New York. My son-in-law Mathew Brailsford became an enthusiastic member of the team when he and Alessandra married in 2018.

Most important was my husband, Andrew Plump. His curiosity is insatiable, his energy boundless. He helped formulate the structure of the book and read the text over and over with lawyerly precision, as he has done every time I have veered away from journalism into book-writing. On weekends and holidays, he traveled with me up and down the length of the Seine, many of its stretches more than once, shooting photographs and videos along the way. We make a great team. He has a great sense of direction; I have a horrible sense of direction. He loves to drive; I hate to drive. He is the best traveling companion ever—on the road and in life. This book is for him.

# Bibliography

AUTHOR'S NOTE: In the absence of footnotes or endnotes, all sources used in writing this book are listed in the Bibliography. All quotations cited are taken from these sources. If a source has been omitted inadvertently, it will be added in a subsequent edition. Concerning translations, for the sake of clarity and style, in some cases I have translated the passages into English myself and cited the original French texts. I hope I have done them justice. In other cases, I have relied upon, and cited, existing English translations of the French texts.

## BOOKS

Ackroyd, Peter. *Thames: Sacred River.* New York: Vintage Books, 2008.

Alexandre, Arnaud, Stéphanie Boura, and Beatrice de Andia. *La Seine et Paris.* Paris: Action Artistique de la Ville de Paris, 2000.

Apollinaire, Guillaume. *Le flâneur des deux rives.* Paris: Gallimard, 1994.

Arthus-Bertrand, Yann. *La Seine vue du ciel.* Triel-sur-Seine: Éditions Italiques, 2009.

Association pour la Promotion des Arts. *Paris sous le ciel de la peinture.* Paris: Association pour la Promotion des Arts, 2000.

Astier, Ingrid. *Quai des enfers.* Paris: Folio, 2012.

Atelier Parisien d'Urbanisme. *Paris, Métropole sur Seine.* Paris: Les Éditions Textuel, 2010.

Atkinson, Rick. *The Guns at Last Light: The War in Western Europe, 1944–1945.* New York: Henry Holt, 2013.

Backouche, Isabelle. *La trace du fleuve: La Seine et Paris (1750–1850)*. Paris: Éditions EHESS, 2016.

Balzac, Honoré de. *The Selected Works of Honoré de Balzac*. Translated by Clara Bell. Ashland, OH: Baker & Taylor Publisher Services, 2013.

———. *The Wild Ass's Skin*. Translated by Herbert J. Hunt. London: Penguin Classics, 1977.

Banse, Laure, and Patrick Lebourgeois. *La vie au fil de la Seine*. Rouen: Éditions des Falaises, 2013.

Berton, Pierre. *Niagara: A History of the Falls*. Toronto: McClelland & Stewart, 1992.

Beaudouin, François. *Paris/Seine: Ville fluviale: Son histoire des origines à nos jours*. Paris: Éditions de La Martinière, 1993.

Beaune, Colette, Olivier Bouzy, Jean-Marc Goglin, et al. *Historial Jeanne d'Arc: De l'histoire au mythe*. Rouen: Beaux-Arts Éditions, 2015.

Bernac, Pierre. *Francis Poulenc et ses mélodies*. Paris: Buchet/Chastel, 2014.

Bernier, François. *Voyages de François Bernier ... contenant la description des états du Grand Mogol, de l'Hindoustan*. 2 vols. Amsterdam: Paul Marret, 1699.

Bertrand, Patrick, and Jacques Dubois. *Les hommes qui ont inventé Le Havre: Un port et une ville 1517–2017*. Rouen: Éditions des Falaises, 2017.

Besse, Françoise, and Jérôme Godeau. *Tableaux parisiens: Du moyen-age à nos jours, six siècles de peinture en capitale*. Paris: Parigramme, 2005.

Binh, N. T., and Franck Garbarz. *Paris au cinéma: La vie rêvée de la capitale de Méliès à Amélie Poulain*. Paris: Parigramme, 2005.

Bourguinat, Elisabeth. *Les rues de Paris au XVIIIe siècle: Le regard de Louis Sébastien Mercier*. Paris: Paris Musées, 1999.

Bowskill, Derek. *River Seine Cruising Guide*. Cambridgeshire: Imray Laurie Norie & Wilson, 1996.

Brennetot, Arnaud, Francoise Lucchini, and Claire Maingon. *La Seine: Une vallée, des imaginaires ... : Perceptions et représentations de la Seine du Moyen Âge à nos jours*. Rouen: Presses Universitaires de Rouen et du Havre, 2016.

Breton, André. *La Clé de champs*. Paris: Le Livre de Poche, 1991.

Budden, Julian. *Puccini: His Life and Works*. Oxford: Oxford University Press, 2006.

Burke, David. *Writers in Paris: Literary Lives in the City of Light*. New York: Paris Writer Press, 2016.

Bussi, Michel. *Mourir sur Seine: Le polar de l'Armada*. Rouen: Éditions des Falaises, 2008.

Busson, Didier, and Sylvie Robin. *Les grands monuments de Lutèce: Premier projet urbain de Paris*. Paris: Paris Musées, 2009.

Les Cartophiles Caudebecquais. *Caudebec-en-Caux: Du Mascaret ... à l'aube du XXIe siècle*. Dieppe: IB4, 2006.

Cendrars, Blaise. *Œuvres romanesques; précédées des poésies complètes*. Paris: Gallimard, 2017.

Chaïb, Jérôme. *La Seine vie et patrimoine. Seine sauvage, Seine domestiquée*. Vol. 1. Rouen: Éditions des Falaises, 2017.

———. *La Seine vie et patrimoine. Seine agricole, Seine industrieuse*. Vol. 2. Rouen: Éditions des Falaises, 2018.

———. *La Seine vie et patrimoine. Seine des loisirs, Seine des légendes*. Vol. 3. Rouen: Éditions des Falaises, 2019.

Charbit, Milena. *Îles de la Seine*. Paris: Éditions du Pavillon de l'Arsenal, 2017.

Chevalier, Louis. *The Assassination of Paris*. Translated by David P. Jordan. Chicago: University of Chicago Press, 1994.

Child, Julia, and Alex Prud'homme. *My Life in France*. New York: Knopf, 2006.

Cobb, Richard. *Death in Paris: The Records of the Basse-Geôle de la Seine October, 1795–September 1801*. Oxford: Oxford University Press, 1978.

Collins, Larry, and Dominique Lapierre. *Is Paris Burning?* New York: Warner Books, 1991.

Cronin, Vincent. *Napoleon*. London: HarperCollins, 1971.

Daguenet, Patrick. *Les séjours de Marie-Antoinette à Fontainebleau (1770–1786)*. Fontainebleau: AKFG Éditions, 2016.

Davenport, William, and Roselle Davenport. *The Seine: From Its Source, to Paris, to the Sea*. London: McGraw-Hill, 1968.

De Carolis, Patrick, and Louis Laforge. *Des racines & des ailes: Paris au fil de la Seine*. Paris: Éditions du Chêne, 2012.

DeJean, Joan. *How Paris Became Paris: The Invention of the Modern City*. New York: Bloomsbury, 2015.

De La Bédollière, Émile. *Le nouveau Paris: Histoire de ses 20 arrondissements*. 1861. Reprint, Paris: Hachette Livre–BNF, 2012.

De La Gournerie, Eugène. *Histoire de Paris et de Ses Monuments*. Tours: Alfred Mame et Fils, 1854.

Delaune, Yves. *Vol au-dessus des Boucles de la Seine Normande*. Saint-Lô: Big Red One and Eurocibles, 2012.

Delvaille, Bernard, André Hardellet, and Serge de Sazo. *Paris, ses poètes, ses chansons*. Paris: Éditions Seghers, 1992.

De Moncan, Patrice. *Paris Inondé: La grande crue de 1910*. Paris: Les Éditions du Mécène, 2009.

Descure, Virginie, and Christophe Casazza. *Ciné Paris: 20 balades sur des lieux de tournages mythiques*. Paris: Éditions Hors Collection, 2003.

Desjeux, Catherine, and Bernard Desjeux. *Seine de vies*. Brinon-sur-Sauldre: Éditions Grandvaux, 2015.

Devisme, Philippe, and Patrick Join-Lambert. *Voies Navigables: La Seine Aval— du Havre à Paris*. Guide Fluviacarte No. 1. Translated by Chris Brown, Julian Walmesley, and Multilingua. Paris: Éditions de l'Écluse, 2011.

———. *Voies Navigables: Seine Amont—de Paris à Marcilly-sur-Seine*. Guide Fluviacarte No. 2. Translated by Neil Allen. Paris: Éditions de l'Écluse, 2012.

Deyts, Simone. *Les bois sculptés des sources de la Seine*. Paris: Éditions du Centre National de la Recherche Scientifique, 1988.

———. *Un peuple de Pèlerins: Offrandes de pierre et de bronze des sources de la Seine*. Dijon: Société Archéologique de l'Est et du Centre-Est de la France, 2003.

Dottelonde, Pierre. *Le Havre: Une identité singulière*. Paris: Le Cherche Midi, 2017.

Dubly, Henry-Louis. *Ponts de Paris à travers les siècles*. Paris: Éditions des Deux Mondes, 1957.

Durand-Ruel, Claire. *L'atelier en plein air: Les impressionnistes en Normandie.* Paris: Fonds Mercator, 2016.

Duteurtre, Benoît. *Le voyage en France.* Paris: Gallimard, 2001.

Duval, Paul-Marie. *Paris antique des origines au troisième siècle.* Paris: Hermann, 1961.

Duvivier, Christophe. *Albert Marquet: Les bords de Seine, de Paris à la côte normande.* Paris: Somogy Éditions d'Art, 2013.

Edwards, Henry Sutherland. *Old and New Paris: Its History, Its People, and Its Places.* Vol. 2. 1893. Reprint, London: Forgotten Books, 2018.

Ehrlich, Blake. *Paris on the Seine.* New York: Atheneum, 1962.

Elder, Marc. *À Giverny, Chez Claude Monet.* Paris: Mille et Une Nuits, 2010.

Fargue, Léon-Paul. *Le piéton de Paris.* Paris: Gallimard, 1993.

———. *Mon quartier et autres lieux parisiens.* Paris: Gallimard, 2018.

Fierro, Alfred, and Jean-Yves Sarazin. *Le Paris des Lumières: D'après le plan de Turgot (1734–1739).* Paris: Éditions de la Réunion des Musées Nationaux, 2005.

Flaubert, Gustave. *Complete Works of Gustave Flaubert.* East Sussex: Delphi Classics, 2013.

———. *Madame Bovary.* Translated by Lydia Davis. New York: Penguin Group, 2010.

———. *Œuvres complètes de Gustave Flaubert: correspondance. Septième série.* Paris: Louis Conard, Libraire-Éditeur, 1873–1876.

———. *Sentimental Education.* Translated by Robert Baldick. New York: Penguin Classics, 2004.

Flaubert, Gustave, and George Sand. *Correspondance.* Paris: Flammarion, 1989.

Fosse, Gérard, Claude Lechevalier, Jean-Pierre Watté, et al. *Lillebonne: Des origines à nos jours.* Lillebonne: Ville de Lillebonne, 1989.

Fournier, Édouard. *Histoire du Pont-Neuf.* Vol. 1. Paris: Libraire de la Société des Gens de Lettres, 1862.

Fraigneau, Amédée. *Rouen Bizarre.* Rouen: Éditions PTC, 2003.

Fraser, James Earle. Unpublished autobiography. Saint-Gaudens Papers. Rauner Special Collections Library, Dartmouth College.

Gaillard, Marc. *The Quays and Bridges of Paris: An Historical Guide.* Amiens: Martelle Editions, 1994.

Gautier, Théophile. *Émaux et Camées.* Paris: Gallimard, 1981.

Gautrand, Jean Claude. *Paris: Portrait of a City.* Cologne: Taschen, 2012.

Gibbons, Helen Davenport. *Paris Vistas.* New York: The Century Co., 1919.

Giesler, Hermann. *Another Hitler.* Leoni: Druffel Verlag, 1978.

Glyn, Anthony. *The Seine.* London: Weidenfeld and Nicolson, 1966.

Gopnik, Adam, ed. *Americans in Paris: A Literary Anthology.* New York: Library of America, 2004.

Grandin, Michel. *Rivières de France: Histoires et portraits.* Paris: Julliard, 1994.

Green, Julien. *Paris.* Translated by J. A. Underwood. London: Marion Boyars, 2005.

———. *The Strange River.* Translated by Vyvyan Holland. New York: Harper & Brothers, 1932.

Hansen, Randall. *Disobeying Hitler: German Resistance After Valkyrie.* Oxford: Oxford University Press, 2014.

Hazan, Eric. *The Invention of Paris: A History in Footsteps.* Translated by David Fernbach. New York: Verso, 2011.

Hemingway, Ernest. *A Moveable Feast.* New York: Charles Scribner's Sons, 1964.

Higonnet, Patrice. *Paris: Capital of the World.* Cambridge, MA: Harvard University Press, 2002.

Hillairet, Jacques. *Connaissance du vieux Paris.* Paris: Le Club Français du Livre, 1965.

———. *Dictionnaire historique des rues de Paris.* Paris: Éditions de Minuit, 1985.

———. *L'Île de la Cité.* Paris: Éditions de Minuit, 1969.

Hoareau, Antoine. *Au pays des sources de la Seine.* Dijon: Editions Clea Micro, 2010.

Horne, Alistair. *Seven Ages of Paris: Portrait of a City.* New York: Vintage Books, 2004.

Hugo, Victor. *Les Contemplations.* Paris: Librairie Hachette et Cie, 1856.

———. *The Hunchback of Notre-Dame.* Translated by A. L. Alger. New York: Dover, 2006.

———. *Les Misérables.* Translated by Christine Donougher. New York: Penguin Group, 2015.

Hureau, Serge, and Olivier Hussenet. *Ce qu'on entend dans les chansons.* Paris: Éditions Points, 2016.

Hussey, Andrew. *Paris: The Secret History.* New York: Penguin Group, 2007.

Jackson, Jeffrey H. *Paris Under Water: How the City of Light Survived the Great Flood of 1910.* New York: Palgrave Macmillan, 2010.

Jacomin, Bernard. *Les Sources de la Seine: Traces fossiles et repèrages astronomiques au Pays des Lingons.* Montigny le Bretonneux: Yvelinédition, 2005.

Janin, Jules. *L'été à Paris.* 1843. Reprint, Paris: Hachette Livre–BNF, 2013.

Jones, Colin. *Paris: The Biography of a City.* New York: Penguin Group, 2006.

Joubert Alain, Marie-Hélène Lemoine, and Dominique Rousselet. *La Seine: Mémoire d'un fleuve.* France: Parc Naturel Régional de Brotonne et la Société d'Éditions Régionales, 1994.

Joyce, James. *Ulysses.* New York: Vintage Books, 1986.

Karpeles, Eric. *Paintings in Proust: A Visual Companion to "In Search of Lost Time."* London: Thames & Hudson, 2008.

Kerper, Barrie. *Paris: The Collected Traveler—an Inspired Companion Guide.* New York: Three Rivers, 2011.

Krebs, Sophie. *Albert Marquet: Peintre du temps suspendu.* Paris: Paris Musées, 2016.

Lachiver, Marcel. *Vins, vignes et vignerons: Histoire du vignoble français.* Paris: Fayard, 2002.

Lacordaire, Simon. *Les Inconnus de la Seine: Paris et les métiers de l'eau du XIIIe au XIXe siècle.* Paris: Hachette, 1985.

Lacour-Veyranne, Charlotte. *Les colères de la Seine.* Paris: Paris Musées, 1997.

Lalandre, Alexandre. *Histoire des ports de Paris et de l'Île-de-France.* Rennes: Éditions Ouest-France, 2004.

Lambert, Guy. *Les Ponts de Paris.* Paris: Action Artistique de la Ville de Paris, 1999.

Lanchon, Yves, and Philippe Marquis. *Le premier village de Paris, il y a 6000 ans: Les découvertes archèologiques de Bercy.* Paris: Paris Musées, 2000.

Lanoizelée, Louis. *Les bouquinistes des quais de Paris.* Paris: L. Lanoizelée, 1956.

Lefeuve, Charles. *Histoire de Paris rue par rue, maison par maison*. Paris: C. Reinwald, 1875.

Lemaître, Pascal, and André Velter. *La Seine des photographes*. Paris: Gallimard Loisirs, 2006.

*La queste del Saint Graal*. Edited by Elizabeth M. Willingham. Turnhout, Belgium: Brepols, 2012.

Léri, Jean-Marc. *Les berges de la Seine: Politique d'urbanisme de la Ville de Paris, 1769–1848*. Paris: Bibliothèque Historique de la Ville de Paris, 1981.

Lesage, Alain-René. *The Adventures of Gil Blas of Santillane*. Translated by Tobias Smollet. Reprint, London: Forgotten Books, 2012.

Lesbros, Dominique. *Paris: Promenades au bord de l'eau: 12 itinéraires de charme le long de la Seine et des canaux*. Paris: Parigramme, 2015.

Levine, Steven, and Claude Monet. *Monet, Narcissus, and Self Reflection: The Modernist Myth of the Self*. Chicago: Chicago University Press, 1994.

Lindbergh, Charles A. *The Spirit of St. Louis*. New York: Scribner Classics, 2003.

Lottman, Herbert R. *The Left Bank: Writers, Artists, and Politics from the Popular Front to the Cold War*. Chicago: University of Chicago Press, 1998.

Mac Orlan, Pierre. *Le quai des brumes*. Paris: Gallimard, 1972.

Magris, Claudio. *Danube: A Journey Through the Landscape, History, and Culture of Central Europe*. New York: Farrar, Straus and Giroux, 1989.

Mallarmé, Stéphane. *Autobiographie—lettre à Verlaine*. Caen: L'Échoppe, 1991.

Masson, Frédéric. *Napoléon intime*. Paris: Tallandier, 2004.

Maupassant, Guy de. *A Parisian Affair and Other Stories*. Translated by Sian Miles. New York: Penguin Classics, 2004.

McCullough, David. *The Greater Journey: Americans in Paris*. New York: Simon & Schuster, 2012.

McGregor, James H. S. *Paris from the Ground Up*. Cambridge, MA: Belknap Press of Harvard University Press, 2009.

Mercier, Louis-Sébastien. *Paris: Including a Description of the Principal Edifices and Curiosities of That Metropolis; with a Sketch of the Customs and Manners of the Parisians Under the Old Regime*. Vol. 1. London: C. Taylor, 1817.

——. *Tableau de Paris*. 2nd ed. 12 vols. Amsterdam, 1783–88.

Mitterrand, François. *Lettres à Anne (1962–1995)*. Paris: Gallimard, 2016.

Moore, William Mortimer. *Paris '44: The City of Light Redeemed*. Oxford: Casemate, 2015.

Nin, Anaïs. *The Diary of Anaïs Nin, 1934–1939*. Vol. 2. Translated by Gunther Stuhlman. Wilmington, MA: Mariner Books, 1970.

Nodier, Charles. *La Seine et ses bords*. Paris: Les Éditions de Paris, 1992.

*Notre-Dame de Paris: Au cœur d'une opération hors-norme*. Allo Dix Huit Hors-Série. L'Association pour le Développement des Œuvres Sociales des Sapeurs-Pompiers de Paris. Mai–Juin 2019.

Omrani, Bijan. *Caesar's Footprints: A Cultural Excursion to Ancient France: Journeys to Roman Gaul*. New York: Pegasus, 2017.

O'Reilly, James, Larry Habegger, and Sean O'Reilly, eds. *Travelers' Tales Paris: True Stories*. San Francisco: Travelers' Tales, 2002.

Pelloux, Patricia, and Pascale Thomas. *Paris: Métropole sur Seine: une concertation XXL*. Paris: Les Éditions Textuel, 2011.

Pessiot, Guy, and Jacques Tanguy. *Rouen photos inédites*. Vol. 1. Rouen: Éditions des Falaises, 2015.

Petitguillaume, Laurent, and Isabelle Bourdet. *Les coulisses du Pont-Neuf.* Paris: Éditions du Chêne, 2010.

Pinchedez, Annette. *Guide du Paris fluvial et maritime*. Colombelles: Éditions du Valhermeil, 2008.

Poulain, A. Georges. *Autour de Vernon*. Vernon: Imprimerie Moderne, 1935.

Powell, Jessica. *Literary Paris: A Guide*. New York: Little Bookroom, 2006.

Prasteau, Jean. *Îles de Paris*. Paris: Arthaud, 1957.

Priestley, John Boynton. *They Walk in the City*. Leipzig: Tauchnitz, 1937.

Privat d'Anglemont, Alexandre, and Alfred Delvau. *Paris inconnu*. Paris: Adolphe Delahays, 1886.

Proust, Marcel. *Contre Sainte-Beuve*. Paris: Édition la Pléiade, Gallimard, 1987.

———. *In Search of Lost Time*. Translated by Lydia Davis. New York: Penguin Classics, 2003.

Puccini, Giacomo. *Il Tabarro*. Translated by Burton Fisher. Boca Raton, FL: Opera Journeys Publishing, 2002.

Quicherat, Jules-Etienne. *Procès de condamnation et de réhabilitation de Jeanne d'Arc, dite la Pucelle*. Vol. 2. Paris: Jules Renouard et Cie, 1844.

Racine, Jean. *La nymphe de la Seine à la reyne, ode*. Paris: Chez Augustin Courbé, 1660.

Ratkovic, Milan. *La légende des bouquinistes de Paris*. Lausanne: L'Age d'Homme, 2000.

Roberts, Andrew. *Napoleon: A Life*. New York: Penguin Group, 2015.

Ronis, Willy. *Sundays by the River*. Washington, D.C.: Smithsonian Institution Press, 1999.

Rosenblum, Mort. *The Secret Life of the Seine*. Boston: Da Capo Press, 2001.

Russell, John. *Paris*. New York: Harry N. Abrams, 1975.

Saint-Juirs [Delorme, René]. *La Seine à travers Paris*. Illustrated by G. Fraipont. Paris: Librairie Artistique de H. Launette et Cie, 1890.

Saint-Pierre, Bernardin de. *L'Arcadie; suivie de la Pierre D'Abraham*. Edited by E. du Chatenet. Limoges: Eugène Ardant et Cie Editeurs, 1883.

Saliot, Anne-Gaëlle. *The Drowned Muse: Casting the Unknown Woman of the Seine Across the Tides of Modernity*. Oxford: Oxford University Press, 2015.

Sartre, Jean-Paul. *The Age of Reason*. Translated by Eric Sutton. New York: Penguin Classics, 2001.

Sauvan, Jean-Baptiste-Balthazar. *Picturesque Tour of the Seine, from Paris to the Sea*. London: Rudolph Ackermann, 1821.

Schürmann, Michael. *Paris Movie Walks: Ten Guided Tours through the City of Lights! Camera! Action!* Branford: The Intrepid Traveler, 1957.

Schweitzer, Jacques. *L'eau à Troyes*. Langres: Éditions Dominique Guéniot, 2007.

Sibout, Cécile-Anne. *Joan of Arc and Rouen*. Translated by Hazel Bertrand. Rouen: Éditions des Falaises, 2015.

Simenon, Georges. *Inquest on Bouvet*. Translated by Eugene MacCown. London: Penguin, 1963.

Skeggs, Douglas. *River of Light: Monet's Impressions of the Seine*. New York: Knopf/ Doubleday, 1987.

Smith, John Frederick. *A Hand Book up the Seine*. London: G. F. Cruchley, 1840.

Speer, Albert. *Inside the Third Reich: Memoirs*. Translated by Richard and Clara Winston. New York: Simon & Schuster, 1970.

Steinmetz, Jean-Luc. *Stéphane Mallarmé*. Paris: Fayard, 2014.

Timoney, Charles. *An Englishman Aboard: Discovering France in a Rowing Boat*. New York: Penguin Group, 2014.

Trout, Andrew. *City on the Seine: Paris in the Time of Richelieu and Louis XIV 1614–1715*. New York: St. Martin's Press, 1996.

Uzanne, Octave. *Bouquinistes et bouquineurs: physiologie des quais de Paris du Pont Royal au Pont Sully*. Paris: Librairies-Imprimeries Réunies, 1893.

Vallas, Jean-Louis. *Ponts de Paris*. Paris: Éditions Albin Michel, 1951.

Verlaine, Paul. *Poems*. Translated by Jacques Leclercq. Westport, CT: Greenwood Press, 1977.

Vernou, Christian. *Ex-voto, retour aux sources: Les bois des sources de la seine*. Dijon: Musée Archéologique de Dijon, 2011.

Vollard, Ambroise. *La Vie et l'œuvre de Pierre-Auguste Renoir*. San Francisco: Alan Wofsy Fine Arts, 1999.

Von Choltitz, Dietrich. *Un Soldat parmi des soldats*. Paris: Éditions Aubanel, 1965.

Walpole, Horace. *The Correspondence of Horace Walpole, with George Montagu, Esq., [and Others]: 1770–1797*. Reprint. Whitefish, MT: Kessinger Publishing, 2006.

Warrell, Ian. *Turner on the Seine*. London: Tate Gallery Publishing, 1999.

Wheeler, Bonnie, and Charles T. Wood, eds. *Fresh Verdicts on Joan of Arc*. London: Routledge, 1999.

White, Edmund. *The Flâneur: A Stroll Through the Paradoxes of Paris*. New York: Bloomsbury, 2015.

*The Works of the Emperor Julian*. Vol. 2, translated by Wilmer Cave Wright. Cambridge, MA: Harvard University Press, 1913. Accessed at www.gutenberg.org.

Zola, Émile. *The Masterpiece*. Translated by Thomas Walton. Oxford: Oxford World's Classics, 2008.

———. *Thérèse Raquin*. Translated by Leonard Tancock. London: Penguin Classics, 1962.

Zola, Émile François, and [Robert] Massin. *Zola: Photographer*. Translated by Liliane Emery Tuck. London: Collins, 1988.

## WEBSITES

Association des Bouquinistes des Quais de Paris. *Les Bouquinistes des Quais de Paris*. www.lesbouquinistesdesquaisdeparis.fr.

City of Paris. *Bouquinistes, les gardiens de l'âme de Paris*. www.paris.fr/actualites/ bouquinistes-les-gardiens-de-l-ame-de-paris-5751.

Géoportail. *Carte-plan des rivières de France*. https://www.geoportail.gouv.fr/ plan/81225/rivieres.

## ARTICLES, ESSAYS, SHORT STORIES, AND DISSERTATIONS

Chanson, H. "The Tidal Bore of the Seine River, France: Le Mascaret de la Seine." PhD diss., School of Civil Engineering, Queensland, Australia, 2000. http://staff .civil.uq.edu.au/h.chanson/mascaret.html.

Corot, Henry. "Fouilles du temple de la *dea Sequana*." *Comptes rendus des séances de l'Académie des Inscriptions et Belles-Lettres* 77, no. 2 (April–June 1933): 289–92.

Deyts, Simone-Antoinette. "The Sacred Source of the Seine." *Scientific American* 225, no. 1 (July 1971): 65–73.

"Emile Zola's Pictures of His Two Lives." *Life* 34, no. 19 (May 11, 1953): 155–62.

"Été 36—la parenthèse enchantée." Special issue, *Historia*, June–August 2016.

"Faits Divers—Arsens Blondin." *L'Impartial*, no. 520 (September 6, 1882): 3.

McGovern, Joe. "*La La Land*: Emma Stone, Ryan Gosling in dreamy exclusive photo." *Entertainment Weekly*. October 28, 2016. https://ew.com/ article/2016/10/28/la-la-land-ryan-gosling-emma-stone/.

Musée Carnavalet. *De la place Louis XV à la place de la Concorde, catalogue d'exposition*. Paris: Musée Carnavalet, 1982.

"1936." Special issue, *Le Monde*, May–July 2016.

Ollier, Brigitte. "Willy Ronis à perte de vues." *Libération*. September 14, 2009. https://next.liberation.fr/culture/2009/09/14/willy-ronis-a-perte-de-vues_581420.

"Paris Antique." Special issue, *Histoire Antique* 10, July–September 2016.

Pénet, Martin. "La Chanson de la Seine." *Sociétés & représentations* 17, no. 1 (2004): 51. doi:10.3917/sr.017.0051.

Pradel, Benjamin, and Gwendal Simon. "Les corporéités de Paris Plages: De la surveillance institutionnelle à l'autodiscipline collective." *Mondes du tourisme*, 9 (2014): 58–67.

Ranum, Orest. "The French Ritual of Tyrannicide in the Late Sixteenth Century." *Sixteenth Century Journal* 11, no. 1 (1980): 63–82. doi:10.2307/2539476.

Schneider, Pierre. "The Well-Loved River." *Horizon: A Magazine of the Arts* 4, no. 6 (July 1962): 53–79.

Syndicat des Bouquinistes Professionnels des Quais de Paris. "Histoire des bouquinistes." *Le Parapet*, no. 53, June 2007. http://www.paris1900.fr/wp-content/ uploads/2011/11/bouquinistes-paris-parapet-n53.pdf.

Thompson, Vance. "The Waterways of Paris." *Outing* 44, no. 3, (June 1904). http:// library.la84.org/SportsLibrary/Outing/Volume_44/outXLIV03/outXLIV03a.pdf.


## FILMS AND FILM SCRIPTS

*A bord du* Go-Ahead, *mémoires de mariniers*. Directed by Aurore Chauvry. Festival Terre d'Eaux, 2014.

*Les amants du Pont-Neuf.* Directed by Leos Carax. Films A2, Gaumont International, Les Films Christian Fechner, 1991.

*An American in Paris.* Directed by Vincente Minnelli. Metro-Goldwyn-Mayer, 1951.

*L'Atalante.* Directed by Jean Vigo. Gaumont Film Company, 1934.

*Boudu Saved from Drowning*. Directed by Jean Renoir. Les Établissements Jacques
Haïk and Les Productions Michel Simon, 1932.

*The Bourne Identity*. Directed by Doug Liman. Universal Pictures, 2002.

*Camille Claudel*. Directed by Bruno Nuytten. Gaumont Film Company, 1988.

*C'était un rendez-vous*. Directed by Claude Lelouch. Spirit Level Film, 1976.

*Charade*. Directed by Stanley Donen. Universal Pictures and Stanley Donen Films, 1963.

*Death in the Seine*. Directed by Peter Greenaway. Erato Films, Allarts TV Productions, Mikros Image, La Sept, NOS Televsion, 1989.

*Diplomacy*. Directed by Volker Schlöndorff. Gaumont Film Company, 2014.

*Everyone Says I Love You*. Directed by Woody Allen. Miramax Films Buena Vista
Pictures, Magnolia Productions, Sweetland Films, 1996.

*Le fabuleux destin d'Amélie Poulain*. Directed by Jean-Pierre Jeunet. Claudie Ossard
Productions and Union Générale Cinématographique, 2001.

*Harmonies de Paris*. Directed by Lucie Derain. Films Albatros, 1929.

*Hugo*. Directed by Martin Scorsese. Paramount Pictures, GK Films, Infinitum Nihil,
2011.

*Inception*. Directed by Christopher Nolan. Warner Brothers, 2010.

*The Intouchables*. Directed by Olivier Nakache and Éric Toledano. Quad Productions,
2011.

*Irma la Douce*. Directed by Billy Wilder. Phalanx Productions and The Mirisch Corporation, 1963.

*Is Paris Burning?* Directed by René Clément. Marianne Produtions and Transcontinental Films, 1966.

*Jules and Jim*. Directed by François Truffaut. Les Films du Carosse and Sédif Productions, 1962.

*La La Land*. Directed by Damien Chazelle. Summit Entertainment, Black Label
Media and TIK Films, 2016.

*Last Tango in Paris*. Directed by Bernardo Bertolucci. Les Productions Artistes Associés and Produzioni Europee Associate, 1972.

*Love in the Afternoon*. Directed by Billy Wilder. Allied Artists Pictures Corporation,
1957.

*Midnight in Paris*. Directed by Woody Allen. Mediapro, Versátil Cinema, Gravier
Productions, Pontchartrain Productions, Televisió de Catalunya, 2011.

*Mission: Impossible—Fallout*. Directed by Christopher McQuarrie. Paramount Pictures and Skydance Media, 2018.

*Un monstre à Paris*. Directed by Bibo Bergeron. EuropaCorp, Bibo Films, France 3
Cinéma, Walking The Dog, uFilm, uFund, Canal+, France Télévisions, CinéCinéma and Umedia, 2011.

*Paris Blues*. Directed by Martin Ritt. Pennebaker Productions, Diane Productions,
Jason Films, Monica Corp., and Monmouth, 1961.

*The Pink Panther*. Directed by Robert Simonds. Columbia Pictures Corporation,
Metro-Goldwyn-Mayer, Robert Simonds Productions, International Production
Company, and the Motecito Picture Company, 2006.

*Le quai des brumes*. Directed by Marcel Carné. Ciné-Alliance, 1938.

*Ratatouille.* Directed by Brad Bird and Jan Pinkava. Don Bluth Productions, Pixar Animation Studios and Walt Disney Pictures, 2007.

*Les rendez-vous de Paris.* Directed by Éric Rohmer. La Compagnie Éric Rohmer, 1995.

*Rive droite, rive gauche.* Directed by Philippe Labro. Films A2 and T. Films. 1984.

*Sabrina.* Directed by Billy Wilder. Paramount Pictures. 1954.

*La Seine a rencontré Paris.* Directed by Joris Ivens. Garance, 1957.

*Something's Gotta Give.* Directed by Nancy Meyers. Columbia Pictures, Warner Bros. and Waverly Films, 2003.

Stone, Peter. *Charade.* Draft Script, October 1, 1962.

*To Catch a Thief.* Directed by Alfred Hitchcock. Paramount Pictures, 1955.

*Victor Victoria.* Directed by Blake Edwards. Metro-Goldwyn-Mayer, Buckhantz-NMC Company, Peerford Ltd., Artista Management, Blake Edwards Entertainment, and Ladbroke, 1982.

*La vie d'un fleuve.* Directed by Jean Lods. Filmtac, 1932.

*A View to a Kill.* Directed by John Glen. Eon Productions, 1985.

*What's New Pussycat?* Directed by Clive Donner. Famous Artists Productions and Famartists Productions S.A., 1965.


## VIDEO AND AUDIO

*En remontant la Seine.* Des Racines et des Ailes. France 3, December 2016. https://www.youtube.com/watch?v=yVUDmEaPaS0.

*Il était une fois la Seine.* Des Racines et des Ailes. France 3, November 2011. https://www.youtube.com/watch?v=aKjSSGpW5iQ.

*Loisirs en Seine.* Two parts. Des Racines et des Ailes. France 3, September 2011. Part 1, https://www.youtube.com/watch?v=kHrTtbAC31w. Part 2, https://www.youtube.com/watch?v=bmfvAlq5l5g.

*The Paris Bouquinistes.* Presented by Kirsty Lang. BBC Radio 4, June 2010. http://www.bbc.co.uk/programmes/b00srktl.

*Source Seine: La Sequanigerminoise.* Directed by Antoine Hoareau. La Cigogne, 2013. http://www.dailymotion.com/video/xx61xu_source-seine-la-sequanigerminoise-version-courte_travel.

*Vikings.* Created by Michael Hirst. History Channel, 2013–18.

*Les visages de la Seine.* Des Racines et des Ailes. France 3, September 2011. https://www.youtube.com/watch?v=fn565fjV6JY.

# Index

Note: Page numbers in *italics* refer to illustrations.

# THE SEINE

*Elaine Sciolino*

# THE SEINE

## *Elaine Sciolino*

DISCUSSION QUESTIONS

1. Elaine Sciolino opens the book with her decision to move to Paris, a time in her life that was filled with heartbreak and uncertainty. As she writes, "I arrived with no sources, no lovers, no family, no friends, no mission except to start fresh in a city all the world loves" (p. 3). Would you ever leave behind all you know in search of happiness and healing? How did Sciolino, as a recently divorced young reporter, find herself and flourish so far from home?

2. The Seine River is always depicted as a woman. Why?

3. Sciolino becomes fascinated with the story of Sequana, a Gallo-Roman healing goddess who ruled over a temple at the sources of the Seine. In one version of the Sequana story, she escapes the clutches of the lascivious sea god Neptune. How might Sequana be seen as an early feminist role model?

4. What would be your own "Sequana" passion project? What did you find most inspirational about the Seine's legacy based on Sciolino's journey from the sources of the river all the way to the sea?

5. In what ways did the Seine play a significant role in Napoléon Bonaparte's life?

6. Napoléon III is credited with saying, "Paris owes its prosperity to the Seine" (p. 32). What role has the river played throughout its history and in everyday life today in fulfilling that saying?

7. How did the Pont Neuf change and shape Paris after its completion in the early seventeenth century?

8. Some of the world's earliest photographs were taken on the river. How has the Seine inspired photographers? Why have so many movies been set in Paris—and on the Seine?

9. Many people live in houseboats along the river. A romantic way to live, or just plain dark and damp?

10. What have the efforts to clean the Seine done to reinvigorate the river? How has the public's interactions with the river changed as it has become less polluted?

11. What value did Sciolino's conversations with the booksellers add to her life in Paris? What did she learn from them about French culture?

12. There are more than one hundred songs about the Seine. What can they tell us about the personality of the river?

13. How and why did the Impressionists become obsessed with painting the Seine?

14. The Seine has also been a river of death and suicide. Explore the dark side of this river.

15. The import of the Seine to Paris has always been monumental. How do Sciolino's stories of various Parisians' interactions with the river, from commerce to wedding photos to leisure, illustrate the importance of the river in a much more intimate way?

16. From the Vikings to Joan of Arc to the World Wars of the twentieth century, the city of Rouen has played a crucial role during important historical moments in France's history. Why is the history of the Seine in Rouen overshadowed by that of Paris?

17. What role did the Seine River play in putting out the Notre-Dame fire? How can the river contribute to rebuilding Paris's most visited tourist site?

18. Paris is called the most romantic city in the world and the Seine has earned a reputation for being the most romantic river in the world. Are these claims valid and why? How has this reputation been perpetuated? Does it have more to do with the river, or the city through which it flows?

19. How does Sciolino see herself and her life's journey in the everchanging nature of the Seine?

| | |
|---|---|
| Meghan Kenny | *The Driest Season* |
| Nicole Krauss | *The History of Love* |
| Don Lee | *The Collective* |
| Amy Liptrot | *The Outrun: A Memoir* |
| Donna M. Lucey | *Sargent's Women* |
| Bernard MacLaverty | *Midwinter Break* |
| Maaza Mengiste | *Beneath the Lion's Gaze* |
| Claire Messud | *The Burning Girl* |
| | *When the World Was Steady* |
| Liz Moore | *Heft* |
| | *The Unseen World* |
| Neel Mukherjee | *The Lives of Others* |
| | *A State of Freedom* |
| Janice P. Nimura | *Daughters of the Samurai* |
| Rachel Pearson | *No Apparent Distress* |
| Richard Powers | *Orfeo* |
| Kirstin Valdez Quade | *Night at the Fiestas* |
| Jean Rhys | *Wide Sargasso Sea* |
| Mary Roach | *Packing for Mars* |
| Somini Sengupta | *The End of Karma* |
| Akhil Sharma | *Family Life* |
| | *A Life of Adventure and Delight* |
| Joan Silber | *Fools* |
| Johanna Skibsrud | *Quartet for the End of Time* |
| Mark Slouka | *Brewster* |
| Kate Southwood | *Evensong* |
| Manil Suri | *The City of Devi* |
| | *The Age of Shiva* |
| Madeleine Thien | *Do Not Say We Have Nothing* |
| | *Dogs at the Perimeter* |
| Vu Tran | *Dragonfish* |
| Rose Tremain | *The American Lover* |
| | *The Gustav Sonata* |
| Brady Udall | *The Lonely Polygamist* |
| Brad Watson | *Miss Jane* |
| Constance Fenimore Woolson | *Miss Grief and Other Stories* |